International Political Economy Series

General Editor: Timothy M. Shaw, Professor of Political Science and Director of International Development Studies, Dalhousie University, Nova Scotia

The global political economy is in a profound crisis at the levels of both production and policy. This series provides overviews and case studies of states and sectors, classes and companies in the new international division of labour. These embrace political economy as both focus and mode of analysis; they advance radical scholarship and scenarios.

The series treats polity–economy dialectics at global, regional and national levels and examines novel contradictions and coalitions between and within each. There is a special emphasis on national bourgeoisies and capitalisms, on newly industrial or influential countries, and on novel strategies and technologies. The concentration throughout is on uneven patterns of power and production, authority and distribution, hegemony and reaction. Attention will be paid to redefinitions of class and security, basic needs and self-reliance and the range of critical analysis will include gender, population, resources, environment, militarization, food and finance. This series constitutes a timely and distinctive response to the continuing intellectual and existential world crisis.

Alfredo Behrens
REGIONAL MANAGEMENT OF ENERGY RESOURCES IN LATIN AMERICA

Robert Boardman
PESTICIDES IN WORLD AGRICULTURE

Bonnie K. Campbell (*editor*)
POLITICAL DIMENSIONS OF THE INTERNATIONAL DEBT CRISIS

Bonnie K. Campbell and John Loxley (*editors*)
STRUCTURAL ADJUSTMENT IN AFRICA

Jerker Carlsson and Timothy M. Shaw (*editors*)
NEWLY INDUSTRIALIZING COUNTRIES AND THE POLITICAL ECONOMY OF
  SOUTH–SOUTH RELATIONS

David P. Forsythe (*editor*)
HUMAN RIGHTS AND DEVELOPMENT
THE UNITED NATIONS IN THE WORLD POLITICAL ECONOMY

Steven Kendall Holloway
THE ALUMINIUM MULTINATIONALS AND THE BAUXITE CARTEL

James H. Mittelman
OUT FROM UNDERDEVELOPMENT

Sharon Stichter and Jane L. Parpart (*editors*)
WOMEN, EMPLOYMENT AND THE FAMILY IN THE INTERNATIONAL DIVISION OF LABOUR

Dennis Pirages and Christine Sylvester (*editors*)
THE TRANSFORMATION OF THE GLOBAL POLITICAL ECONOMY

Structural Adjustment in Africa

Edited by

Bonnie K. Campbell

Professor of Political Science
Université du Québec à Montréal

and

John Loxley

Professor of Economics
University of Manitoba

St. Martin's Press   New York

© Bonnie K. Campbell and John Loxley 1989

First published in the United States of America in 1989

Printed in Great Britain

Library of Congress Cataloging-in-Publication Data
Structural Adjustment in Africa/edited by Bonnie K. Campbell and
John Loxley.
p. cm.–(International Political Economy Series)
Some chapters translated from French.
Contents: The Devaluation Debate in Tanzania/by John Loxley–
The World Bank and the IMF in Zimbabwe/by Colin Stoneman–The
IMF, World Bank, and Reconstruction in Uganda/by John Loxley–
From 'Revolution' to Monetarism/by Eboe Hutchful–Structural
Disequilibria and Adjustment Policies in the Ivory Coast;
Structural Disequilibria and Adjustment Programmes in Madagascar/
by Gilles Duruflé–Production and Commercialization of Rice in
Cameroon/by Dominique Claude–The Politics of Adjustment in
Morocco/by David Seddon.
ISBN 0–312–03553–5
1. Africa–Economic Policy. 2. Economic Stabilization–Africa.
I. Campbell, Bonnie K., 1946–   .II. Loxley, John. III. Series.
HC800.S78 1989
338.96–dc20   89–34361
                                                            CIP

This book is dedicated to Salim, Camille, Christopher and Alicia

Contents

* These chapters were translated under the direction of Bonnie K. Campbell.

List of Maps and Tables

List of Acronyms

BCEAO	Banque Centrale des Etats de l'Afrique de l'Ouest
CCCE	Caisse Centrale de Coopération Economique
CFA franc	Communauté financière africaine franc (former Colonies françaises d'Afrique franc)
CFAO	Compagnie française de l'Afrique occidentale
CFCI	Compagnie française de Côte d'Ivoire
CADA	Credit Assistance to Agriculture
CASI	Credit Assistance to Industry
DP	Democratic Party, Uganda
DRC	Domestic Resource Cost
EECI	Energie Electrique de Côte d'Ivoire
EFF	Extended Fund Facility
ERP	Economic Recovery Programme
FAC	Fonds d'Aide et de Coopération
FMG	Malgache franc
IBRD	International Bank for Reconstruction and Development (World Bank)
ICCO	International Cocoa Agreement
IDA	International Development Association
IMF	International Monetary Fund
LIBOR	London Interbank Offered Rate
NDR	National Democratic Revolution
NEP	New Economic Policy (Soviet Union 1921–27)
NESP	National Economic Survival Programme (Tanzania)
NIC	Newly Industrialising Country
NRA	National Resistance Army (Uganda)
NRM	National Resistance Movement (Uganda)
PAMSCAD	Programme of Action to Mitigate the Social Costs of Adjustment **or** Programme of Action and Measures to address the Social Costs of Adjustment, Ghana
PDCs	People's Defence Committees, Ghana
PME	Petites et Moyennes Entreprises (Small and Medium Sized Businesses)
PNDC	Provisional National Defence Council, Ghana
SADCC	Southern African Development Coordination Conference

List of Acronyms

SAL	Structural Adjustment Loan
SAP	Structural Adjustment Programme
SDR	Special Drawing Right
SEMRY	Société d'expansion et de modernisation de la riziculture de Yagoua (Cameroon)
TAG	Tanzania Advisory Group
UNICEF	United Nations Children's Fund
UPC	Uganda People's Congress
WDCs	Workers' Defence Committees
ZANU-PF	Zimbabwe African National Union-Patriotic Front

Moroccan parties and organisations:

CDT	Democratic Labour Confederation
FDIC	Front pour la Défense des Institutions Constitutionnelles
Ilal Aman	Split from the Party of Liberation and Socialism (the former Communist Party)
Istiqlal	Independence Party
MP	Mouvement Populaire
PCM	Moroccan Communist Party
PDC	Parti Démocratique Constitutionnel
PDI	Democratic Party of Independence
PND	Parti National Démocratique
PPS	Parti de Progrès et du Socialisme (former Party of Liberation and Socialism)
RNI	Rassemblement National des Indépendants
UC	Union Constitutionnelle
UMT	Union Marocaine de Travail
UNEM	Union Nationale des Etudiants Marocains
UNFP	Union Nationale des Forces Populaires
USFP	Union Socialiste des Forces Populaires

Exchange Rates

		June 1981	*June 1988*
Cameroon	CFA Francs per $US	285.90	307.10
Ghana	Cedis per $US	2.75	188.67
Ivory Coast	CFA Francs per $US	285.90	307.10
Madagascar	CFA Francs per $US	285.90	1430.38
Morocco	Dirhams per $US	5.454	8.378
Tanzania	Shillings per $US	8.308	97.187
Uganda	Shillings per $US	77.750	60.000*
Zimbabwe	$Z per $US	0.6989	1.814

* In 1987 a currency reform converted old currency to new at a rate of 100:1.

Acknowledgements

We wish to thank the School of Economic Studies of the University of Leeds where John Loxley was Visiting Professor during the year 1987–88, and the Université du Québec à Montréal for its support in the final preparation of this volume. We would also like to express our sincere appreciation for the excellent secretarial support provided by Nilambri Ghai, Betty McGregor, Louise Mireault and Jean Wilson.

Notes on the Contributors

Bonnie K. Campbell is Professor of Political Science at the Université du Québec à Montréal where she was appointed in 1973. She has done extensive research on the political economy of the Ivory Coast. Her work on this subject is published in a wide variety of journals and in the form of an essay in *West African States* (edited by John Dunn, Cambridge UP, 1978), in *Contradictions of Accumulation in Africa, Studies in Economy and State,* which she co-edited with Henry Bernstein (California: Sage, 1985) and *Political Dimensions of the International Debt Crisis*, which she edited (London: Macmillan, 1989). She is also the author of *Libération nationale et construction du socialisme en Afrique (Angola/Guinée-Bissau/Mozambique)*, (Montréal: Editions Nouvelles Optique, 1977) and *Les enjeux de la bauxite: la Guinée face aux multinationales de l'aluminium,* (Montréal: Presses de l'Université de Montréal and Geneva: Institut universitaire des hautes études internationales, 1983). Bonnie K. Campbell was Book Review Editor of the *Canadian Journal of African Studies* and is presently a member of the Editorial Board of that Journal, as well as being an Overseas Editor of the *Review of African Political Economy* (Sheffield, UK) and *Cahiers d'études africaines* (Paris).

Dominique Claude is a high-ranking civil servant in an international organisation, who has done advisory work in half a dozen African countries concerning agricultural policies, notably with respect to food security.

Gilles Duruflé holds a Master's degree in philosophy, a Doctorate in mathematics, and works presently as an economist. He was employed for many years as a research consultant for the Société d'études pour le développement économique et social SEDES, Paris, a French semi-public consultancy body. While with the SEDES, he did a great deal of field research in Senegal, Ivory Coast and Madagascar, and produced many reports for a wide range of institutions including the Ivorian Government, UNDP, the French Ministry of Cooperation, the EEC, the French Ministry of Planning, and so on. He is now working as an economic consultant for the Bureau d'informations et de prévisions économiques (BIPE), Paris. Gilles Duruflé is the author of *L'ajustement structurel en Afrique (Sénégal, Côte d'Ivoire, Madagascar)*, Paris, Karthala, 1988, and co-author of *Les effets sociaux et économiques des projets de développement rural*, Manuel d'évaluation, Paris, Ministry of Cooperation, 1988.

Eboe Hutchful holds a PhD from the University of Toronto (1973) and is presently Associate Professor in Political Science, Trent University, and Adjunct Professor, Scarborough College, University of Toronto. He taught previously at the University of Ghana, Legon, and the University of Port Harcourt in Nigeria. He is the author of *The IMF and Ghana* (Zed Press, 1987) and of a forthcoming study on oil, ecology and public policy in Nigeria. He has researched and written on military politics, debt and structural adjustment, and the environmental aspects of the oil industry in Nigeria. In addition to contributions to several books, his publications have appeared in such journals as the *International Social Science Journal*, the *International Journal of the Sociology of Law*, the *Review of African Political Economy*, and *Alternatives*.

John Loxley is Professor and Head of the Department of Economics, University of Manitoba. He specialises in teaching Development Economics and International Finance. He has taught in Uganda and Tanzania and acted as an economic advisor to the Governments of Tanzania, Uganda, Madagascar, Mozambique and Manitoba. He is the author of *Debt and Disorder: External Finance for Development* (Boulder, Colorado: Westview Press, and Ottawa: North-South Institute, 1986), and of numerous other publications on development. He is a member of the editorial board of the *Review of African Political Economy* and of the advisory board of the *Canadian Journal of Development Studies*.

David Seddon is Reader in Development Studies at the University of East Anglia. Before joining the School of Development Studies and Overseas Development Group in Norwich in 1973 he taught in the Department of Sociology and Anthropology at the School of Oriental and African Studies in London. Research and consultancy assignments have enabled him to carry out fieldwork in various parts of Asia, the Middle East and Africa, but the involvement with Morocco dates back to 1968, when he carried out his doctoral research in northeast Morocco for a PhD at the London School of Economics. His publications include *Moroccan Peasants* (1981) and many articles on the political economy of Morocco. He currently writes the quarterly report on Morocco for the Economist Intelligence Unit and has a chapter on 'Structural adjustment and Moroccan agriculture in the 1980s' in a forthcoming book on *Structural Adjustment and Agriculture*, edited by Simon Commander. He is a member of the editorial working group of the *Review of Middle East Studies* and of the *Review of African Political Economy*.

Colin Stoneman qualified as a scientist with BSc and PhD degrees in Chemistry. He taught chemistry at the University of Hull, England for 15 years; after requalifying as an economic statistician, he began work on various aspects of the impact of foreign capital on economic development, in particular in Zimbabwe in 1981, since when he has been in the Centre for Southern African Studies at the University of York, England. He has visited Zimbabwe two or three times a year since 1983, and writes the quarterly reports on that country for the Economist Intelligence Unit. His most important publications include: *Education for Democracy* (Co-editor with David Rubinstein); (Harmondsworth: Penguin, 1970, 1972) *Zimbabwe's Inheritance* (editor); (London: Macmillan, 1981) Foreign Exchange Study: Final Report for the Government of Zimbabwe, (with L. Pakkiri and R. Davies, and in association with Coopers & Lybrand Associates), (London: Coopers & Lybrand, mimeo., February 1982) Southern African Development Co-ordination Conference (SADCC): *Indicative Industrial Development Plan* (with Richard Moorsom and Sam Wangwe; for the Commonwealth Secretariat, IDU/SADCC/41, September 1987) *Zimbabwe's Prospects* (editor); (London: Macmillan, 1988) *Zimbabwe: Politics, Economics and Society* (with Lionel Cliffe), to be published in the 'Marxist Régimes Series' (London: Frances Pinter, 1989).

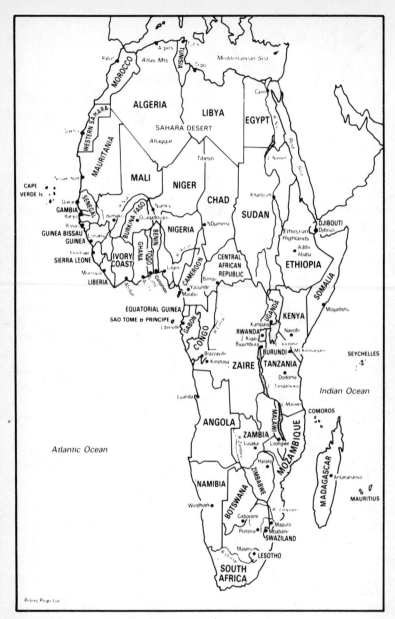

Map 1 *The Peters Projection of Africa*

Extracted from the *South Atlas*, designed by Arno Peters, and published by South Publications Ltd, with the kind permission of South Publications Ltd, Lasa.

Introduction

JOHN LOXLEY AND
BONNIE K. CAMPBELL

The conditions under which African governments have had to respond to the global crisis of the early 1980s have had the effect of locking them into new forms of dependent relationships with western governments and international financial organisations. In particular, the acute balance of payments crises suffered by most African states in recent years, and the accompanying disruption of local production, have undermined the continent's ability to service foreign debt incurred in better times. Indeed, many countries have been forced to go even deeper into debt in an effort to stave off economic collapse and/or to attempt to stimulate economic recovery. In particular, they have turned to the International Monetary Fund and the World Bank for balance of payments loans. Usually, they have done so reluctantly, and because they have exhausted other possibilities of obtaining finance. Sometimes, banks, bilateral donors and other sources of funding insist that African governments borrow from the international institutions as a condition for maintaining their own contribution to balance of payments assistance. Their enthusiasm for this flows from the fact that Fund/Bank assistance carries with it the requirement that borrowers pursue economic policies acceptable to the international institutions, a requirement which explains the reluctance of most governments to draw on this assistance except as a last resort. It is through such policy conditionality that most structural adjustment programmes in Africa are implemented.

Since 1980 almost forty African governments have turned to the IMF for balance of payments support, while half this number have received World Bank structural adjustment loans. The bibliography at the end of this volume is but a partial guide to African experience under this new form of international tutelage. Never before have the international financial institutions wielded such pervasive influence on policy formulation in Africa: not since the days of colonialism have external forces been so powerfully focused to shape Africa's economic structure and the nature of its participation in the world system.

1

Structural adjustment, as advocated by the international institutions, seeks to restore growth and stability by recasting relative prices, domestic expenditures and the type and degree of state intervention in the economy. Adjustment programmes are couched in narrow economic terms, as a series of changes in a number of key policy parameters, such as the exchange rate, the supply of credit, the tax regime, the price to producers of export commodities or the retail price of food. The policy variables involved are broadly the same regardless of the country or government seeking assistance, only the details of adjustment vary. Yet behind this 'technical' façade, which justifies policy changes by reference to 'efficiency', appropriate specialisation based on comparative advantage, and fiscal prudence – seemingly unobjectionable, neutral terms – lie a number of unstated, but contestable, ideological presuppositions; and what are represented as policy changes designed simply to improve 'economic' rationality often have far-reaching and highly controversial political and social consequences. Little wonder then, that structural adjustment initiatives have given rise to both academic debate and political struggles of some intensity.

Much of the early academic exchange concerning structural adjustment programmes in Africa was largely abstract, or at best anticipatory, as it revolved around the *plans* of the World Bank as formulated in the Berg Report.[1] These proposals have, with some amendment, now become the blueprint for Bank inspired adjustment programmes. When first mooted, they were criticised a) for promoting export-oriented growth strategies which, it was thought by some, would serve only to congest already weak world markets; b) for advocating the promotion of 'progressive' farmers and regional inequality in the interests of immediate growth; and c) for launching a frontal attack on state intervention.[2] It was not that the critics had any illusions about the ability or desire of many African governments to pursue growth oriented, inward-looking, distributionally progressive development strategies (as their critics, such as Sender and Smith charged).[3] Rather, it was felt that the Berg approach might deny *some* governments of that option. At the same time, by drawing on a distorted interpretation of how the newly industrialised countries had successfully adopted export-oriented strategies, which effectively ignored the centrality of the interventionist role of the state,[4] the Bank appeared to be exaggerating the likely growth effects of its own strategic recommendations.

In retrospect, it is apparent that the debate over the Berg Report and subsequent Bank statements on structural adjustment, although couched in terms of *policy* alternatives, is a continuation of the debate over appropriate development *theory*. On the one hand, the Bank believes that market-oriented, private sector led strategies are capable of generating sustained economic progress in Africa, free from the kind of chronic imbalances which have characterised recent experience. Marxist theorists of the classical, or Warrenite school,[5] share this optimism and interpret post-Independence economic policies in Africa as being detrimental to the development of the forces of production and to the emergence, ultimately, of a revolutionary proletariat. Critics of both feel that this optimism is misguided, and that some version of dependency theory, albeit of a more subtle, sophisticated variety than earlier, discredited 'neo-Smithian' approaches, more accurately portrays Africa's likely prospects from further integration into the world economy and from exposure to unbridled free enterprise. This debate is an on-going one[6] to which, it is hoped, this book might make some modest contribution. For, although the main object of this volume is to throw light on the origins of crisis in Africa, to examine the specific nature of policy adjustments designed to deal with crisis, and to offer some assessment of the record of adjustment to date in a representative sample of African countries, its findings will inevitably have relevance for this larger theoretical issue.

The case studies in this volume cover both francophone and anglophone Africa, and countries in north, south, east and west Africa. They reveal a great diversity of experience in terms of the origin, degree and nature of crisis. They also underscore the very different relationships which different governments have with the international financial institutions, and also reflect the weight of changing alliances within governments over time. Countries such as the Ivory Coast, and to a lesser degree, Morocco, have had less difficulty accepting orthodox policy conditionality, at least in the initial stages of reform, because it by and large converged with the policy outlook of the governments involved. For others, such as Ghana, Tanzania, Madagascar, Uganda and Zimbabwe, resort to the Fund represented a clear compromise in terms of policy and was strongly resisted by factions of the government. Zimbabwe stands alone as an economy sufficiently healthy to avoid continuing dependence on the Fund, but even there a brief flirtation in 1982 was quite costly to progressive government policies in the area of social policy.

It is, indeed, the distributional impact of orthodox programmes that underlies the resistance of African governments to applying the Fund/Bank type of cure to the problems they face. It is to be emphasised, however, that resistance tends to be selective, to protect the political base of the government and is often accompanied by compliance in other areas designed to bring certain sections of the economy/society to heel. What may appear to be contradictory policy positions may, therefore be rooted in the logic of political strategy. Where urban workers are strong politically and reasonably well organised, they are likely to react violently to the equally violent assaults on their living standards which these programmes usually entail. Sudden, large shifts in purchasing power away from urban workers towards the export sector, have caused political upheavals in Morocco, and in several other African countries not covered in this volume, for example Zambia, Egypt and Tunisia. That this has not been the experience generally is explained by the weakness of urban workers elsewhere, who have suffered dramatic declines in living standards and whose families have had to resort to a variety of survival strategies which have placed them under enormous daily stress. In some cases, governments have attempted to ameliorate the worst effects of income decline through raising minimum wages (for example Tanzania, Uganda and Mozambique) or by focusing very specifically on revitalising basic social services and ensuring some minimal access to these by ordinary workers and peasants (for example Uganda and, very recently and only as an afterthought, Ghana). Countries which have been able to raise food output and hence reduce the main source of inflationary pressure in African economies, have experienced fewer political pressures in implementing reform programmes. This has been the case at certain times in Ghana, Ivory Coast and Tanzania.

The second major cause of concern with orthodox programmes is, however, their underlying strategic focus on export orientation and the fact that they neglect the crucial food sector, so that where improvements have been experienced in food output, this has been generally by accident of nature and *not* by the design of policy reform. Food policy tends to be confined largely to removal of consumer subsidies and is a major cause of the urban discontent mentioned above. Whether or not this measure stimulates an increase in food production depends on how subsidies were administered, on the severity of non-price constraints in the food sector, and on the nature of accompanying policy reform. Where, as in Tanzania, the food subsidy was financed out of the recurrent budget of the government, its removal did not raise producer prices but instead reduced the budget deficit. In Madagascar, on the other hand, subsidy removal led to an immediate increase in the producer price of rice. This, however, conflicted with the main thrust of IMF/ Bank reform policies which were designed to shift the terms of trade in favour of export crops, and at the same time, did nothing to remove the non-price constraints on expanding food production. These weaknesses are generally built into orthodox adjustment programmes as applied to Africa. They find reflection in spirals of inflation caused by food output lagging behind demand as the terms of trade are shifted to export crops. As food prices rise and reduce the competitiveness of export crops, the state is pressured to devalue in order to restore the differential. In time, the consumer price index again responds to food shortages and the cycle repeats itself.

In the CFA zone, in which governments are not able to vary the exchange rate, the rate of inflation has generally been much lower than in those parts of Africa with more flexible exchange rate regimes. Incentives for exporters are administered essentially through the subsidy mechanism financed by tariffs on imports. This administered adjustment to effective exchange rates reduces the inflationary potential of the system, although the basic problem of competing strategic options, of export orientation versus production for the domestic market, still remains.[7] The cost of greater price stability is, however, new forms of dependent relationships with France, and greatly reduced discretion over monetary and fiscal policy.[8]

That there are no simple solutions to the food problem in Africa is demonstrated by the study in this volume of the Semry project of the Cameroon. Here is an example of a World Bank project designed to raise rice output and peasant incomes which, although not part of a structural adjustment programme, embodies many of the policy conundrums faced by those programmes and which reveals how domestic and foreign influences combine to frustrate food policies, especially when they are reliant on foreign capital for their implementation. As a result of contradictory pressures emanating not only from domestic class structure, mediated through the state, but also from external influences, the prices received by peasants are so low, and the rents paid by them so high, that they are forced to engage in other labour activities and, where possible, by-pass formal marketing channels. The project has, therefore, assisted the process of class differentiation and gender discrimination and, at the same time, given rise to pressures to shift the focus of sales from the domestic to the export market. Raising the domestic price of rice is unacceptable to the government because of the political pressure it would generate in the urban areas. Thus, what might have appeared to be a perfectly sound idea on paper has been distorted by the complex social and economic forces working upon it in practice.

The emphasis on export promotion in orthodox adjustment programmes has consequences beyond those for the supply of food. To begin with, in the case of some commodities, such as cocoa, coffee and cotton, of great importance to several of the countries in this volume, the widespread adoption of Fund/Bank programmes has led to an expansion of world supply and a corresponding decline in world prices. In consequence, the programmes of individual countries, several of which suffered already from an over-optimistic estimate of how quickly output and exports would respond to price incentives, were founded on quite unrealistic projections of trends in world prices. By 1987–88 it was apparent that this exaggerated optimism characterised programmes which hitherto, had considered quite successful, for example those of the Ivory Coast and Ghana. Furthermore, in some of the countries in question, especially Madagascar and Ghana, the push to expand exports is a major contributing factor to extensive and possibly irreversible damage to highly sensitive hardwood forest environments.

The combination of an emphasis on export promotion with a clear ideological prejudice on the part of Fund and Bank programmes in favour of reliance on market mechanisms and the promotion of the private sector, has other important implications for the structure of client countries. In some cases this is clearly leading to the growth in the influence of foreign capital, for example in the Ivory Coast, and is the result not merely of World Bank influence, but also of government policies of deliberately courting foreign capital. On closer examination, though, the Ivorian example does not appear to be a vindication of World Bank strategy. Favourable conditions have been created to open up the country for foreign capital, by privatisation and the strengthening of incentives in sectors in which multinationals dominate, without creating conditions which promote the expansion of local interests; neither has foreign capital been regulated in the national interest, so that there are clear limits to the potential of this strategy in terms of promoting growth and balance of payments stability. Although increased activities of foreign companies do not appear to be a general phenomenon given the ambivalent, if not unequivocally hostile, attitude of certain African governments to international capital over the past fifteen years, other African countries appear to be attracting foreign capital in certain, specific sectors of the economy, for example in the mining and energy sectors of Ghana. In yet other African countries this policy combination has the effect of putting pressure on governments to open up their fledgling domestic manufacturing industries to competition from abroad in a bid to make them more efficient. World Bank advice is particularly slanted in this direction and, as the chapters on Madagascar and Zimbabwe show, would be quite pernicious if followed, destroying the manufacturing sectors of both economies, by the premature removal of protective tariffs. The latter chapter demonstrates the essentially ideological nature of what the Bank presents as scientific tools of economic analysis, and reiterates the case for African states retaining discretion in matters of industrial policy in order to promote development based on *dynamic* as opposed to *static* comparative advantage.

These and the many other criticisms of orthodox programmes to be found in this volume (concerning, for example, the internal consistency of programmes, the speed and timing of adjustment and the impact on internal demand) raise the question of why governments which subscribe to quite different strategic goals than those advocated by the Fund/Bank turn to them for assistance in the first place. In some cases, the answer seems to be that they do so for purely tactical reasons, in order to promote short-term recovery considered vital if longer-term policies of national economic integration and/or some form of socialism are to be at all feasible. Where this is the ostensible reason, for example Uganda, Tanzania, Ghana and Mozambique, there is usually great controversy over the move as there is no guarantee that the threats to longer term strategic options can be resisted. Also, of course, there are always sections of the dominant ruling groups who favour the longer-term strategies of the Fund and Bank and who do not see the taking of assistance from them as being simply tactical. What emerges from the chapters on Tanzania and Uganda, however, is that those who oppose dealing with the international institutions often have no practical alternatives to offer. This is especially true of those opposing the use of one specific policy instrument, namely devaluation. This instrument raises particular debate in Africa as, in the hands of Fund/Bank advisers, it has been used bluntly, crudely and with costly implications to many people (not to mention governments). At the same time, the record of governments refusing to offset, or in extreme cases actually consciously promoting, over-valued exchange rates is a dismal one. The case is made that devaluation can help stimulate economic recovery and may, at the same time permit governments to pursue progressive social expenditure policies and reasonably progressive incomes policies if due regard is paid to, and careful control exercised over, its distributional consequences.

The principal incentive to turn to the Fund and Bank is, of course, the opportunity they afford for reducing the import constraint which is so binding in African economies. In this respect, their loans are no more important than the access they provide to the formal restructuring of debt. In recent years, however, it has become apparent that multilateral debt is itself becoming a major problem for many African countries. World Bank group debt incurred shortly after independence is now falling due while borrowings from the Fund during the crisis of the early 1980s must now be repaid. These types of debt cannot be restructured. Furthermore, while some creditor governments have written off official debt to low-income Africa, this does not extend to officially guaranteed bilateral commercial debt and does nothing for middle income countries, like Morocco and the Ivory Coast, which owe large sums of money to private creditors.[9] It is clear from many of the case studies in this volume that longer term development and current consumption levels in Africa are both being sacrificed because of the efforts of governments, under considerable international pressure, to maintain debt repayment obligations.

The failure of current strategies for dealing with the African debt crisis is growing more obvious from year to year. Since early 1987, both Nigeria and Zambia have moved to impose a ceiling on the percentage of exports they are willing to pay for debt servicing, while in May 1987 the Ivory Coast introduced a debt moratorium as a means of drawing attention to its plight. Such developments have had the effect of forcing the international institutions to change their policies towards African debt over the past six years, and it is important to recognise that this has been the case. These institutions are not as static or unyielding as they are sometimes portrayed; they do respond to pressure, albeit slowly and perhaps reluctantly, and especially where the interests of their major shareholders are deemed to be at risk, or where the costs of avoiding global disruptions are considered relatively slight. Additional special funding for low-income countries, most of which are in Africa, has been provided by the international institutions while the 1988 Toronto summit paved the way for the 'menu' approach to African debt and, especially, more favourable terms of debt restructuring from the Paris Club. Yet, while this provides some immediate relief for the poorest countries of Africa, none of these initiatives provides any permanent solutions to the debt problem since they mainly refinance debt, putting it off to the future; and little has been done to ease the burden of the larger debtors, presumably because of the risk of 'moral hazard' this might carry with respect to the debts of major borrowers outside Africa. It is to be noted that among the larger African debtors, Nigeria, the Ivory Coast and Morocco, were designated 'highly indebted countries' under the 1985 Baker Plan, which was designed to head off the debt crisis by infusing large additional inflows of credits from both international agencies and commercial banks. The latter flows did not materialise in Africa, any more than they did in most other highly indebted parts of the world, and the Baker initiative appears to have been replaced by an equally unsatisfactory 'muddling along' on a case by case basis, at the cost of great hardship to large sections of society in the debtor countries.[10]

What is unambiguous is that structural adjustment policies and current debt strategies are closely intertwined. The main purpose of these policies is to strengthen the external accounts of African countries so that they can nurse down their external liabilities. At the same time, the necessity to pay debts, which many observers now see as unpayable, reduces the ability of African governments to institute alternative approaches to structural adjustment programmes.

There is no blueprint for what form alternative adjustment programmes might take, but some rough parameters may be spelled out. They would concentrate on guaranteeing minimum consumption levels, which would mean that ensuring adequate food supplies would be the main priority. Similarly, they would seek to provide a minimal level of health care, education and water supply. They would lay down a foundation for self-sustaining growth based on dynamic specialisation as far as available investment resources would permit, and would exploit to the full opportunities for local and regional integration. Ultimately, this would give rise, not to an autarkic development strategy, but to a gradual transformation of the structure of foreign trade, based on dynamic comparative advantage. This might entail closing down or significantly modifying or scaling down uneconomic 'white elephant' projects, of which there are many throughout Africa. It would draw heavily on local initiative and reinforce the use of local resources in a way that is ecologically sound.

Central to this approach would be a policy for appropriate training and education, and a science policy geared to local resource conditions and to local production possibilities.

Implementation of the strategy might be achieved using state or collectively-owned industries, private enterprise or a mix. It will require at a minimum, however, that the state does not abdicate responsibility for development policy to the market and to private enterprise. Finally, if a political consensus is to be achieved around adjustment programmes, then provision must be made for greater public participation in their design, implementation and review. Even in those countries claiming to adopt IMF/Bank adjustment programmes for tactical reasons, and which have expressed some interest in developing alternative approaches, there has been little or no popular participation in the exercise. To the very important question of the economic sustainability of these programmes, and that of the possible inconsistency between adopting short term tactics and maintaining long term strategic options, is added, therefore, that of the political sustainability of programmes which are, even if with the best of intentions, imposed upon the people.

Notes

1. World Bank, *Accelerated Development in Sub-Saharan Africa: An Agenda for Action* (Washington DC: 1981).
2. See John Loxley, 'The World Bank and the Model of Accumulation', in Jonathan Barker (ed.) *The Politics of Agriculture in Tropical Africa* (California: Sage, 1984), and Martin Godfrey, 'Export Orientation and Structural Adjustment in Sub-Saharan Africa', IDS *Bulletin* vol. 14 (Sussex: January 1983) no. 1.
3. J.B. Sender and S. Smith, 'What's Right with the Berg Report and What's Left of its Critics?', Institute of Development Studies, University of Sussex, (1984) discussion paper no. 192.
4. Manfred Bienefeld, 'Efficiency, Expertise, NICs and the Accelerated Development Report', IDS *Bulletin*, vol. 14, (Sussex: January 1983) no. 1.
5. See Bill Warren, *Imperialism: Pioneer of Capitalism* (London: Verso, 1980) and John Sender and Sheila Smith, *The Development of Capitalism in Africa* (London: Methuen, 1986).
6. See, for instance, Henry Bernstein and Bonnie K. Campbell (eds), *Contradictions of Accumulation in Africa* (California: Sage, 1985).
7. See for instance the important article by Thomas J. Bassett, 'The World Bank in Ivory Coast', *Review of African Political Economy*, vol. 41 (September 1988).

8. For an insightful discussion of these restrictions, see Jean Coussy, 'La Zone Franc au cours des trois dernières décennies, (1960–1988)' (St Anthony's College, Oxford: April 1988) mimeo.

9. It is an indication of the terrible toll the crisis is taking on the people of Africa that Morocco was downgraded by the World Bank from a middle-income country to a low-income country in 1988.

10. For a discussion of the Baker Plan, see Roy Culpeper, 'Beyond Baker: The Maturing Debt Crisis', North-South Institute, Ottawa, Briefing Paper, May 1987. For Africa, See John Loxley, 'The African Debt Crisis', in Sean Moroney (ed.), *Africa Handbook 1988* (New York: Facts on File Publications, 1988).

1 The Devaluation Debate in Tanzania*

JOHN LOXLEY

INTRODUCTION

The protracted dispute between Tanzania and the International Monetary Fund, which lasted over half a decade, was widely publicised internationally. It has been the subject of numerous articles in newspapers and scholarly journals so much so that it might be thought that the subject has been thoroughly exhausted. To one who was intimately involved in advising on policy formulation in that country between 1981 and 1984, however, it seems that there is still more to be said; not all the issues have been aired fully, nor have all the nuances been adequately or sometimes accurately explored.

In particular, little is known publicly about the debate which took place within Tanzania on the appropriate negotiating position to be taken with the Fund. While there were those who believed that the Fund's terms should be accepted as offered, these were few and far between. The consensus in Tanzania was that the IMF terms were unnecessarily onerous and potentially far too destabilising politically. There was, therefore, general support for rejecting the 1981 IMF policy package. Within this consensus, however, there were quite sharp differences of policy emphasis, the key issue being whether or not exchange rate depreciation was necessary or desirable as a tool of economic stabilisation and adjustment. What follows will examine the arguments put forward within Tanzania on this issue and will deal only peripherally with the various IMF proposals themselves. Nonetheless the debate has great relevance for other countries in Africa which are considering IMF assistance because exchange rate depreciation is a fairly standard IMF prescription for Sub-Saharan Africa countries.[1] Moreover, Tanzania's resistance to devaluation has informed policy at one time or another in at least two neighbouring countries, Zambia and Uganda, and has been adopted by a wide variety of groups throughout Africa as the appropriate response to those advocating exchange rate adjustment. In the light of such influence, it seems sensible to subject this position to close scrutiny.

13

BACKGROUND TO THE DEBATE

The dimensions of the economic problems of Tanzania in the early 1980s are well known and have been described at length elsewhere.[2] In short, with the exception of the short-lived coffee boom in 1976–77 the country had been experiencing low (or negative) GDP growth and falling per capita incomes since the mid-1970s. By 1981 the rate of inflation was double the level it had reached two years earlier. Domestic output was constrained by a severe shortage of imported goods despite a drawing down of foreign reserves to dangerously low levels, a heavy reliance on expensive trade credits and mounting payments arrears. The volume of imports declined steadily as did the relative importance of imports in GDP. A large and growing external payments gap developed as export earnings fell. By 1982, the value of exports was less than 40 per cent that of imports, the gap being filled largely by foreign aid which was becoming more difficult to sustain, let alone increase. The external deficit reflected a serious decline in domestic savings as the share of both public and private consumption rose in the face of falling per capita incomes. Real levels of per capita consumption, however, fell by 13 per cent between 1979 and 1982[3] and shortages of goods were widespread as capacity utilisation in most industries fell dramatically between 1976 and 1982.[4]

Although Tanzania's fiscal performance was generally sound in the 1970s, it deteriorated significantly after 1979. A large fiscal deficit resulted from constrained imports and poor growth, as well as from rising military expenditures and put pressure on prices through expanded borrowing from the banking system.

The causes of these severe economic difficulties were to a very large extent external in nature. With the exception of the coffee boom period, the external terms of trade fell by between 33 and 40 per cent between 1970 and 1981–82; Tanzania experienced serious drought in the 1970s; suffered a major war with the Amin regime in Uganda in 1979 and paid heavily for the break-up of the East African common market.[5] In addition, however, there can be no question that policy shortcomings contributed to the difficulties. Domestic policy generally neglected agriculture, leading to periodic food crises and a trend decline in agricultural exports and emphasised the building of highly import-dependent industrial and transportation sectors. It also failed to move quickly to offset external shocks, which were not compensated for in the form of additional foreign capital inflows. As Svendsen argued 'it is by now fairly generally accepted that it makes little sense to speak of *either* external *or* internal causes. It is the unfavourable combination of external shocks with internal policies, which in their sum has put the country in its present situation.'[6]

It was against this background that Tanzania turned, reluctantly, to the IMF for balance of payments assistance. From the beginning negotiations were very difficult with Tanzania rejecting what it saw as the unnecessarily harsh austerity demanded by the Fund and this led to a much publicised attack on the IMF by President Nyerere in which he asked the question: 'When did the IMF become an International Ministry of Finance? When did nations agree to surrender to it their power of decision taking?'[7] Perhaps as a result of this statement, which drew considerable support from other Third World members of the Fund, Tanzania subsequently negotiated a relatively 'soft' agreement with the Fund in September 1980,[8] one which did not call, for instance, for devaluation of the Tanzanian shilling. This opened the way for negotiations with the World Bank for a Structural Adjustment Loan (SAL). Unfortunately, Tanzania was unable to comply with credit and import ceilings laid down by the IMF because of weaknesses in the programme concerning under-estimation of tax revenue response lags, and of accumulated arrears, as well as an overestimation of the amount and speed of World Bank credit inflows.[9] After only one drawing, the agreement was suspended. Since World Bank SALs were tied to the existence of an IMF stabilisation programme, Tanzania also lost this source of financing. By the time negotiations resumed in 1981 the Fund had shifted its general policy stance on conditionality, demanding much harsher terms from Third World borrowers; a reflection at the international level of the coming to power of the monetarist Reagan government. Subsequent IMF demands on the Tanzanian government were considered dangerous to the stability of the government and included 90–240 per cent devaluation, immediate increases in *real* producer prices of 45 per cent for exports and 25 per cent for food; the abolition of the maize subsidy, thereby raising consumer prices of maize by more than threefold; price controls were to be removed while urban nominal wages were to be frozen for a year and interest rates increased to positive real levels. This package hardened opposition to the Fund in Tanzania and caused a breakdown in negotiations.[10]

In an effort to break the subsequent deadlock with the IMF, the government of Tanzania agreed in 1981 to the appointment of a neutral three-person advisory group financed under a World Bank credit. This was the first time such a mechanism had been utilised to help design adjustment policy independently of the international institutions. The Tanzania Advisory Group consisted of two Canadians and a Swedish chairperson, each known to be sympathetic to Tanzania yet, importantly, each known also to be of the highest integrity and with a proven track-record of success in institution building in Africa and/or their own countries. They were assisted by a group of technical staff, both expatriate and Tanzanian, all with extensive experience in Tanzania, who were appointed on contract to the Tanzanian government. The composition of the TAG and its support staff and their relationship to Tanzania and its government warrants emphasis because some of those within Tanzania who disagreed with some of the key recommendations of the TAG seek to discredit the group by describing them quite misleadingly as 'World Bank experts'.[11]

Unfortunately, the TAG was established only after very strong battle lines had been drawn and a good deal of animosity generated between the Tanzanian leadership and the IMF. This and the fact that the Fund was not involved in the appointment of the TAG, probably meant, in retrospect, that any attempt at mediation was doomed from the start. On no issue was this more evident than that of devaluation. It was a source of considerable distress to some in the Tanzanian leadership that the TAG concluded that some exchange rate depreciation would be necessary for Tanzania to begin to extricate itself from its problems. This smacked too much, for some, of an IMF type solution even though the TAG recommendations as a whole were very different from those traditionally associated with the IMF. The Ministry of Planning, under whose wing the TAG secretariat was located, was particularly resistant to this policy recommendation and worked hard to prevent its adoption. Indeed, the government's Structural Adjustment Programme, which was based on the TAG Report, omitted all reference to exchange rate depreciation while assuming that large foreign capital inflows would be forthcoming – a scenario strongly rejected by the TAG Report itself which saw devaluation, correctly as events proved, as a *sine qua non* for obtaining multilateral financing. In his assessment of the report, the Minister of Planning at that time castigates the TAG team for putting excessive reliance on IMF/World Bank assistance, 'a hope which could not be realized', but he fails to mention that it was not realised because initially the government, at the strong urging of his ministry, adopted an exchange rate policy which was unacceptable to the international institutions and, in the opinion of TAG, quite unsustainable over any period of time.

THE ARGUMENTS AGAINST DEVALUATION

The arguments *against* devaluation were that it would *not* improve the balance of payments, and that it would generate inflation thereby causing political tension over income shares and erosion of the budget balance. Furthermore, a devaluation would not succeed in reducing the *real* exchange rate to some target level, because the inflation it generated would lead rapidly to an appreciation of the real rate, requiring in turn further devaluation and causing, therefore, a never-ending spiral of devaluation – inflation – further devaluation. The remainder of this section will elaborate on these arguments.

Elasticity pessimism was at the core of the belief that devaluation would not lead to an improvement in the balance of payments. Supply response would take at least a year for crops such as cotton and tobacco and between five and six years for tree crops such as coffee, tea, cashew nuts and sisal, and would be uncertain because of cost inflation induced by devaluation. Nor should we expect devaluation to raise officially recorded exports by reducing smuggling for, the critics argued, the incentive to smuggle was based on a desire to acquire luxury goods which were not available in Tanzania. There might be prospects, however, for the expansion of manufacturing exports but these would be best realised *not* by a general devaluation but by a selective one, that is, through dual or multiple exchange rates.[12]

One should also not expect the *demand* for foreign exchange to be reduced by devaluation. The vast majority of Tanzania's imports were of intermediate and capital goods, and total imports were already well below socially acceptable minimum standards; devaluation would not (and should not) lead, therefore, to reduced foreign exchange expenditures on imports.[13]

In addition, since the parallel market was driven by the motive of capital flight, one should not expect this to be sensitive to changes in the exchange rate either. In short, devaluation could not be expected to lead to any short-run improvement in the balance of payments. Its long-run impact on the balance of payments would depend crucially on its short-run impact on the rate of inflation and, therefore, on the structure and level of incentives.

Critics argued that devaluation would inevitably be inflationary as those whose real income and consumption levels it affected adversely, especially urban workers, would fight to protect their living standards. Inflation was seen, therefore, as a *social* phenomenon, not a simple monetary one. But if inflation was the inevitable result of devaluation, then the efficacy of the policy measure itself would be undermined. Attempts to alter relative prices and income distribution, in real terms, would be frustrated. A well known article by Nicholas Kaldor[14] makes this point quite forcefully and is quoted frequently by the critics of devaluation in the Tanzanian debate.[15] Moreover, it is argued, devaluation-induced inflation would tend to offset devaluation-induced improvements in the budget by making more expensive the imported and domestic goods bought by government. Thus, devaluation would not necessarily improve an adverse fiscal balance; this would depend crucially on its inflationary impact.

THE ARGUMENT FOR DEVALUATION

Ironically, the TAG was very sympathetic to these structuralist arguments which it too developed, quite independently of the critics,[16] but it drew somewhat different policy conclusions. The group believed that the Tanzanian shilling had become *so* overvalued in real terms that a general devaluation was warranted; that the inflationary impact of such a move would be minimal, if the adjustment was handled properly; that the distributional effects could be managed in such a way that they would *not* be regressive; that devaluation *would* improve the fiscal situation and, moreover, that it would lead to an immediate improvement in import capacity.

What is interesting is that the Kaldor article accepts that there will be situations in which a general devaluation is warranted; namely, when 'the cost of production of a country's staple exports . . . had got seriously out of line with world prices expressed in terms of local currency at the prevailing rate of exchange'.[17] This, most surely, was the case in Tanzania where the shilling had appreciated by almost 70 per cent in real terms between 1970 and 1980,[18] where the real producer prices of coffee, cotton, cashew nuts and tobacco had fallen by 46.2 per cent, 34.5 per cent, 63.2 per cent and 50 per cent respectively over the same period. These declines were well in excess of the very large deterioration in the external terms of trade during that time (31 per cent). By 1982 the government was having to subsidise most major export commodities. Clearly, this was an untenable situation.

TAG did not believe, however, that devaluation alone would improve the economic situation. To be effective and sustainable, the exchange rate depreciation would need to be accompanied by, or preferably (but unrealistically) *preceded* by, a significant inflow of foreign exchange to improve import capacity.[19] This in turn would provide the necessary incentive goods, intermediate inputs and transportation required to remove the physical impediments to supply expansion. The perceived sources of balance of payments support were the IMF, the World Bank and some switching from project to programme aid by bilateral donors.

If external finance could be mobilised quickly in sufficient quantity the Group believed that the inflationary impact of devaluation would be minimised. If consumer goods were made available quickly, either from imports or preferably from a revived manufacturing sector, TAG believed that farmers *would* switch some output from the black market. Textiles, soap, cooking oil, matches, cigarettes, beer *and* shoes were important to peasants and should not be considered 'luxuries'; all were manufactured locally but were in extremely short supply in 1981–82. Furthermore, if these and relevant price incentives were in place, TAG believed that some short-run *expansion* in output was possible, from more intensive cultivation of existing tree crops[20] *and* from enhanced planting of annual crops. Certainly, the expansion in manufacturing output induced by the availability of inputs would itself have a fairly immediate impact on overall growth. The greater this type of output increase, the less would be the inflationary pressure of devaluation. The Group argued strongly, therefore, for 'the front-end loading' of balance of payments support.

The TAG also believed that the likely inflationary impact of a suitable rate of depreciation (the meaning of which is yet to be discussed) had been exaggerated by the critics. They felt that by 1981 price controls had been seriously eroded and official rationing mechanisms had begun to break down. While this process was not complete, there is no question that local prices of imported goods were set more by reference to the black market rate of exchange than by the official rate. This being so, it was felt that a *formal* devaluation would, to a large extent, simply reduce the huge rents being earned by those buying at the official rate and selling on the black market;

that is, it would switch transactions from the unofficial to the official market without necessarily raising prices, or at least, not to the degree envisaged by critics.

Finally, the TAG felt that devaluation would reduce the budget deficit and that this too would reduce inflationary pressures. A devaluation would eliminate the subsidisation of export crops and raise import duties. The anticipated recovery of the manufacturing sector would, in turn, raise revenue from income, sales and excise taxation. The local currency proceeds of balance of payments support would combine with these factors to more than offset the increase in budgetary costs caused by devaluation.

For all these reasons TAG was sanguine about the inflationary impact of devaluation and felt that the critics had exaggerated the likely problem by underestimating both the prevalence of black market consumer pricing and the supply inducing effects of producer price changes and, especially, of additional balance of payments support linked to devaluation.

On the question of the *distributional impact* of devaluation, TAG shared the concerns of the critics of devaluation over the possible hardship which might be imposed on urban workers whose real incomes already had fallen quite significantly. They felt that the projected expansion of output would facilitate the shifting of incentives to the tradable goods sector and that lower-paid workers could be protected, to a large extent, by an increase in the minimum wage. It was assumed that the reduction of black market rents and of parastatal inefficiencies would also ease the burden on urban workers; beyond that, the urban burden would be shared in an equitable manner. In addition, other elements of the TAG proposals were designed to safeguard the living standards of less well-off Tanzanians; namely, the retention of the subsidy on maize-meal and an increased relative emphasis in government recurrent spending on basic needs and infrastructural rehabilitation at the expense, largely, of military spending.

The TAG group did not share the view of devaluation critics that urban workers were strong enough to protect their real wages and, in the process, generate inflation. On the contrary, experience in Tanzania had demonstrated the utterly weak bargaining position of urban workers and their powerlessness to prevent substantial falls in real wages and employment. The TAG group's concern was that the distributional implications of devaluation be put on the political agenda and that concrete policy measures be taken to prevent the full short-run burden of adjustment from falling on the urban worker only. Thus, they rejected the view of the critics that the effects of devaluation were *inevitably* inequitable. They also rejected, incidentally, the apparent view of the IMF that the burden should *properly* fall disproportionately on the urban worker; use of the world 'apparent' is required because, as Helleiner has argued 'the Fund's missions resolutely refused to analyze matters of distributional equity or the broader much-publicised aspirations (and considerable successes) of the Tanzania government with respect to the reduction of poverty'.[21]

THE CONSEQUENCES OF DELAYING DEVALUATION

For the most part, the critics of devaluation were responding to proposals of the IMF for a sudden very large devaluation accompanied by the removal of the maize subsidy, a freeze on urban money wages and a reduction of government spending. They quite properly vigorously opposed such a programme. The TAG likewise advised against this approach and, apart from recommending a very different strategy of distribution, also proposed a very different *pace* of adjustment. This involved a much *lower* rate of exchange rate depreciation than that proposed by the IMF, but a rate sufficiently large to enable the government to pay increased producer prices in real terms *and* to reduce the budget deficit while protecting basic needs expenditures. After an initial adjustment in the rate, the idea would be that there would be fairly frequent, small adjustments. Such a strategy, it was felt, would also minimise inflationary pressures.

Eventually, the government of Tanzania followed this strategy, but only after strenuous opposition from the critics of devaluation who succeeded in *excluding* the policy measure from the government's Structural Adjustment Programme (SAP). In this, they not only prevented any possibility of a settlement with the IMF/IBRD and, therefore, of the country achieving the capital inflows assumed by the SAP; they indirectly and unwittingly contributed, in this writer's view, to the government pursuing quite *inequitable* adjustment policies.[22] Since these are serious charges, they need elaboration.

There were two glaring deficiencies in the position put forward by the critics of devaluation. First of all, they had no discernible programme for raising the foreign exchange required for economic rehabilitation and recovery and, secondly, they had no concrete proposals for dealing with the inflationary fiscal deficit of the government. On the first they spoke of the need to encourage export promotion without specifying where the additional foreign exchange required to make it a possibility would come from. While arguing, correctly, for import-saving they acknowledged that this, too, often involved an enhanced demand for imports in the short-run, but again the possible sources of funding for this were generally not mentioned.[23] At best, there was a plea for Northern European donors to put pressure on the IMF for it to support Tanzania's adjustment programme without insisting on a devaluation of the shilling.[24] It was clear by 1982, however, that the donors would do no such thing; on the contrary, they were pressing Tanzania to devalue as a means of coming to terms with the IMF. In effect, therefore, the alternative, no-devaluation approach provided, at best, prolonged austerity, with the economy being placed, as one of its proponents put it, on a 'war economy' footing.[25] No consideration was given to the *political* acceptability of such a programme over the medium-term, although even by 1982 there were 'widespread frustrations with government policy'.[26]

The second deficiency of the no-devaluation approach was that, although it accepted the necessity for increased price incentives for export crop producers,[27] it provided no policy guidance on how the resulting large and growing (inflationary) fiscal imbalances were to be rectified. Yet, it was conceded that fiscal balance *was* also necessary.[28] This ambiguous policy must, to some extent, be held responsible for abolition of the maize subsidy and the imposition of user charges for education and a poll tax for social services and local government in the 1984 budget, and for a general contraction in real state spending on basic needs between 1981 and 1984. Though to some extent offset by an increase in wages, these fiscal measures were clearly regressive. It has been calculated that the purchasing power of the minimum wage fell from 8 kg of maize flour per day to just 2 kg between 1983 and 1985.[29] This is not to say that proponents of no-devaluation necessarily supported or condoned these inequitable developments; rather, their intransigence on the exchange rate issue in earlier years and the ambiguity of their overall position helped prolong the crisis, thereby enabling more conservative elements to prescribe such measures as being necessary. The ultimate irony is that the 1984 budget was also accompanied by further devaluation of the shilling. If more timely action had been taken on the exchange rate, however, the conservative fiscal measures of 1984 might possibly have been avoided.

THE TAG PROGRAMME

As it was, the recommendations of TAG, excluding devaluation, were accepted by the government more or less in their entirety and formed the basis of the government's own Structural Adjustment Programme – SAP.[30] In many respects, and especially given the relative lack of adjustment experience in Africa at the time it was written, the SAP was a unique programme. It was certainly quite a different programme from any likely to be recommended by the IMF or the World Bank at that time. To begin with, it had a heavy emphasis on food security and the reduction of food imports.[31] Secondly, it encouraged the development of greater local linkages around the industrial sector.[32] Thirdly, the SAP aimed to reduce dependence on aid and assert greater government control over the quantity and quality of aid.[33] Given these recommendations, it is clearly a misrepresentation for the Minister of Planning at that time to claim that pursuit of TAG policies meant the forfeiture of strategies of self-reliance.[34] Furthermore, this claim represents a very distorted view of recent history in Tanzania. The TAG report followed on the heels of a National Economic Survival Programme (NESP), drawn up by the Ministry of Planning, which emphasised both self-reliance and export expansion, but which contained few specific instruments to achieve either. It relied, principally, upon directives to state entities and moral exhortation to peasants and workers. But directives *per se* were of little value in a situation of acute goods shortages and the mobilisation of workers and peasants on a purely political basis was, by 1981, almost futile in Tanzania. Exhortation had met with some success in stimulating food production in the mid-1970s but after years of austerity and falling living standards, and in a context of widespread shortages of consumer goods, equipment and supplies, not to mention transport bottlenecks, the ability of the state to *mobilise* people by exhortation was greatly reduced and the physical capacity of people to respond was limited. As a strategy both of stabilisation and self-reliance the NESP was, therefore, a failure and it cannot be claimed fairly that the SAP undermined the NESP.

Moreover, the TAG report retained exactly the same policy objectives as the NESP but recognised the necessity for a blend of *both* price incentives and direct intervention to achieve the goals of output growth, financial balance and enhanced self-reliance. Furthermore, it emphasised the centrality of the import constraint in Tanzania but, unlike NESP, accepted the necessity for substantial balance of payments support if economic recovery was to proceed quickly. Exchange rate adjustment was considered important, therefore, for improving incentives, achieving domestic financial balance and relieving the import constraint.

The SAP was also quite different from orthodox programmes in allowing for a mix of material *and* moral incentives for workers,[35] aiming to 'safeguard the system of workers' involvement and extend it over time'[36] within a more general commitment to 'extending popular participation in the control of institutions'. In this context, the partial reliance upon moral incentives was to be founded not merely upon exhortation but upon profound institutional reform designed to extend the power of workers.[37] The SAP was also cognisant of the distributional implications of adjustment and contained a commitment to equity, the preservation of basic needs expenditures, the protection of jobs and the compensation of those affected by unavoidable layoffs.[38] For these reasons, it is equally incorrect to argue that 'socialism and self-reliance' had been abandoned under SAP[39]; rather, SAP and especially the TAG Report underlying it, is better seen as an attempt to revive an economy racked by crisis and to do so in a way which kept policies of socialism and self-reliance on the political agenda.

Regrettably, the credibility of the SAP was undermined seriously by the position taken initially by the government on devaluation, for it guaranteed that additional inflows of foreign exchange would not be forthcoming and as a result SAP targets of export recovery, economic growth, fiscal improvement and basic needs protection *could* not be met and were not met.[40] Had SAP included the relatively modest (compared to IMF demands) provision for devaluation recommended by TAG, Tanzania *might* have been able to sway the donor community to its side in its dispute with the IMF and hence break the deadlock. Inflexibility on the single issue of devaluation, therefore, resulted in Tanzania missing the opportunity to gain international acceptance of an adjustment programme 'the class implications of which (were) radically different from those implied by the Fund/World Bank proposals'.[41]

THE 1986 IMF AGREEMENT

As the economic situation inevitably worsened, the government eventually had no option but to devalue, a capitulation which must have damaged the credibility of that faction of the government which had advocated 'no devaluation'. Thus, in June 1983, the shilling was depreciated by 20 per cent and again in 1984 by 35 per cent. However, by waiting so long and by divorcing SAP from this measure, Tanzania left itself open to the claim by the IMF that these devaluations were too little too late. There can be no question that by this time the IMF was clearly the intransigent party as Tanzania had undertaken a much greater degree of policy reform than was commonly associated with IMF programmes elsewhere in Africa. Indeed, there is evidence that even the World Bank felt that the Fund was being unjustifiably difficult, given Tanzania's willingness to adjust policy.[42] The suggestion that the Fund wished to teach Tanzania a lesson for being so openly critical of its policies was given credence by the comment of a senior Fund official to the author (in the presence of a TAG member) in 1985 to the effect that in the Tanzania case the Fund was simply being 'bloody-minded'. It took the resignation of President Nyerere before the Fund began serious negotiations with Tanzania, culminating in the 1986 agreement.

It is instructive that the eventual agreement with the IMF was much less demanding than the 1981 package, so much so that the new President was able to claim that it constituted 'a victory for Tanzania'.[43] The relative ease of the 1986 agreement cannot be explained simply in terms of the Tanzanians having already carried out extensive reforms prior to 1986: it reflects to some degree a conscious effort on the part of the IMF to regain influence in Tanzania by being more accommodating, within a broader context in which it was, in any case, backing away from some of its cruder, 1981 monetarist positions which in practice had not led to much success in Africa.[44] For these reasons, and because the government itself was organised, with a clearly worked out position, Tanzania was able to wring concessions from the IMF on the extent and pace of exchange rate depreciation. The IMF initially argued for an exchange rate of sh150 to the US$ but settled, eventually, for sh40. Tanzania resisted pressure to privatise the parastatal sector and rejected the IMF's call for an urban wage freeze and the cutting of free public services. The decontrol of prices was to be stretched out over three years (with one third being decontrolled in 1986) and even then the prices of twelve key commodities would remain controlled. Tanzania retains discretionary controls over the allocation of foreign exchange within a more liberalised framework which allows exporters the retention of 50 per cent of foreign earnings for intermediate and capital goods and approved consumer goods imports.[45]

Within the framework of IMF conditionality, these concessions are quite significant and indicate a degree of continuity in the government's cautious approach to stabilisation measures. They were unquestionably important in generating a consensus in favour of an agreement with the Fund although, understandably, there is still considerable ambivalence within Tanzania about the reform package and the devaluation debate, in particular, is likely to be an ongoing one.

The main shift in policy paving the way for the Fund agreement was the explicit commitment to a more liberalised exchange rate made in the government's Economic Recovery Programme.[46] It was argued by Tanzania, and accepted by the Fund, that achieving an 'equilibrium' rate would take time; it was envisaged that this might be accomplished by mid-1988. As progress is made in this direction, import controls will be liberalised and the tariff structure rationalised, this being a continuation of measures first introduced in 1983–84. Indeed, there is precious little in the IMF agreement or in the 1987–90 Policy Framework Paper[47] which is new in policy terms. Rather, these policy statements and the budgets of 1986 and 1987[48] are better seen as extensions of reform efforts embodied in the SAP of 1982 but, hopefully, within a more logical and coherent macroeconomic framework.

The emphasis throughout the current reform phase is one of caution and realism. A modest GDP growth of 4 per cent per annum or 1 per cent per annum in per capita terms is the minimum target. It is recognised that dealing with the balance of payments deficit will take time. The current account deficit (excluding government transfers) is slated to fall only from 178 per cent of merchandise exports in 1986–87 to 134 per cent in 1989–90. A 'sustainable balance of payments position' might be reached in the early 1990s.[49] This caution seems to reflect the view that the country's balance of payments problems are structural in nature requiring a variety of policy and institutional solutions, including exchange rate changes, to take effect over a number of years. The commitment to increase the relative share of export earnings to producers to reach at least 60–70 per cent of f.o.b. prices and that of decontrolling consumer prices are likewise ones to be reached over a period of years as they touch upon important questions of institutional structure and performance. There is, therefore, no crude head-long rush into simplistic liberalisation and privatisation solutions, but rather a more pragmatic and cautious approach to problems of management and resource allocation. While some agricultural estates are being privatised, the commanding heights of the economy will undoubtedly remain in public, co-operative or peasant hands into the foreseeable future. Even those who would like to see more foreign private investment in Tanzania tend to see this taking the form of joint ventures with parastatals.[50]

The main object of the agreement from Tanzania's point of view was, of course, to secure a significant inflow of freely-usable foreign exchange, a goal which seems to have been realised. While the IMF credit is quite small, an SDR 64.2 million Stand-by Facility and an SDR 20 million Structural Adjustment Facility, it allowed Tanzania access to a $100 million World Bank rehabilitation credit and a $50 million Special Joint Financing credit from Germany, Holland, Switzerland and the UK. Overall, the agreement enabled Tanzania to secure donor pledges of $800 million per annum between 1986–87 and 1988–89 of which about $30 million per annum was fresh aid and $400 million per annum old aid, release of which had been made conditional upon an IMF agreement.[51] In addition, it paved the way for Tanzania's first Paris Club rescheduling covering at least $600 million in debt payments and arrears falling due between October 1986 and September 1987[52] and a resumption of the flow of suppliers' credits which apparently had been cut off by banks in 1984.[53] Remarkably, by October 1987, Tanzania was able to negotiate a $50 million revolving credit for coffee exports from a syndicate of international commercial banks from five different countries. This is Tanzania's first-ever syndicated bank loan, advanced at the very time that international banks were withdrawing from the Third World market.

It is envisaged that these capital inflows will complement policy and institutional reform to permit a sustained expansion of domestic supply. It remains a moot point whether or not a more accommodating approach to exchange rate adjustment would have secured them four years earlier and allowed adjustment to take place at a lower social cost in terms of reductions in real income and in the provision of public goods.

It is far too early to assess the effectiveness of the 1986 package and in particular the more flexible exchange rate policy but some preliminary observations can be made. To begin with, in 1986 for the first time in years, the growth of GDP exceeded that of population and this continued into 1987. In part this was due to favourable weather conditions, but the gradual improvement in the terms of trade facing farmers must have played a part, as evidenced by the more than 100 per cent increase in cotton output, from 103 000 to 215 000 tonnes. The output of sisal, tea and coffee also increased (although the *export* of coffee did not, due to transportation problems)[54] as did that of maize. The growth in maize production was dramatic resulting in Tanzania becoming a net exporter to the tune of 60 000 tonnes in 1987 whereas in previous years imports had reached 150 000 tonnes. This recovery in growth undoubtedly eased the social and distributional costs of adjustment and seems to confirm, to some degree at least, that supply in Tanzania is price elastic.

An important corollary of the above is that, to this point in time, the adjustment programme has not led to a persistent increase in the rate of inflation, as some critics argued it might. On the heels of two significant devaluations and the liberalisation of key consumer prices (including the abolition of the sembe subsidy) the rate of inflation rose, initially, from 27 per cent to 42 per cent from 1983 to 1984. By the following year, however, as food production expanded, and as imports of consumer goods rose through liberalised own – foreign – exchange transactions, the rate dipped to 24.5 per cent, its lowest level since 1979.[55] It now appears to be in the range of 30 per cent per annum and the recovery programme anticipates it will fall to less than 10 per cent per annum by 1989–90. The ability of the government to bring down the inflation rate, in the context of further exchange rate adjustment, and the further decontrol of consumer prices and foreign exchange transactions, will depend critically upon maintaining food production, raising export proceeds, real imports and industrial output, and controlling public sector borrowing. These will not be easy tasks. The increase in food output was partially the result of shifting domestic terms of trade in favour of food production. The current phase of adjustment shifts them strongly in favour of export production. It is not known how this will affect food output.[56] Also, transport bottlenecks still appear to be a major problem which may take some years to rectify, while industrial output recovery has apparently been sluggish. To some degree these problems may reflect the pronounced shift towards consumer goods imports which has resulted from exchange liberalisation measures. Ndulu[57] estimates that high rent yielding, consumer and luxury goods rose from 29 per cent of privately financed imports in the month before liberalisation to 50 per cent by the first quarter of 1985. Notwithstanding the important incentive effect of such imports (consumer goods imports had been suppressed to below 10 per cent of *total* imports for much of the 1970s) this increase is a cause for some concern given the pressing need for infrastructural and industrial recovery.[58] It may be that rents on such items have, in any case, been squeezed by consumer price liberalisation and by further devaluations but, regardless, a close watch needs to be kept on the nature of no-forex imports and on (the more tightly controlled) imports from export retention funds.

The disbursement of foreign loans and grants has also been a problem impeding output recovery. In 1986–87 these fell 10–20 per cent below target due, it appears, partly to bureaucratic aid procedures in Tanzania but, more importantly, to problems encountered by local companies in raising or affording local cover for commodity aid.[59] This problem is commonly encountered in Africa and reflects an inconsistency between the foreign inflow, the exchange rate and supply recovery components of IMF programmes and their domestic credit and demand restraint components. For the most part, these are irritants which could be avoided by a more careful budgeting of domestic credits to sectors capable of generating rapid supply responses to enhanced access to foreign exchange.

Disbursement problems appear also to have frustrated efforts to meet enhanced development spending targets. Higher import costs, the stagnation of coffee exports and the loss of local proceeds of food aid sales (because of good harvests) have also put financing pressures on the development budget which are expected to persist in the near future, unless the administration of tax collection can be improved significantly. The fiscal deficit has, however, been reduced steadily over the past two years as a percentage of GDP and bank financing of the deficit fell by 70 per cent between 1985–6 and 1986–7 and is slated to fall by a further 40 per cent in 1987–8.[60]

Finally, despite some large increases in the last two years, real wages continue to be well below their 1980 levels and government can expect on-going political pressures from urban labour to rectify this.

After six years of significantly adjusting economic policy, Tanzania faces the prospect of several years more of difficult reforms and, at best, only moderate increases in per capita incomes can be expected for many years to come. While these increases, if realised, would represent a great improvement over past performance in recent years, the likely modest pace of economic improvement in the face of widespread hardship and impoverishment, will undoubtedly generate difficult internal political pressures. Moreover, the fragility of world commodity markets (made even weaker, it should be noted, by the widespread adoption by Third World countries of IMF programmes promoting export supply) and the fickleness of aid donors offer a weak foundation upon which to erect any reform programme. Yet, alternative approaches to building a firm foreign exchange base, such as promoting industrial exports or the bringing on stream of oil and gas production (both possibilities in Tanzania) require longer term initiatives. The hope is that the reform efforts introduced since 1982 will provide Tanzania with a breathing space in which the economy can be revamped in these and in other, structurally, beneficial ways. Already, success on the food production front is a major accomplishment but it needs to be complemented by break-throughs on the more narrowly defined balance of payments front.

It would also be a mistake to interpret the Tanzania reforms as *necessarily* implying an abandonment of socialist ideals. To the degree that such ideals persist in Tanzania, and many would argue that they had been eroded substantially by the early 1970s, the reform programme does not *inherently* undermine them. The movement away from state control has been accompanied by a revitalisation of the co-operative movement as much as (if not more than) it has by a recovery of the private sector. In some areas, for example retailing and small transport, private ownership may be the only feasible solution at this point in time while in others, for example, sisal and certain export trade areas, the performance of the public sector has been so bad that its replacement will be both popular and productive. Reform of the remaining, dominant, parastatal sector need not exclude more participatory forms of management and, given the inability of the system to afford rapid improvements in real wages and salaries in the near future, workers may be in a good strategic position to press for non-wage concessions and in the process, widen the scope of democracy in Tanzania.

What *is* certain is that the biggest threat to what remains of Tanzania socialism has emanated from the economic crisis itself, for disillusionment was widespread in the early 1980s. It was, unquestionably, the recognition of this which led the party and the government to adopt the reform programme in the first place. The fact that the programme was initiated by President Nyerere and that he and his close political associates continue to dominate the Central

TABLE 1.1 *Tanzania: Economic Indicators 1979–86*

	1979	1980	1981	1982	1983	1984	1985	1986
Real GDP % growth p.a.	1.2	0.8	-1.1	1.3	-0.4	2.5	2.3	3.8
Real GDP per capita	-2.1	-2.5	-4.4	-2.0	-3.7	-0.8	-1.0	0.5
Inflation rate % p.a.	13.0	30.2	25.6	28.9	27.1	36.0	24.5	30.0 (est.)
Budget deficit (overall) Tsh m	4 740	5 184	4 795	5 185	4 404	5 047	6 560	6 400 (budget)
Balance of payments current account deficits $m (excl. government transfers)	-478	-637	-503	-606	–	–	-555	-538
External debt $USm	–	2 011	2 189	2 391	2 584	2 594	3 609	–
Annual external debt servicing % exports	–	17.0	–	–	–	22.0	55.0	50.4 (scheduled)
Exports as % imports	49.1	46.8	48.0	36.9	43.3	40.5	34.7	33.1
Real import volume	100.0	85.0	65.0	56.0	39.0	43.0	48.0	56.2
Terms of trade (barter) 1975=100	95	89	79	79	81.7	84.4	81.9	102.4
Exchange rate Nominal sh/$	8.25	8.20	8.32	9.51	10.32	–	–	32.3
Real effective 1978=100	92.9	106.8	139.6	165.6	171.0	181.3	(216.4)	–
Real coffee producer price index 1977/78=100	74.0	76.3	64.7	61.2	47.8	40.4	59.0 (est.)	82.0 (est.)
Coffee exports 000 tonnes	45 429	43 540	73 273	53 477	–	55 000	46 000	–
Minimum wage index–real terms	100	97	97	75	59	59	47	47

SOURCE: Government of Tanzania (June 1987), Ndulu (1987), Stewart (1986), *Africa Research Bulletin* (1987) and own calculations.

Committee of the Party seems to indicate that Tanzania will continue to approach reform cautiously and, reasonably progressively.[61]

CONCLUSION

The written record does not reflect accurately the extent to which the single issue of the exchange rate dominated the rift between Tanzania and the IMF in the years 1981 to 1983. Nor does it capture the absolute intransigence of the critics of devaluation to a movement, of any size, in the exchange rate. Over time, the public position of the critics has become modified in tune with that of the Tanzania government itself; that is, that there is now no opposition to the *principle* of devaluation, only to its size, timing and accompanying supportive policy measures. Yet this was *not* the position of the critics in those early years: their opposition went well beyond that and was almost absolute. It led, directly, to the government pursuing producer price policies which were incompatible with budgetary or consumer price stability and can be held partially responsible, therefore, for the consequent attack on basic needs expenditure designed to balance the budget. Above all, the closed-mindedness on the exchange rate issue probably contributed to the long delay in reaching agreement with the IMF and helped prolong, therefore, the balance of payments and production crisis. It is ironic that, eventually, the critics arrived at a position on the exchange rate which was virtually indistinguishable from that of the TAG team some years earlier. Regrettably, in the meantime, implacable opposition to exchange rate adjustment had become identified in Tanzania with a 'left-wing' perspective and in the process blinded its proponents to the distributional and growth consequences of this position, which, in the view of this author at least, were quite costly to ordinary Tanzanians.

Notes
*Thanks are due to Gerry Helleiner for his helpful comments and suggestions.

1. See John Loxley, 'Alternative Approaches to Stabilisation in Africa', in Gerald K. Helleiner (ed.), *Africa and the International Monetary Fund* (Washington DC: IMF, 1986) p. 124.

2. See R.H. Green, 'Political-Economic Adjustment and IMF Conditionality: Tanzania 1974–81', in John Williamson (ed.) *IMF Conditionality* (Washington: Institute for International Economics, 1983); Brian Van Arkadie, 'The IMF Prescription for Structural Adjustment in Tanzania', in Karel Jansen (ed.), *Monetarism, Economic Crisis and the Third World* (London: Frank Cass, 1983); Frances Stewart, *Economic Policies and Agricultural Performance: The Case of Tanzania* (Paris: OECD, 1986); Benno Ndulu, 'Stabilisation and Adjustment Programmes and Policies – Tanzania' (Helsinki: World Institute for Development Economics Research, 1987).

3. World Bank, *Tanzania: Country Economic Memorandum* (Washington, DC: 1985) p. 15.

4. Ibid. p. 159.

5. See R.H. Green, D.G. Rwegasira and B. Van Arkadie, *Economic Shocks and National Policy Making: Tanzania in the 1970s* (The Hague: Institute of Social Studies, 1980).

6. Knud Erik Svendsen, 'Tanzania's Recent Macroeconomic Policies', report to the Swedish International Development Agency (September 1984).

7. J.K. Nyerere, 'No to IMF Meddling', extract from new year messages to the diplomats accredited to Tanzania, *Development Dialogue* (1980) no. 2.

8. The fact that Tanzania's Minister of Finance at that time was also to chair the annual meetings of the Fund and the World Bank in September 1980, may also have helped the government obtain a fairly 'soft' agreement.

9. Van Arkadie, op.cit.(1983) p. 136.

10. R.H. Green, 'Stabilisation in Sub-Saharan Africa and the IMF. A Critical Review and Prolegomenon, – As illustrated by Tanzania', mimeo (1984); and John Loxley, 'Tanzania: Origins of a Financial Crisis', in J. Torrie (ed.), *Banking on Poverty: The Global Impact of the IMF and the World Bank* (Toronto: Between the Lines, 1983).

11. Kighoma Malima, 'The IMF and World Bank Conditionality: The Tanzania Case', in Peter Lawrence (ed.), *World Recession and the Food Crisis in Africa* (London: ROAPE and James Currey, 1986). The TAG Report referred to here was entitled an *Interim Report on a Structural Adjustment Programme For Tanzania* (1982).

12. Ajit Singh, 'Tanzania and the IMF: The Analytics of Alternative Adjustment Programmes', *Development and Change*, vol. 17, (July 1986) no. 3, pp. 435–436.

13. Malima, op. cit. (1986) p. 132.

14. Nicholas Kaldor, 'Devaluation and Adjustment in Developing Countries', *Finance and Development*, vol. 20 (June 1983) no. 2.

15. See Singh, op. cit. (1986) and also his 'The IMF-World Bank Policy Programme in Africa: a Commentary', in Lawrence (ed.), op.cit (1986).

16. See John Loxley, 'Some Considerations on Exchange Rate Theory and Policy', *Tanzania Advisory Group. Working Paper* (December 1981) no. 5, and Van Arkadie, op. cit. (1983).

17. Kaldor, op. cit. (1983) p. 36.
18. Loxley, op. cit. (1981).
19. In addition, of course, to a whole series of institutional reforms designed to facilitate export growth and diversification and the more rational use of scarce foreign exchange.
20. Kaldor, op. cit. (1983) p. 37, also makes this point.
21. Gerald K. Helleiner, 'Stabilisation, Adjustment, and the Poor', *World Development* vol. 15 (1987) no. 12.
22. The devaluation debate was not helped by the 1982 ILO/JASPA Mission which was split over the issue and which ended up taking a non-position. This mission did help focus attention, however, on the erosion of basic needs and the deterioration in income distribution caused by the crisis. See ILO, *Basic Needs in Danger: An Oriented Development Strategy For Tanzania* (Addis Ababa: ILO, JASPA, 1982).
23. See Malima, op. cit. (1986) pp. 137–138.
24. See Singh, *Development and Change*, op. cit. (1986) pp. 449–450.
25. Ibid.
26. Walter Biermann and John Campbell, 'The Chronology of Crisis in Tanzania, 1974 to 1986', (London: Institute for African Alternatives, September 1987) mimeo, p. 16.
27. Malima, op. cit. (1986) p. 132.
28. Ibid. p. 138.
29. Vali Jamal, 'Economics of Devaluation: The Case of Tanzania', *Labour and Society*, vol. II (September 1986) no. 3.
30. Government of Tanzania, *Structural Adjustment Programme for Tanzania* (Dar es Salaam: June 1982).
31. Ibid pp. 16–17.
32. Ibid. p. 24–25.
33. Ibid. pp. 52–53.
34. See Malima, op. cit. (1986) p. 138. The TAG Report provided explicitly for reserving some investment funds for promoting the basic industrial strategy though this item does not appear in the SAP.
35. *Structural Adjustment Programme for Tanzania*, op. cit., pp. 26,43.
36. Ibid. p. 42.
37. In earlier drafts of the TAG Report and in sharp contrast to the SAP, these proposed institutional reforms were spelled out in some detail. The main deviation of the SAP from the TAG report is, however, that it assumed that enhanced foreign assistance would be forthcoming in the absence of an exchange rate adjustment, whereas the TAG recognised that this would *not* be the case in practice.
38. *Structural Adjustment Programme for Tanzania*, op. cit., pp. 6, 13, 24.
39. Biermann and Campbell, op. cit. (1987) p. 27.
40. See Ndulu, op. cit. (1987) pp. 31 ff.
41. Cheryl Payer, 'Tanzania and the World Bank', *Third World Quarterly*, vol. 5 (October 1983) no. 4.
42. This is apparent from correspondence between the Bank and the Fund in possession of the author.
43. Biermann and Campbell, op. cit. (1987) p. 26.

44. John Loxley, 'The IMF, the World Bank, and Sub-Saharan Africa: Policies and Politics', in Kjell J. Havnevik (ed.), *The IMF and the World Bank in Africa: Conditionality, Impact and Alternatives* (Uppsala: Scandinavian Institute of African Studies, 1987). An important element in this more accommodating IMF stance was the removal of the IMF team leader who had been quite intransigent in earlier negotiations.

45. The retention scheme was initiated in 1982 and the rate of retention for non-traditional exports has since been raised from 5–15 per cent of exports to 50 per cent.

46. Government of Tanzania, *Economic Recovery Programme* (Dar es Salaam: May 1986) p. 15.

47. Government of Tanzania, *Policy Framework Paper 1987/88 to 1989/90* (Dar es Salaam: June 1987). See also Government of Tanzania, *Programme for Economic Recovery* (Dar es Salaam: June 1987).

48. See *Africa Research Bulletin*, Economic Series (Exeter: 31 July 1986 and 31 July 1987).

49. *Policy Framework Paper* op. cit. (1987) p. 5.

50. See, for example, C. George Kahama, T.L. Maliyamkono and Stuart Wells (eds), *The Challenge for Tanzania's Economy* (London: James Currey, Portsmouth: Heinemann and Dar es Salaam: Tanzania Publishing House, 1986) pp. 313 ff.

51. *Africa Research Bulletin* (31 July 1986) p. 8288.

52. Ibid. (31 October 1986) pp. 8402–8403.

53. Biermann and Campbell, op. cit. p. 27.

54. *Africa Research Bulletin* (April 1987) p. 8639.

55. See Ndulu, op. cit. (1987).

56. There is an assumption underlying IMF and World Bank pricing policies for *export* crop producers that food and export crops are *complementary*. Bassett (1987) argues that this is a gross generalisation and oversimplification. Using data from Northern Ivory Coast he argues that there are often severe non-price constraints on food production and that a complex relationship often exists between food and export production. See Thomas J. Bassett, 'The World Bank in Ivory Coast', *Review of African Political Economy*, vol. 41 (September 1988).

57. Ndulu, op. cit. (1987) p. 36.

58. It is not clear from Ndulu's paper what has happened to the sum of such imports in *total* imports. His figures relate only to the privately financed *share* of such imports.

59. *Africa Research Bulletin* (31 July 1987) p. 8750.

60. See Benno J. Ndulu, 'Notes on Medium Term Development Issues: Tanzania' (University of Dar es Salaam: 1988) mimeo.

61. At the same time the new President, Mwinyi, seems capable of implementing the politically difficult institutional reforms within the progressive framework set by the Party, as evidenced not only by the nature of the IMF agreement negotiated under his tenure but also by such recent initiatives as the expansion of the number of women in senior ministerial appointments from 3 to 5 (*Africa Research Bulletin*,

Political Series, 15 April 1987 p. 8425). As usual, the politics of Tanzania are complex and defy simplistic formulation. It should be noted, however, that even those very despondent about the Fund programme have not written off, altogether, the possibility that current policies represent a tactical retreat from, not a strategic defeat of socialism in Tanzania. See Haroub Othman and Ernest Maganya, 'Tanzania: The Pitfalls of the Structural Adjustment Programmes', (London: Institute for African Alternatives, September 1987) mimeo.

2 The World Bank and the IMF in Zimbabwe

COLIN STONEMAN

INTRODUCTION

Zimbabwe became a member of both the World Bank and IMF shortly after independence in 1980. It is therefore one of their newest members, although followed by Mozambique and Angola which were in effect forced into membership as a result of the failure (or destruction) of their early socialist experiments.

Zimbabwe too espoused a socialist policy, but, in the words of (then) prime minister Mugabe, 'My Government, committed as it is to socialism . . . recognises the existing phenomenon of capitalism as an historical reality, which because it cannot be avoided has to be purposefully harnessed, regulated and transformed as a partner . . . '[1] Part of the policy therefore was an attempt at harnessing the capitalist world's main financial institutions to provide development aid and balance of payments support in the process of socialist transformation. How seriously one takes that process is of course a matter of debate,[2] but it is nevertheless clear that Zimbabwe intended to pursue an economic policy at odds with World Bank ideology in a number of respects, even if we choose to identify the overriding impetus as economic nationalism rather than socialism.

There was thus a tension from the start with Zimbabwean policy focused primarily (though not exclusively) on developing and rectifying imbalances in the internal economy, and with international organisations by contrast exerting influence towards opening up an economy that had been partly isolated. In this chapter we examine the nature of relationships between Zimbabwe and the international institutions and, in particular, expose the essentially ideological foundation of economic techniques applied by the Bank (in particular) in its analysis of structural adjustment policies in that country. Since these techniques are used widely in Africa and elsewhere by the Bank this critique has a relevance which goes well beyond the immediate case study.

POST-INDEPENDENCE EXPANSION

Social Policies

Zanu-PF's 1980 election manifesto, and its programme once elected, were much less radical than had been expected. Whether this was because control had already passed to more urbanised middle-class elements or because the constraints imposed by the Lancaster House constitution were decisive, is still occasionally debated.[3] It is reported that president Samora Machel of Mozambique advised prime minister Mugabe not to repeat Mozambique's mistakes, driving out the whites and precipitating South African destabilisation by premature revolutionary fervour.

However that may be, the dominant policy was one of reconciliation between the races and the rival parties, including blacks who had collaborated with the white regime. In practice this meant that a structure of extreme inequality of wealth and income was left intact, with modification only at the lower end.

Thus minimum wages were introduced for all workers including domestic and agricultural labourers, with the latter groups initially at only Z$30 (US$47) per month, and industrial workers at Z$70 (Z$85 from January 1981). Even the latter figure, however, was well below the poverty datum line for a family of six. Free primary, and heavily subsidised secondary schooling,[4] and a free health service for all earning less than Z$150 (US$235) were also introduced. Rapid economic growth – over 12 per cent in both 1980 and 1981 was expected to pay for this 'levelling up', making an attack on the incomes of the 5 per cent who earned half the total income unnecessary. (Few whites earned less than Z$750 a month in 1980.)

Expenditure on health almost doubled in real terms between 1980 and 1982, and the health vote rose to a peak of 5.6 per cent of the budget in 1981–82, but in the next financial year with the attempt to follow an IMF-type stabilisation programme there was a cut in real terms and its budget share fell below 5 per cent.

Expenditure on education also rose rapidly, again almost doubling in real terms between 1980 and 1982; thereafter it rose only 16 per cent over the next four years. As a percentage of national income it peaked in 1983–84, but its budget share may have peaked in 1982–83. The rise was mainly a consequence of the increase in school enrolments occasioned by wider access, a population bulge, and catching up by children and young adults who had missed education because of the war. Primary schooling became almost universal (from about 70 per cent before the liberation war), and enrolments in the first form of secondary school multiplied nearly eight fold to 170 000 between 1980 and 1986. Total enrolments rose from 1.3 million in 1980 to 2.8 million in 1986. The consequent increase in demand for teachers was the main cause of pressure on the budget, but this was held back both by low salary settlements and inadequate teacher training; the proportion of untrained primary school teachers rose from 9 per cent to 47 per cent in 1985; even in secondary schools, where the number of teachers increased five-fold, 32 per cent were untrained in 1985.

Inequality of wealth was little affected: the key factor here was the Lancaster House provision which effectively prevented radical land reform, because land for resettlement of some 400 000 excess families in the overcrowded and ecologically inferior communal areas had to be bought from the 5000 white 'commercial farmers', who owned the better half of the land, on a willing-seller willing-buyer basis. In practice, even with the miserly British aid, this meant that only a small programme could be afforded, with plans announced to resettle 165 000 families over a three year period.

As for the top end of the income distribution, fairly rapid inflation (10–15 per cent) coupled with a freeze on top salaries had a small but significant narrowing effect (soon reduced by job redefinitions and fringe benefits). But guaranteed agricultural prices benefited rich commercial farmers as well as peasants. As about half the whites left over the years following independence, the elite became racially mixed, effectively guarding against possible future 'levelling down' policies.

So it cannot be claimed that government had a very radical policy favouring the poor before conditionality began to bite; but it *was* attempting a policy of redistribution with growth and, had growth continued, a measure of levelling up would probably have occurred.

World Bank Loans

Between 1981 and 1987 Zimbabwe received nine loans from the World Bank and four IDA credits, totalling US$646 million. Three supported the reorientation of agricultural services towards the communal areas, two the manufacturing sector, three the transport sector, two energy development, and others supported urban development, small-scale industry and family health.

Although many of these were plainly beneficial, some involved indirect interventions with long-term structural consequences of a regressive nature. In the manufacturing sector there was an export promotion project worth US$70.6 million (discussed at the end of this chapter) and we analyse the industrial rehabilitation loan and the associated Jansen study in detail below. The Bank also played a key role in guaranteeing the enormous loans for the Hwange thermal power station, and there was also a direct IFC loan to the Wankie Colliery Company to help produce the needed coal. This project which was framed under the Smith regime so as to promote energy self-reliance from neighbouring countries to the north, was pushed through at a time of government inexperience; it is privately admitted in government circles that it would be extremely unlikely to be approved now, both for financial reasons, and because of the need to promote imports from other SADCC countries if exports to them are to rise. The total project cost was Z$850 million, and already the unfavourable terms negotiated under sanctions are having serious consequences on the balance of payments, and the electricity cost is more than double the cost of hydroelectricity.

Thus Zimbabwe gained independence of its SADCC partners in favour of increased reliance on a South African company, Anglo-American Corporation, then the majority owner of the Wankie Colliery Company, and still the manager. It is also of significance that Zimbabwean industry lost a major cost advantage, as electricity prices doubled and then doubled again within three years of independence. (By contrast the retail price index rose about 50 per cent over the same period.)

THE SLUMP AND ADJUSTMENT

In 1982 Zimbabwe was hit by three simultaneous crises: the world slump, involving declining demand, at a falling price, for Zimbabwe's exports; the first year of a three-year drought, estimated officially to have cost Z$680 million in that year alone; and (probably South African inspired) insurgency in Matabeleland which almost destroyed the nascent tourist industry and raised defence costs. The years 1982–84 therefore saw Zimbabwe under severe pressure to adjust along lines laid down by IMF conditionality even though the main causes were exogenous and might have been expected to prove temporary.

But the first example of possible IMF pressure begins back in the 1980–81 boom period. During 1981, reports began to circulate linking South Africa's destabilising activities towards Zimbabwe with the current negotiations with the IMF. The simplest version of the thesis held that in urging restrictions in government spending, devaluation and so forth on the Zimbabwe government, the IMF was reinforcing South Africa in its efforts to prevent the restructuring and rapid development of the Zimbabwe economy.

On the face of it the events of 1981 supported this view: South Africa had withdrawn locomotives on loan early in the year and was holding up Zimbabwean trade directly through inadequately explained delays and bottlenecks inside South Africa. This particularly affected exports, losing the country between Z$5 and Z$7 million a week in 'delayed exports' according to widely accepted reports at the time. Zimbabwe's post-independence drive to retool and invest after 15 years of sanctions was sucking in imports on a greatly increased scale (+47 per cent in 1980, +26 per cent in 1981 despite the end-of-year restrictions), so a rapid increase in exports was essential. The IMF had encouraged Zimbabwe in, if not profligate ways, at any rate attempts to redevelop rapidly. Thus within a year of joining from an 'underborrowed' position, Zimbabwe was drawing on a stand-by arrangement and was, therefore, in the position of being dictated to in its economic policies. The IMF apparently took the opportunity to urge a range of policy directions that were contrary to Zimbabwe's professed aims of redistribution, socialism, and increased self-reliance. It may of course be entirely coincidental that what many believe to be the thoroughly inappropriate policy prescriptions of the IMF, happen to steer Zimbabwe away from a course that would have displeased South Africa; but whether there was collusion or not, South Africa can conclude that its destabilisation of Zimbabwe in 1981 produced valuable, if limited gains. It is not clear that it was seeking more dramatic results in any case.

But what of the IMF itself? We know that in 1982 South Africa received a substantial loan from the IMF which was smoothly approved, despite opposition from Third World countries. We know also that Zimbabwe followed a familiar course in first resisting IMF conditionality, then, as the balance of payments continued to deteriorate, introducing a number of elements in the package (such as devaluation, reduction of subsidies), denying that this was under IMF pressures, and then being allowed to continue drawing funds under the stand-by arrangement. But if the IMF took advantage of the problems caused by South Africa, this is not sufficient to demonstrate that there was any collusion. Indeed on the face of the record, there was no export crisis in mid-1981.[5] However, significant *tonnage* declines did occur in June to October,[6] *corresponding to value declines in bulkier commodities*. So although Zimbabwe's exports did *not* fall 25 per cent as alarmist predictions suggested at the time, *belief* that this might be the case was in the air whilst IMF reviews were continuing, and it *would* have been the case but for excellent planning on the Railway Priorities Committee coupled with boom output of sufficient high value commodities as well as the bulk ones, so that substitution possibilities did exist.

A common consequence of IMF programmes with their emphasis on price responsiveness and devaluation, is to worsen income distribution. Thus in Zimbabwe, IMF-inspired policies may have vitiated the declared aim of promoting greater equality. Towards the end of the Smith regime a World Bank table showed Zimbabwe as having the second widest income distribution in the world. Since then, minimum wages have been raised and higher wages frozen (or subjected to smaller increments); but as Riddell[7] concludes, there is little real evidence of narrowing: 'Between mid-1980 and mid-1982 the ratio of average wages to minimum wages remained constant, the absolute gap widening by Z$890 a year. And since mid-1982 no policy changes have led to a narrowing of these gaps.' With the exception of a minority (about 20 per cent) involved in production for the market, farmers in communal areas suffered real falls in income because of the droughts; and comparing resettlement farmers to those on the minimum urban wage: 'between these different groups, inequalities in income have not only increased substantially since Independence but these inequalities have been the result of government legislative action.'[8]

This government action included an effective suspension of the land resettlement programme after three years during which only about 36 000 families had been resettled (half the rate necessary to prevent the population in the overcrowded communal areas from increasing) and many on inferior land. The programme was later restored, but remains so constrained by orthodox policies of financial restraint that it is now of little more than token significance (the current five-year plan envisages resettlement of 15 000 families per year). Also serving to reverse the tentative moves to narrow income distribution was the reduction in subsidies on basic foodstuffs which caused rapid rises in the prices of maize meal, cooking oil and meat.

Over the period May 1982 to September 1983 the price of beef rose by 30 per cent and then a further 30–55 per cent, that of maize meal rose 50 per cent and then a further 40–45 per cent, bread rose 25–30 per cent, milk 50 per cent and vegetable oils 25 per cent. In addition, as part of the IMF agreement, there were increasing restrictions on the expansion of government and private credit in 1983, and bank rate rose from 4.5 per cent to 9 per cent in 1981.

So far as health and nutritional status is concerned, Davies and Sanders in work for Unicef [9] have catalogued the rapid improvement up to 1982, followed by a levelling off (and some possible first signs of actual deterioration) in the years that followed. Thus, free health care was introduced in 1980 for those earning less than Z$150 per month, at a time when the industrial minimum wage was Z$85; the qualifying figure remained unchanged at Z$150 into 1987, when the minimum wage had risen to Z$158; that is, rises in the money value of wage levels (corresponding *at best* to stagnation in real earnings) have now excluded all workers and their families from free health care. Of course this latter period also corresponded to the years of drought and world depression; but the point that is being made is that funds were *not* unavailable to maintain the needed improvements in health and education, and to improve the structure and capacity of industry – *on the contrary* they were denied because government was not reducing the budget deficit in the face of rising needs occasioned by drought relief and South African destabilisation.

On the other hand, the IMF has failed to hold Zimbabwe to some elements of its conditionality; although the Z$ was devalued (and has since continued to decline following the introduction of a new formula allowing it to float down against a basket of relevant trading currencies), there has been stiffening resistance to liberalisation of trade and foreign exchange. Because of tighter direct controls, imports rose only 6 per cent in money terms in 1982, and fell 2 per cent in 1983 (with inflation running at around 20 per cent); this was a result of reduced allocations as determined by available export earnings, designed to give a small visible trade surplus in 1983. Nevertheless inclusion of invisibles still left an overall deficit, and action was taken against this in March 1984 in a package of measures which included the suspending of all profit repayments on foreign investment and the acquisition by the government of the 'pool' of foreign assets owned by residents (and more contentiously, by nominee companies on behalf of ex-residents). These measures automatically produced a suspension of the then current stand-by arrangement whilst the second programme review was in session, thus preventing any further borrowings. After restoration of the flows during 1986, new (milder) restrictions were imposed in mid-1987 in the face of increasing (and increasingly damaging) diversion of foreign exchange away from industry into debt-servicing. Nevertheless contact with the IMF has continued.

A general conclusion that we may draw from all this is that Zimbabwe, subject as it is to rather large swings in its export earnings caused by world market conditions over which it has very little (if any) control, may be prepared to compromise with the IMF to some degree so as to borrow to smooth out the variations in earnings. Where, however, it sees IMF demands for 'liberalisation' in pursuit of short-term balance as threatening its ability to maintain long-run expansion, it is able to prefer direct controls to achieve the balance, even if at a temporarily lower level of activity because of denial of IMF funding. Unlike many poor countries it has this choice thanks to a diversified and basically sound economy.

WORLD BANK IDEOLOGY: STATIC COMPARATIVE ADVANTAGE

Just as Lawrence Harris has argued for the IMF,[10] the World Bank's overall intention, and increasingly effect, is to promote the construction of a single world market, substantially on the basis of the present world division of labour. Despite a number of development-oriented projects (and rhetoric), the Bank is strongly opposed to the fundamental structural changes that are necessary for development (let alone for socialism), and is therefore degenerating into an agent for promoting the interests of the dominant capitalist powers. This role is mediated through an ideology that is claimed to be a value-free science, and its associated methodologies.[11] These contentions will be supported in the following sections, first at a general level, then by a detailed examination of two World Bank-sponsored studies on Zimbabwe's manufacturing sector.

Let us begin by referring to 'the main insight of static trade theory – that international prices, for a small country, represent opportunity costs'.[12] Now the use of international prices to determine opportunity costs of local industry is undoubtedly correct, in the short run. But the run is short on two counts: firstly developing countries are more interested in *developing*, that is moving away from the present equilibrium position rather than moving towards a more efficient but possibly stagnant equilibrium at existing comparative advantage; and secondly, world prices are often unstable, or subject to market imperfections, or both.

The first consideration leads us to a familiar set of arguments about the static costs of policies that are concerned with dynamic aspects of economic efficiency. Beyond conceding that such static costs may of course possibly exceed any dynamic advantages that are being sought, and may thereby prevent their realisation, we will not pursue this controversy further here.[13]

As for the consequences of instability and imperfections in the world market, it would clearly be unproductive for any country to continually shift resources about in response to continuously varying opportunity costs as determined by world commodity markets; and where monopoly power is present, a quite false idea may be given of true (or longer-run) opportunity costs. Suppose for instance that through the existence of an international cartel (such as OPEC amongst oil producers), international prices dictated that a country like Zimbabwe should invest in a highly capital-intensive industrial plant (oil-from-coal, in this example). This could appear to be sensible in the short-run, solely because of the inflated price. But it would compound the inefficiency of world (oil) production and it would be susceptible to the break-up of the cartel. On the other hand, suppose that Zimbabwe, through the availability of natural resources, adequate capital investment, and the development of skills in the labour force, had become the world's most efficient producer of a particular commodity (this is by no means a far-fetched scenario for steel, if markets can be guaranteed). Should this industry be closed down because imperfections in the world market (for example a cartel attempting to destroy competitors, or overcapacity on a world scale coupled with a world slump and extensive dumping) were temporarily dictating very low prices?

This leads us to the ideological loading of approaches focusing on comparative advantage and in particular the DRC (domestic resource cost) approach. It is taken for granted that economic efficiency is the only criterion, or (on a variant) that the *costs* of other government aims (for example, equity, socialism) are to be referred to a hypothetical 'efficient' alternative in which all non-economic aims are ignored. Like social cost-benefit analysis in general it is thus an example of a methodology which separates ends and means, the former being selected on some normative criteria with 'science' entering only to decide on the most efficient means of achieving such ends. The ends may be no more adequately formulated than stating that economic development (or growth) is required, along with, if possible, equity. (Efficiency criteria would then usually dictate the neglect of the latter.)

As this approach does not need to inquire into the causes of the problems that exist (*why* is a country poor? *why* is it unequal?), its criteria of efficiency take the parameters of the status quo for granted. Hence its reference not merely to the world market, but to the particular prices that happen to be thrown up by it at any time. Thus, the definition of DRC is in terms of the value of domestic resources employed in earning or saving a unit of *foreign exchange*. But supposing that integration with the world market is a part (one does not need to embrace dependency theory uncritically) of the problem? Then a major part of any solution (as opposed to an efficient accommodation to realities), may be a reduction of this influence on certain aspects of economic policy. Criteria other than the DRC would then become appropriate.

In summary, the central problem for poor countries and regions is how to increase *internal* specialisation and trade, *not* how best to fit in with the existing international division of labour. The use of the comparative advantage criterion may have a role to play here, but it must be used with great caution. In fact its ideological role in the hands of the World Bank derives in part from a successful confusion between the correct argument which tells us not to try to grow bananas in Britain, and the incorrect one that tells us not to try to make steel in Zimbabwe. It may be the case at present that because of inadequate skills, poor local infrastructure, few upstream and downstream companies to buy from and sell to or obtain services from, calculations of comparative advantage in steelmaking or engineering come out badly for Zimbabwe. *But that is merely a restatement of the problem of development.* The comparative advantage argument is circular: Zimbabwe is underdeveloped so it has a comparative disadvantage in developed activities and so should avoid them!

WORLD BANK METHODOLOGY: THE DOMESTIC RESOURCE COST APPROACH

The identification of a country's comparative advantage is often formalised through the calculation of domestic resource costs

(DRCs). The accepted definition of the DRC for a particular activity is:

> The value of domestic resources (evaluated at 'shadow' or opportunity cost prices) employed in earning or saving a dollar of foreign exchange (in the value-added sense) when producing domestic goods.[14]

It is clear that, to be useful, the cost of domestic factors of production in the numerator must be related to the dollar value of foreign exchange earned or saved (in the denominator), through an appropriate exchange rate. Therefore central problems of the methodology concern the obtaining of appropriate social (or shadow) prices, and the exchange rate used, either to convert the cost of domestic factors of production into international prices, or (as in Jansen's approach) to convert world prices for tradable outputs and inputs into local currency terms.

Much of the experience with the use of DRCs to measure allocative efficiency derives from a series of studies carried out by the National Bureau of Economic Research in New York. Nine country volumes were published,[15] along with two 'synthesis' volumes[16]; I shall mainly refer to the one by Bhagwati. After writing about the difficulty of setting up a wholly adequate framework of analysis, Bhagwati introduced the DRC approach as follows: 'In place thereof, we have resorted to a technique that the country authors recognize clearly as rather simple (and perhaps simplistic)'.[17] If one activity has a higher DRC than another it then follows that it is producing less value added at international prices than is the other, for the same input of domestic resources, and a marginal shift from the former to the latter would be more efficient:

> . . . in other words, the existing, initial allocation with differential DRCs in the two activities is inefficient. This argument is clearly based on the main insight of static trade theory – that international prices, for a small country, represent opportunity costs.[18]

After referring to the difficulties of estimating shadow prices, Bhagwati continues:

> Furthermore, it must be recognized that the demonstration of wide differentials in DRCs among different activities is not equivalent to arguing that the losses therefrom must also be correspondingly

large: (1) the shift of resources from a higher DRC activity to a lower DRC activity may run into increasing costs; and (2) the expansion of output in the lower DRC activity may run into reducing output prices (as, for example, exports are increased to clear the supplies). In general equilibrium analysis, moreover, we should be prepared for three complications. First, as resources are shifted from a number of activities to other activities, in a shift to optimal equilibrium (e.g. free trade for a small country), the associated shift of prices may imply that, at the changed techniques, an activity that was higher DRC than another in the suboptimal equilibrium may become lower DRC than the other in the optimal equilibrium. Second, evaluation of the activity at, say, c.i.f. international prices in the suboptimal equilibrium may have to give way to its evaluation at f.o.b. prices in the optimal equilibrium. Third, the relative expansion and contraction of different activities in the optimal equilibrium as compared to the suboptimal equilibrium cannot be forecast in general from the mere examination of the relative DRCs in the initial suboptimal equilibrium, in consequence.[19]

He then claims that they nevertheless give ' . . . a reasonable clue to the wide variations in the social returns to different activities in the system' but almost immediately partially retracts by referring to the unreliability – under three heads – of the sorts of data that go to make up DRC estimates, and urges the reader to read:

the fine print on the untidy methods used to derive the DRC estimates, appearing neatly in their tabulated form . . . . [as a corrective] to the tendency to consider these estimates as yielding more than a rough-and-ready guide to differential returns among activities.[20]

In a footnote (which might have been aimed at the Jansen Report), referring to: ' . . . enthusiastic inferences from these arrays of ERPs and DRCs about which industries should be expanded and which contracted, and where a planning commission is wrong in its choice of targets, and so on . . . ' he advocates the use of such estimates much more 'weakly' as evidence of misallocation . . . without pretense that the numbers tell you anything more than that.'[21]

The retraction is then further reinforced by a reference to the earlier caveats and the recognition that:

the view that all DRCs would be equalized in the absence of distortions, if only the foreign-trade regime allowed international opportunity costs to be reflected in domestic decision-making, is not really convincing.

Because of changing technological know-how, factor supply changes, variations in international prices and so on, even economies with 'optimal policy frameworks' would experience disequilibrium, and:

> The variations in DRCs that would be observed in any one cross section at a single point in time cannot therefore be meaningfully attributed to the inefficiencies in the trade regime. This would be 'economic overkill'.[22]

> > Bhagwati next argues that nevertheless:

> > . . . it does not seem unreasonable to assume that the process of freer competition for imports under a more liberalized trade regime . . . would have served to bring pressure to bear in reducing the wide variations in DRCs both within and between industries. The process of careful qualification and scepticism should not be carried too far.[23]

He thus quotes Krueger to the effect that in Turkey the ' . . . wide variation in DRCs on the import-substitution side is indicative of the degree to which encouragement of import-substitution has been indiscriminate.'[24] Once again, however, and despite these almost unexceptionable statements, he seems to get cold feet, for the next paragraph begins:

> Recall, however, that inferences of 'large' welfare losses from large variations in DRCs between industries are not persuasive in the face of such objections as: What would one do with the increased output from the expansion of the low-DRC industries? or, The factors utilized in one industry may be highly specific to that industry so that there may be rapidly increasing costs to expansion of outputs in the low-DRC activities.

However, wide variations of DRCs amongst firms *within* industries do strongly suggest that ' . . . there is no easy way out of the conclusion that the pattern of investment allocations was less than optimal'.[25]

This continual oscillation between advocacy and denigration shows both a desire to accept a technique which appears to legitimise free-market ideology, and an honest recognition of the flaws in the argument on which the approach is based. At the least practitioners should recognise the warnings against uncritical use of DRCs. We will now therefore investigate whether the Jansen Report meets the necessary high standards, or whether it falls to criticism from inside its own camp; we then query whether the Belli Report has taken sufficient account of such criticisms of Jansen or whether it too falls at the first fence.

THE WORLD BANK AND THE COMPETITIVENESS OF ZIMBABWEAN INDUSTRY

The 'Jansen Report',[26] on the international competitiveness of Zimbabwe's industry, was commissioned in 1982 in connection with the first loan that Zimbabwe received from the World Bank; the 'Belli Report',[27] *An Industrial Sector Memorandum*, followed four years later.

Now both reports were highly critical of Zimbabwe's past and present industrialisation and foreign-exchange policies, so it is important to appreciate at the outset that *even in the reports' own terms* the overall results they obtained were quite favourable towards Zimbabwe's achievements:

> Although Zimbabwe manufacturing may not be clearly efficient in an absolute sense, it is very efficient compared to other manufacturing sectors in Africa and many other developing countries.[28]

Whereas the overall DRC was estimated at 1.27, similar studies had given 1.95 for Ghana, 1.83 for the Cameroon, and 1.34 for Ivory Coast.

As the last-named country is frequently praised by the World Bank for its relatively open policies,[29] it should have seemed all the more remarkable that Zimbabwe should show a *better* result, after nearly two decades with a relatively closed economy, during which it added to its industry a range of more sophisticated processes requiring more protection as infants in any case. Belli's solution is to express surprise at the success (despite the system), and then to pass to a catalogue of what it sees as disadvantages of the system (some real, some already solved, some merely disadvantages to the operation of capitalism), without ever mentioning any advantages.[30] All World Bank or IMF reports in the end turn what evidence they have to recommending the standard free-market package, modified only slightly for a country's specificity.[31] Even if one were to accept that this package was appropriate for a country (like Zambia) in serious trouble after a commodity collapse and failed industrialisation strategy (although this could of course be challenged), it does not necessarily follow that it would be appropriate for a country with a significantly more successful industrial record. One is therefore tempted to ask how successful Zimbabwe's policies would have to be before the World Bank would be obliged to alter its prescription.

My detailed criticisms of 'Jansenism' follow in the next section, and fall under two main headings: *misuse of the methodology* and *neglect of the reservations* made by more sophisticated practitioners of the methodology such as Bhagwati.[32]

THE JANSEN REPORT

Methodology

The Jansen study attempted to survey the ten main branches of manufacturing industry, investigating 122 firms representing 62 per cent of net output in 1981. (In fact as it restricted attention to only three products per company it covered only a tiny fraction of the 6200 products listed in *Products of Zimbabwean Industries* in 1980).[33] The efficiency of these firms relative to international competition was judged by calculating their domestic resource costs. Where these were above unity Zimbabwe would, according to the ideology, gain by closing down such firms and devoting the resources so freed to ones with DRCs below unity.

The methodology of the Jansen Report is thus very simple (or simplistic?); DRCs are calculated by dividing the cost of domestic factors of production ('in social prices') by value added (revenue less costs of tradable inputs, both costed in terms of 'social prices', that is, f.o.b. export prices for exportable output, whether or not actually exported, c.i.f. import prices for importable inputs or output of import substitutes).

Let us take these components in turn. Although the report argues that 'Domestic factors of production – land, labour and capital – are evaluated with respect to their social opportunity costs',[34] in fact, this was not the case. Because of data and time constraints, shadow wage rates were not calculated; market wages were assumed to represent accurately the opportunity cost of labour. Private rates of return on capital were also *assumed* to equal social rates of return.[35] Thus it cannot truly be claimed that either labour or capital are actually costed in social terms: if private prices of these factors exceed social prices by 10 per cent (a fairly conservative estimate), then the DRCs are overestimated by the same amount.

Also, in converting the international prices to domestic prices, the appropriate exchange rate is, as the report states, that rate which would result in an overall balance of the external accounts if all restrictions on trade and capital movements were removed.[36] Such a hypothetical rate is extremely difficult to calculate where controls have been in force for a number of years.

> If one assumes that the exchange rate was more or less in equilibrium in that year (1965) and takes into account adjustments in the exchange rate that were made during this period, the Zimbabwe dollar does not appear to have been significantly overvalued in 1981.[37]

Not only is the assumption once again questionable (for there was already a moderate level of protection in 1965), but the calculations leading to the conclusion are nowhere given. No other observer has denied that the dollar was overvalued in 1981–82 (estimates ranged to 50 per cent), and indeed, a devaluation of about 30 per cent occurred in late 1982 and early 1983.[38]

As every 10 per cent overvaluation of the dollar as used by the researchers will raise DRCs by an equivalent amount, it is of critical importance, if any conclusions are to be drawn, that one should have confidence in the calculation of this exchange rate; this cannot be the case in this instance.

Thus we must conclude that the Jansen Report falls short of acceptable standards in terms of its own methodology. Its findings of DRCs above unity for Zimbabwe were arrived at only by *both* overvaluing the social price of domestic factors and undervaluing the social price of value added in the output of Zimbabwean industries.

The Ideology of Jansen

The Jansen Report resorts to just the sort of 'economic overkill' castigated by Bhagwati by attributing variations in DRCs to the inefficiencies in the trade regime. Indeed Jansen goes further, at one point[39] even stating that market imperfections are 'considered to be entirely the result of government policy'.

There is a crude propagandistic flavour, with repeated references to the efficiency of market allocation, the 'efficiency criterion' (with other criteria associated with equity or other government aims explicitly seen as trades-offs against efficiency), and the existence of market imperfections. This latter phrase is in effect redefined from its technical economic meaning to mean something akin to 'government interference with the market'; there is no recognition either of the natural monopoly inevitable in a small market, nor of the requirements of planning industrialisation with a time-frame of more than a year or two.

As the report is clearly aimed at non-economists, this loose use of technical terms hardly seems fortuitous. Jansen, like the World Bank, advocates a larger role for the market, including the world market; in the context of an 'efficiency analysis', 'market imperfections' becomes a loaded term implying that there is no alternative but a change in government policy in the direction of trade liberalisation.

Jansen's Recommendations

As the overall DRC for Zimbabwe's manufacturing industry was calculated at only 1.27,[40] it could hardly be claimed that Zimbabwe should not be manufacturing, but should concentrate on mining or agriculture. However, with a spread of 0.66 to 3.62 amongst the branches of manufacturing industry, the *possibility* of serious inefficiency in some activities is raised. And in some of these branches individual companies scored still higher (up to 5.44) on the DRC scale.

There is no question of dismissing such figures as meaningless, but with Bhagwati we should seek what lessons are to be drawn; we may also consider the different perspective offered on pages 45–6.

First, however, let us look at the recommendations made by Jansen. To take metal and metal products (Group 9) as an example: this group scored the highest overall DRC at 3.62. This could however be reduced by various adjustments. Thus excluding Zisco it fell to 2.69; by assuming 25 per cent currency overvaluation it fell to 2.89; on adjusting for 86 per cent capacity utilisation it fell to 3.31; and by considering all capital costs to be sunk it fell to 2.01. This latter adjustment to the DRC (yielding a value, DRC(SR) still above unity) is supposed to indicate that there would be gains from closing down the firm or sector *immediately*, simply writing off the capital investment, as it is unable even to cover its variable costs. No calculations involving two or more of these adjustments together appear to have been made: it appears possible that if all are made to the sector excluding Zisco the result is about 1.10, implying only a marginal financial gain from immediate closure; naturally some companies will be below this figure, probably below unity, others will be above. In fact the sub-sectors of heavy metal equipment, light metal products, agricultural equipment and industrial electrical equipment, all develop average DRCs below unity (or very near) allowing for capacity utilisation and devaluation (in fact agricultural implements had an *unadjusted* value of 0.91). Only iron and steel and non-ferrous metals, and household electrical equipment stay obstinately above 1.0.[41] The report's comments on the former of these two concedes that:

> A major reason for the poor performance of the firms in this activity is the fall in the world prices for steel and metallic minerals.

Nevertheless:

> . . . the country would save foreign exchange by closing them down instead of running down their fixed capital. The ensuing massive layoffs of workers would be undesirable, but a study of alternative product lines and more efficient use of existing plant and machinery should be undertaken.

When would such a study *not* be good advice? The important point concerns the long-run prospects for industry rather than short-run savings during a world slump. But ' . . . these figures indicate the magnitude of the inefficiency and losses generated by their operation'.[42] These statements ignore Bhagwati's explicit caveats already quoted above.[43]

The final chapter of the report is entitled 'Policy Recommendations'. The main recommendation at first sight seems sensible, because it addresses the problem where the report is on the strongest ground, that is the variation of DRCs amongst firms *in the same sub-sector*. If two firms are making the same product by broadly the same methods, but one has a DRC of 0.9, the other 2.1, then something is probably wrong with the latter firm. However, before forcing it into bankruptcy as Jansen recommends, further investigation of its problems might be sensible. For instance the latter firm might be in the early learning stages of a process of exploiting a new technology expected to make it more efficient than the other (a microcosm of the whole economy in fact).

Some other recommendations are not directly linked to the DRC methodology, but form part of any World Bank type package: abandon price controls and subsidies, remove minimum wage and other legislation concerned with labour control, phase out exchange and import controls, and so forth.[44] Finally, 'The losses in efficiency that are occurring under the present set of policies have no offsetting benefits in terms of satisfying other government objectives and have been shown to be extremely costly'.[45] This statement occurs on the final page of the Jansen Report. *Almost every aspect of it is wrong.* It is wrong in its own terms, that is in terms of the evidence presented in the report; it is wrong in terms of DRC methodology, because it misuses it and ignores the reservations made by more sophisticated practitioners; and finally it is wrong because it ignores the fact that the process of industrialisation is very much more than a process of looking for the position of greatest efficiency in the short-run.

THE WORLD BANK'S INDUSTRIAL SECTOR MEMORANDUM: THE BELLI REPORT

Introduction

The Belli Report[46] is the first substantial in-house analysis of Zimbabwean manufacturing industry by the World Bank. Although its intent was to improve upon the analysis of the widely discredited Jansen study, which was rejected by the Zimbabwe government, its recommendations are in all respects exactly those which someone with no knowledge of Zimbabwe, but familiarity with the World Bank, would have predicted.

In its consideration of how the present structure of manufacturing industry has arisen, the Belli report acknowledges that the *effective* start of industrialisation occurred during the Second World War under natural protection and some state initiatives in the steel and textile industries; that the federation with what are now Zambia and Malawi from 1954–63 benefited Zimbabwean industry internally through widening its market, and externally through tariff protection; and that the enforced protection during the UDI period resulted in the creation of about half of present industry producing some 6000 distinguishable products as compared with some 600 before UDI. What the report plays down[47] is that this was a process involving a high measure of both protection and state control and initiative (in key respects if not always in detail). It also attempts to play down the importance of the UDI period, when protection and control were most visible, by emphasising that a half of industry was in place beforehand (implying wrongly that this had arisen primarily through market forces)[48] and that structural changes inside the manufacturing sector during UDI were slight.[49]

The scientific and objective tone of the Belli report is in fact spurious, for the essence of the scientific method is the rejection or modification of hypotheses in the light of conflicting experience. However, as in the case of Jansen, the Belli mission seems to have started from a received and inviolable theory, so that the task it set itself became one of fitting facts that could not be ignored into the framework, without modifying it in any way. At its weakest, when it is obliged to report that Zimbabwe has had success with policies of a type that it recommends should be abolished, the report can do no better than state that this success is surprising! Equally, no mention is made of countries which have had failures with World Bank policies, or those which have had success with opposite policies.[50]

As with Jansen the over-riding criterion employed is that of *short-run efficiency*: present policies are judged inefficient because the market would dictate a different pattern of relative prices and resource allocation. Considerations of equity, of a desire to construct a socialist society, even of the need for structural change for development, are implicitly relegated to a subsidiary category whose main characteristic is that of imposing costs above the level of a market outcome. This implies an underlying assumption that the basic structure of the economy is sound: all that is needed is to allow market forces to favour those activities for which a comparative advantage already exists. The report, in other words, denies the need to promote structural change (despite this being an oft-repeated government aim), either for social justice or for the purpose of developing comparative advantage in new areas. The primary aim of the Belli report is thus to accelerate the process of reintegrating the Zimbabwean economy into the world market system in such a way as to make any attempt at an independent policy (even of economic nationalism, let alone of socialism) impossible.

Belli's Results and Recommendations

As the conceptual and methodological weaknesses of the Jansen Report had been severely criticised[51] and as the report was rejected by government, the World Bank understandably wished to distance itself from Jansen; however it clearly wanted to retain the conclusions, and to quote the results of the earlier study where it was unable to repeat the field work.

The Belli Report is therefore by and large only implicitly critical of Jansen,[52] despite quoting significantly more favourable DRC values from its own field work; although this changes the specific recommendations, the general ones are untouched. Thus Zisco, which on Jansen's figures should have been written off immediately,[53] is now judged to be potentially very efficient with a significant comparative advantage (that is DRCs below unity) if appropriate adjustments are made to the crude figures.[54]

The report gives a number of reasons why it obtained such a startlingly different result from Jansen, including the subsequent devaluation and her failure to calculate proper shadow prices. But if a reinvestigation of Zisco can change a DRC of 4.4 to a DRC of less than unity, how reliable should we regard her other calculations? And even if they were accurate how useful are they if they are so sensitive to change? And what weight should we attach to her overall DRC figure for manufacturing industry of 1.27? Should it really have been about 0.9? Or 0.5? Nevertheless (despite privately expressed embarrassment) the Belli report explicitly admits to drawing on the Jansen study, and indeed falls back on it repeatedly.

The report reiterates at various points a range of familiar World Bank nostrums, without any clear relevance to Zimbabwe's particular circumstances, oblivious of the possibility of any alternative worldview to its own. On page xvi we are also informed that the system created a 'foreign exchange shortage', as if the main cause were not inadequate world demand (or low commodity prices) for Zimbabwe's exports. To suggest as a solution the pricing of most would-be purchasers of foreign exchange out of the market by seeking a market-clearing rate for foreign exchange[55] is not only naive, but no more a real solution for the shortage than would be a 'solution' to a food shortage that reduced demand by raising prices until people starved. A real solution requires higher export earnings, and there are other ways to achieve this.

Static Comparative Advantage Again

The Belli Report shares with Jansen an obsession with static comparative advantage (which is what DRCs really measure) to the near exclusion of longer run considerations. It is accepted that it is common for governments to protect industry, but the reasons for this are not discussed. Neither the exception to neoclassical theory of infant industry protection, nor structuralist, nor socialist theories of industrialisation are mentioned.[56] Equally one could not guess that 'model' countries, like Japan and South Korea at early stages of their development (to say nothing of the socialist countries), consciously decided to create new comparative advantages through protection; that is they invested heavily in industries which had high DRCs at the expense of existing ones with lower values. In arguing against the present system, the report implies that it might have been necessary during UDI, but that those conditions no longer obtain. This may well be true, but it misses the point that if the high degree of protection and the discretionary (as opposed to market determined) allocation, were responsible in large measure for the economic success (as we would argue), there is no reason why these elements cannot be used now under more favourable conditions. The boot should really be on the other foot, for it is the report's recommendation that a free-market, export-led strategy could generate the type of success seen in South Korea, that assumes conditions that no longer obtain. Aside from the fact that the *internal* components of the South Korean strategy were far from free market, few would maintain that the favourable world market conditions enjoyed by that country in the crucial take-off period of the 1960s obtain now, or that (unlike the case with planned allocational mechanisms), developing countries can do anything significant about it.

JANSEN AND BELLI IN PERSPECTIVE

In effect these two reports present the pattern of DRCs amongst branches of manufacturing industry in Zimbabwe as a 'hit list'. The arguments in Jansen amount to the claim that *any* shift from a high DRC firm to a lower DRC firm will increase efficiency; that is the spread of DRCs is (by definition) too large. Whereas Bhagwati (see note 10) is aware that at the most only marginal changes can be indicated, Jansen's arguments lead to the conclusion that in the end all resources ought to be employed in the single activity with lowest DRC. If this ridiculous conclusion (implicit also in Belli) is rejected, where does one stop on the way towards such an outcome? The report offers no guidance; it might be quite soon, or it is even possible that Zimbabwe might have *already* gone too far towards this extreme. *Any* position of differential DRCs is open to the arguments they make.

For international competitiveness the Belli report suggests that either the most capital-intensive new machinery has to be imported, or real wage-rates have to be squeezed down to the levels of the main Far Eastern competitors. Both options are inconsistent with Zimbabwe's socialist aims in the short run. Devaluation could increase the competitiveness of industry, but at the expense of making imports more expensive, reducing living standards, and transferring income from importers and their customers (industrialists and consumers of industrial products) to exporters (largely foreign-owned mining, ranching and plantation companies and settler farmers). We would recommend broadly the adoption of what this report describes as 'A second best alternative',[57] by an extension of present policies to promote exports at roughly the present exchange rate.

As the report states, import, price and investment controls would have to be retained in this case; it sees this as a negative factor because of 'the distortions that they introduce' – that is, relative to world market prices.[58] We would however accept that these controls could be simplified and reformed in several ways, both so as to increase the efficiency of their operation and also so as to allow the introduction of more economic analysis into the decision-making process.

The Jansen and Belli reports sit so centrally in the mainstream of World Bank and IMF advice that their major procedural failings merge imperceptibly, through the ignoring of Bhagwati's caveats, into the ideologically loaded nature of World Bank methodology in general. This methodology, in subtler hands and with painstaking data collection, can certainly derive reliable knowledge on *static* comparative advantage (and thereby provide a useful guide to short-run efficiency); there is, however, no methodology that can reliably handle *dynamic* comparative advantage, dealing as it should with several dimensions of the future: the gaining of economies of scale by infant industries, learning by doing, technological change internally and externally, short- and long-term changes in world markets, and so forth.

The essential policy thrusts of the Jansen and Belli reports have been endorsed by two more recent World Bank studies of Zimbabwe. These argue that the growth performance of the country needs to be improved by cutting back the budget deficit and by introducing foreign exchange liberalisation and further devaluation.

Criticisms of Zimbabwe's economic record and policies are certainly justified in a number of respects. Compared with either the socialist countries or the capitalist NICs, the rise in both per caput incomes and manufacturing value added since the Second World War are unimpressive.[59] The present course indeed seems unlikely to lead over the next 30 years to a dramatic transition of the type that has occurred in those countries. However, before the World Bank's diagnosis is accepted and the remedy swallowed, it should be observed that even so Zimbabwe was one of the most successful of all African countries during the 1980s (more so than more open economies like Kenya, Ivory Coast, Zaire, South Africa) when all Africa was afflicted by debt and world slump; in addition it suffered worse than most from four years of drought. It can by no means be ruled out that mediocre as recent performance has been, it would have been much worse had World Bank policies been adopted.

Finally, we should query the proposition that the only alternative strategy to the status quo is the World Bank's proposal. Present policies are in fact showing signs of solving the forex constraint, with non-traditional manufactured exports rising a claimed 65 per cent in 1987. Ironically part of the cause of this was a US$70.6 million export-revolving fund made available by the Bank in 1985, which is undoubtedly aiding Zimbabwe's long-run ability to reduce reliance on primary commodities. However, negotiations for an extension of this fund so as to include agricultural and mineral exports have been stalled for two years, with the World Bank demanding liberalisation of the trade regime before making the loan available. That is it could be argued that the Bank is holding back on the loan precisely *because* it might help present policies to succeed. Support for this cynical view of Bank policy comes from private communications suggesting internal dissent inside the Bank, with hardliners preventing an agreement until Zimbabwe agrees to far more radical shifts in policy than moves to liberalisation (such as abandonment of socialism as an aim).

Meanwhile in 1987 Zimbabwe lost patience and borrowed substantially on the commercial market (mainly British and Australian banks) so as to set up the new fund without Bank support.

CONCLUDING THOUGHTS

The above criticisms should not be taken to mean that all World Bank advice is worthless and should be disregarded altogether: efficiency *is* of vital importance despite its frequent misuse to promote a free-market ideology; Zimbabwe's economy *does* have a number of serious structural problems, and many institutional forms are indeed more related to the needs of UDI than Zimbabwe's present aspirations. But it is those aspirations, and the most efficient way of achieving *them*, that is Zimbabwe's main concern, and *not* the best way of accommodating itself to a niche that might be assigned to it in the world market.

More fundamentally, we might ask what Japan's pattern of DRCs was 35 years ago? Or South Korea's 25 years ago? What evidence there is suggests that even negative value-added (implying large negative DRCs) was tolerated for short periods. Naturally such policies can fail through inefficiency running out of control; the historical evidence from nearly all presently industrialised and industrialising countries seems to be that a dynamic policy involving the *shift* of the position of equilibrium (including the pattern of comparative advantage) has been an essential component of eventual success, and that finding the most efficient accommodation to the existing equilibrium, in the manner recommended by the World Bank and the Jansen Report, has therefore not been important.

Devaluation may well be necessary for a trading country if the currency becomes seriously overvalued. The current measure of overvaluation of the Zimbabwe dollar is not generally thought to be excessive (and the Belli Report does not claim this[60]), but the World Bank is not so much concerned with the actual rate as with how it is determined: it wishes to see it freed from the type of state control that can use determination of the rate as part of the planning process, by allowing it to be fixed by the market.[61] Many developing countries have grown rapidly with overvalued currencies, and the reason may be precisely because of the consequences that the World Bank opposes: that the overvaluation imposes an implicit tax on agriculture and exporting, in favour of industry and the domestic market. If one is content with a structure that is largely reliant on agriculture and the export of primary commodities, that is certainly an inefficient policy; if however one is attempting to industrialise and to develop an underdeveloped internal market, it becomes part of the necessary price that has to be paid, analogous to the postponement of consumption implicit in every investment decision. Higher export earnings are undoubtedly necessary, but the point being argued here is that export promotion can be planned as *part* of a policy of transformation, whereas the free-market approach would expect the export 'tail' to wag the development 'dog', with development for most of the population being at the mercy of the unreliable process of 'trickle down'.

In attempting to establish an alternative paradigm, therefore, we may justifiably argue that the pursuit of dynamic comparative advantage makes it *necessary* to look beyond static comparative advantage; however we would be foolish to regard this as *sufficient*.

Zimbabwe's freedom of manoeuvre, like that of many small poor countries, is very limited. It is not, however, completely constrained. There is some encouragement to be drawn from the fact that despite the combination of a drastic fall in its ability to import because of a combination of higher oil prices, a world slump in export demand, and South African disruptions, many fundamentals of Zimbabwe's economic policy remain intact: not only have the recommendations of the Jansen Report not been followed, but on the contrary, a significant expansion of Zisco is under way; foreign exchange control rather than the market remains the prime means for balancing payments and allocating foreign exchange to importers. However this is still a far cry from a genuinely self-reliant socialist strategy, or even a coherent economic nationalist one: too many ingredients are merely carried over from the earlier siege regime when their ultimate intention was of course very different. Mere opposition to IMF/World Bank pressure to open the economy to world market forces is not enough, and will be subject to progressive erosion especially in future economic downturns. What is needed is a coherent alternative policy, similar in spirit to Tanzania's counter-proposals to those of the IMF.[62] Neither the Transitional Development Plan nor the First Five-Year National Development Plan provided this.

Notes

1. R.G. Mugabe, Foreword, *Transitional National Development Plan, 1982/83 – 1984/85* (Harare: Ministry of Finance, Economic Planning and Development, 1982) vol.1. p. i.
2. See for example Rob Davies in Colin Stoneman (ed.), *Zimbabwe's Prospects* (London: Macmillan, 1988).
3. See for example chapters 3 (by Rob Davies) and 5 (by Colin Stoneman) in Stoneman (ed.), *Zimbabwe's Prospects* (ibid.).
4. The school fees are still quite high in relation to average earnings. In 1985 a survey by A. Riddell showed that in district council schools parents paid Z$73 per year out of total expenditure of Z$215 (34 per cent), whilst in Group A (urban) schools they paid Z$178 out of Z$598 (30 per cent).
5. In 1981 as a whole, exports (excluding gold) were up 12.8 per cent on 1980 at Z$888 million (only a small decline in real terms) but lagging badly on imports which rose 26 per cent.
6. Central Statistical Office, *Monthly Digest of Statistics* (Harare: CSO, April 1982).
7. Roger Riddell, 'Zimbabwe: The Economy Four Years after Independence', *African Affairs*, vol.83 (October 1984) no. 333, p. 468.
8. Ibid. p. 469.
9. R. Davies and D. Sanders, 'Adjustment Policies and the Welfare of Children: Zimbabwe 1980–1985', in *Adjustment with a Human Face: Country Case Studies* (New York: Unicef, 1987).
10. L. Harris, in Peter Lawrence (ed.), *The World Recession and the Food Crisis in Africa* (London: James Currey, 1986).
11. It should be emphasised that not all World Bank people accept this ideology in entirety and a minority actively disagree; this may explain some of the inconsistencies in the Belli report (note 27). However the ideology certainly constitutes the dominant view.
12. J. Bhagwati, *Anatomy and Consequences of Exchange Control Regimes* (New York: National Bureau of Economic Research, 1978) p. 88.
13. See Roger Riddell, *Foreign Aid Reconsidered* (London: James Currey/ ODI, 1987) ch. 12.
14. J.R. Behrman, *Foreign Trade Regimes and Economic Development: Chile* (New York: National Bureau of Economic Research, 1976) p. 387.
15. One, the study on Chile, is in note 14; the other countries studied were Turkey, Ghana, Israel, Egypt, the Philippines, India, South Korea and Colombia.
16. Anne O. Krueger, 'Liberalization Attempts and Consequences' (New York: National Bureau of Economic Research, 1978); Bhagwati, op. cit. (1978) p. 88.
17. Bhagwati, op. cit. (1978) p. 87.
18. Bhagwati, op. cit. (1978) p. 88.
19. Bhagwati, op. cit. (1978) p. 88.

20. Absent, incidentally, from the Jansen Report, as we shall see in discussion of the report.
21. Bhagwati, op. cit. (1978) p. 89 and his note 15, p. 122.
22. Bhagwati, op. cit. (1978) pp. 89–90.
23. Bhagwati, op. cit. (1978) p. 90.
24. Krueger, op. cit. (1978) p. 225.
25. Bhagwati, op. cit. (1978) p. 91.
26. Doris J. Jansen, *Zimbabwe: Government Policy and the Manufacturing Sector*, a study prepared for the Ministry of Industry and Energy Development, executive summary and two main volumes (April 1983) mimeo. (Unless otherwise stated, further references are to the main report, vol. I.)
27. *Zimbabwe: An Industrial Sector Memorandum*, World Bank Report no. 6349–ZIM, of a mission to Zimbabwe in October–November, 1985, led by Pedro Belli (World Bank, 22 May 1987).
28. Jansen, op. cit. (1983) p. 7.
29. See for example B.A. den Tuinder, *Ivory Coast: The Challenge of Success* (Baltimore and London: Johns Hopkins University Press 1978); also see John Loxley, 'The IMF, the World Bank, and Sub-Saharan Africa: Policies and Politics', in K.J. Havnevik (ed.), *The IMF and the World Bank in Africa: Conditionality, Impact and Alternatives* (Uppsala: Scandinavian Institute of African Studies, 1987), pp. 56–59.
30. Recognition of different aspects of the success is expressed on pages xv, 1, 10, 26, 28, 40, 52, 64–6 and 74. Catalogues of the disadvantages of the system occur throughout but particularly on pages xvi, xx, xxi, 35, 36, 37, 40, 51, 52 and 74. Claims that problems (for example the high degree of monopoly) are attributable to the system, neglect alternative explanations (such as the small size of the domestic market). Admissions that the system works quite efficiently in preventing the consequences of some of the disadvantages occur on pages 44, 46 and 63–4. Advantages of the system and the disadvantages of liberalisation are mentioned nowhere.
31. This includes devaluation of the currency, liberalisation of the foreign-exchange and import-control regimes, removal of discrimination between sectors of the economy and branches of manufacturing industry, reduction or removal of subsidies, and generally bringing the relative price structure more into line with the world market and reduction of the state's role in the economy.
32. See the discussion in the preceding section on World Bank methodology.
33. The text is not clear, at one point stating that only 33 products were studied; this would strengthen the case made here considerably.
34. Jansen, op. cit. (1983) pp. 14–15
35. Jansen, op. cit. (1983) pp. 27–28, emphasis added in both cases.
36. As recognised by the World Bank in its 1985 memorandum, this is easier said than done: despite having a sound economy a country may have some citizens with a strong interest in expatriating funds, and attempts to do this might produce very misleading signals. See World

Bank, *Zimbabwe: Country Economic Memorandum: Performance, Policies and Prospects*, World Bank Report no. 5458–ZIM (28 October 1985) p. 66.

37.   Jansen, op. cit. (1983) p. 26.

38.   We may note in passing the irony that Jansen, whilst sharing the usual World Bank desire to argue that the currency was overvalued (so as to strengthen the arguments for devaluation) was here obliged to argue that this was not the case, for otherwise the empirical basis for her arguments for fundamental changes in government policy would disappear!

39.   Jansen, op. cit (1983) p. 19; a fuller treatment of this point is given in Roger Riddell, *A Critique of 'Zimbabwe: Government Policy and the Manufacturing Sector'* (Harare: Confederation of Zimbabwe Industries, July 1983) mimeo, p. 12.

40.   And as the dollar was probably overvalued by about 30 per cent in 1981 a more correct average DRC may have been below unity!

41.   Jansen, op. cit. (1983) vol. II, Table C.1, p. 84; and note that none of this discussion queries the actual values obtained by Jansen; our criticism on pp.51–2 above would suggest that there are grounds for thinking that the report has systematically biased its DRCs upwards in two main ways.

42.   Jansen op. cit. (1983) p. 109.

43.   See above, pp.46–50 and in particular Bhagwati, op. cit. (1978), pp. 89–91.

44.   Riddell, op. cit. (1983), makes this point forcefully on pp. 21–2.

45.   Jansen, op. cit. (1983) p. 134.

46.   Belli Report, op. cit. (1987).

47.   It is of more than passing interest that Belli's main source for Zimbabwe's industrial history is in fact Jansen.

48.   There is some evidence of differing views amongst members of the team on a number of issues (see also note 30): in this particular case we find the significance of the pre-UDI period (and its supposed free market character) being argued on pages xv and 71, with this view being explicitly or implicitly contradicted on pages 8, 84 and 96.

49.   Belli Report, op. cit.(1987) p. 12; in fact the Table 1.8 referred to in the text shows that the proportion of total gross output in manufacturing industry accounted for by the metals and metal products branches rose from 14.5 per cent to 22.1 per cent between 1967 and 1975, an increase in share of more than 50 per cent! This is a major change in a key sector for self-sustaining industrialisation and depended on both state action in underwriting the expansion of the steel industry, and continued protection of a range of metal products industries that few developing countries have yet developed.

50.   For example over the last thirty years growth has been extremely rapid both in several East European countries and in South Korea and Taiwan; about the only other thing that these two sets of countries have in common is that their economic policies have been diametrically opposed to World Bank recommendations in several crucial respects.

51. Riddell, op. cit. (1983); Colin Stoneman (1983) mimeo.
52. Apart from the implications of the very different results obtained for Zisco, it criticises the failure to use shadow prices (p. 66) and the unavailability of c.i.f. prices used in the Jansen calculations (p. 58), stating that the figures dependent on them 'should be used with a good deal of care'.
53. That is it was in the worst category, with a DRC of 4.4, in which immediate closure without running down of the sunk capital investment was indicated. Jansen did not in fact recommend closure here (a political non-starter), but made it plain that her figures pointed unequivocally to this; at the very least it was suggested that no further investment or even renovation was appropriate.
54. The average DRC (before such adjustments) was calculated as 1.55, but it falls to 0.85 if restricted to domestic sales.
55. Especially in a context of politically or racially motivated reasons for capital flight.
56. Protection, however, is seen by at least one member of the team as having played a large role in Zimbabwe's development (p. xiv, 3, 4 and 60) but this is contradicted in several other places; see especially p. 12 and the discussion in note 30 above.
57. Belli, op. cit. (1987) p. 81.
58. Although the latter do represent short-term opportunity costs for Zimbabwe, they are by no means market equilibrium prices, being heavily influenced by cartelisation, trade agreements and protectionism, and the operation of monopoly power by TNCs. They will most probably give the wrong signals for a country seeking to change its economic structure and create comparative advantage in new areas.
59. Zimbabwe's present per caput income is around US$500 per annum. Most of the countries mentioned had incomes below African levels 30 years ago; now they are in the range US$2–4000.
60. See Belli, op. cit. pp. 38–39.
61. As we have seen (note 36) it allows that non-economic reasons for capital flight may require the maintenance of controls on capital transactions.
62. Loxley, in P. Lawrence (ed.), *The World Recession and The Food Crisis in Africa* (London: James Currey, 1986) p. 15.

3 The IMF, the World Bank and Reconstruction in Uganda

JOHN LOXLEY

INTRODUCTION

A recurring theme in critiques of the IMF and World Bank policies for stabilisation and adjustment is that such policies undermine national economic integration and self-reliance by promoting the greater internationalisation of trade and capital flows.[1] At issue here is the question of the appropriate strategy of economic development and the extent to which countries borrowing from the international institutions to manage immediate crises forfeit control over choice of long term economic strategy. Critics contend that integration into the international economy on the basis of static comparative advantage exposes Third World countries to instability and to constrained long term growth possibilities. IMF and IBRD policies of reducing state intervention in the economy and of allowing market forces and world prices to dictate resource allocation serve, it is claimed, to reassert the logic of the (in Africa's case) colonial division of labour and promote the interests of international capitalism at the expense of the ordinary people of the Third World. The Fund and the Bank are seen, therefore, as agents of imperialism whose role is that of ensuring the most favourable conditions for the accumulation of capital at the international level. Governments dealing with them are seen, in the extreme, as conspiring against the best interests of the people they claim to serve.[2]

It is against the background of this interpretation of their role that one must situate the 1987 agreement between the Government of Uganda and the IMF and World Bank. Whatever ambiguity might surround the policies of Yoweri Museveni's National Resistance Movement government, its vision of appropriate long term economic strategy and its views on the danger of loss of autonomy in domestic policy formulation are crystal clear. The NRM is committed to the creation of an independent, integrated and self-sustaining economy,[3] and its essential ideology is 'anti-imperialist: we are against foreign domination. We are against our economy being used to service other people's economies to our detriment . . . '[4]

This paper seeks to explain why the NRM government chose to subject the economy of Uganda to IMF and World Bank conditionality given the apparent conflict between its declared economic strategy and that implicit in the policies insisted upon by the international institutions as a requirement for access to their loans. The options facing the NRM government cannot be understood, however, without first analysing the economic policies of previous governments and their impact on the economic situation inherited by the NRM.

BACKGROUND TO THE CRISIS

The Amin Years 1971–79

It is customary to trace the origin of the economic crisis in Uganda to the coming to power, through a coup d'état, of Idi Amin in 1971. Certainly, as we shall see, it is only after that date that many common economic indicators begin to turn downwards. Yet it is not possible to understand the Amin years in isolation from the economic, social and political structure of the country as it evolved both in pre-independence times and in the early years of independence under the Obote I government.

Colonial Uganda was based on peasant production of cotton, coffee and food while international trade and finance was in the hands of European capital and management, and domestic trade, outside of co-operatives and state marketing boards, was controlled by the Asian merchant class. Though still essentially an agricultural export-import economy, by 1971 Uganda had an embryonic industrial base accounting for over 10 per cent of monetary GDP and a significant mining sector. Asian capital was important in manufacturing (especially in sugar and textiles) while international capital dominated mining and some industries (for example, meat, breweries, cigarettes). In order to strengthen the role of national capital the Obote government had initially established state institutions to compete alongside Asian and European capital. These were largely owned and controlled by the Uganda Development Corporation (established in colonial times) which operated quite efficiently though often in partnership with Asian/foreign private capital. As time went by, however, the Obote I government became frustrated at the slow pace of African control over business and it resorted, increasingly, to the partial or outright nationalisation of certain key businesses, for example, in banking and insurance. In doing so, the Uganda People's Congress (UPC) government opted not to encourage the growth of Buganda private enterprise, the Baganda being the tribe benefiting most from the colonial division of labour and the most capable (in terms of capital) of developing a rapid capitalist presence to replace Asian and foreign capital had suitable incentives been made available by the state.

Obote further alienated the Baganda by abrogating the constitution in 1966 and by forcibly removing the Kabaka of Buganda from his position as president of the country. It was this combination of political and economic restrictions on the Baganda that led them initially and, as it tragically turned out, quite mistakenly, to welcome the Idi Amin coup in 1971.

The Amin years marked a major turning point in economic policy and laid the foundations of the economic chaos inherited by the NRM. Economic policy during 1971–79 was characterised by enhanced state intervention, often in arbitrary and contradictory ways, by the extensive use of direct controls, the undermining of market incentives, the erosion of official market transactions and the unhinging of foreign exchange, monetary and fiscal balance.

The immediate object of state intervention was the 'final solution' to the dominance of Asian merchant capital, that element of capital most visible to Africans and the one most seen to be standing in the way of accumulation by Africans. In launching the 'Economic War' in 1972 Amin expelled 50 000 Asians in under three months confiscating their huge productive and personal assets. Ownership of most of the 5500 businesses was transferred to individuals, instantly creating an African merchant class, while the larger, more complex enterprises and Asian houses were transferred to the parastatal sector.[5]

Initially popular, the measure was to prove disastrous for the economy for the Asian expulsion entailed an abrupt loss of skilled personnel in both private and public sectors. In addition, the new African merchant class was not stable in its composition as no fewer than four redistributions of property took place to 1979 and several thereafter.[6] Under Amin, redistribution was quite random as was the personal violence which often accompanied it, except to the extent that gradually, over 50 per cent of the property found its way into military (essentially northern) hands. The consequence of this uncertainty of ownership was that the guiding principle of business became short term rapaciousness with no thought for maintaining the property in good condition or of reinvesting for longer term accumulation. This myopia was fed by a chaotic broader economic environment which encouraged speculation, black marketeering and racketeering. As a result, during the Amin years the capital assets of the economy, productive and infrastructural, decayed badly, real output fell significantly and monetary imbalances became acute.

Further nationalisation of foreign enterprises in 1975 swelled the parastatal sector which was already too large given the management capacity of the state. Likewise, pervasive use of direct controls bore no relationship to the likelihood of their efficient implementation, but rather found rationale in the rents to be syphoned off by state officials in bribery, corruption and illicit dealings. In particular, a fixed exchange rate (tied to the SDR), fixed producer prices and controlled retail prices, in a context of production and foreign exchange shortfalls, gave rise rapidly to black markets and much higher unofficial prices. Thus, while the cost of living faced by farmers in 1978 (low income consumer price index excluding food) was over six and a half times that of 1971, the official coffee price was less than three times its 1971 level, thereby effectively halving real returns to production of Uganda's principal export crop. Deterioration in physical infrastructure, a significant reduction in the vehicle fleet and delays in crop financing were additional factors reducing production and exports. Other export crops fared equally badly while the notoriety of the Amin regime destroyed entirely the lucrative tourist industry and led to the drying up of concessional foreign assistance by bilateral aid donors. As a result, real imports in 1979 were only a third of those of 1971, external debt almost tripled, debt arrears reached $100 million and net foreign reserves fell to almost zero. (See Table 3.3.) Large, but unmeasured, quantities of scarce foreign exchange were spent on weaponry during this period.

Because Uganda relied so heavily on imports, the monetary sector of the economy was thrown into disarray. Real monetary GDP, which had grown at an average of 5.2 per cent per annum between 1963 and 1970[7] fell to −2 per cent per annum in 1970–78. In spite of the coffee price boom in the midst of this period, *official* coffee exports in 1978 were only about a half of their 1970 level, having declined in every year during this period; cotton export volume fell by over 80 per cent, tea by 58 per cent, copper by 50 per cent, tobacco

TABLE 3.1 *Percentage Declines in Production: Selected Manufactured Goods 1971–78*

Sugar	95
Soap	94
Beer	35
Cement	79
Corrugated iron sheets	86
Steel lugots	59
Matches	93
Vegetable oils	100
Fabrics	49

by 60 per cent. Industrial production fell drastically, as Table 3.1 shows, with average capacity utilisation for the sector as a whole falling well below 30 per cent. This in turn undermined production incentives for farmers and encouraged unofficial imports.

Some of the decline in recorded monetary output was, of course, accounted for a burgeoning of unofficial transactions and black marketeering became established as a way of life with huge profits being earned by state officials and those benefiting from state largesse. Nevertheless, the tax base of the economy was eroded significantly and, even though the real incomes of many civil servants declined drastically and social services were cut back, budget deficits increased steadily during the period (moderated only by the coffee price boom), with consequent increases in the money supply.

The social costs of Amin's 'economic war' were borne not merely by the Asian community, foreign capital and export farmers. Urban wage earners suffered so badly that they virtually ceased to exist as a distinct proletariat group. In the eight years of Amin's rule the minimum wage rose by only 54 per cent[8] while the relevant price index rose ninefold.[9] The real wage fell, therefore, by 83 per cent to well below survival levels. Indeed corporate liquidity crises meant that often no wages were paid at all. Workers survived by relying more heavily on subsistence production, by holding down two or more jobs, by sending dependents out to work and by engaging in petty trading, theft or corruption. Women were particularly hard hit by the crisis often having to undertake petty trading as well as holding down a regular job, carrying the burden of housework and dealing with the acute problem of shortages of goods and deterioration in health care and other social facilities. Since public sector employment actually rose during Amin's years, productivity declined significantly, tardiness and absenteeism understandably became the order of the day and discipline collapsed.

The extent to which farmers suffered in these years cannot be evaluated since the scope of the unofficial market is not known. Food producers in the vicinity of larger urban centres may have derived benefits from higher food prices, but even there it is likely that merchants and transporters were the major beneficiaries. What is clear is that food production held up well during this period (except in a few drought prone northern areas) and subsistence production appears to have flourished. It is this ability of both farmers and urban dwellers to fall back on subsistence that prevented even greater disaster during these years and in the even more chaotic years which followed.

From 'Liberation' to January 1986

The Amin government was overthrown in April 1979 by a combined force of the Tanzanian army and the United National Liberation Front. In the process, several major towns and the capital city suffered extensive war damage and the country's fleet of vehicles was reduced by a further 40 per cent. Even worse, widespread looting followed the victory; hospitals, schools and government departments lost vital equipment and supplies so that even routine tasks became impossible. The widespread disruption in the economy led to a fall of over 20 per cent in GDP in 1979–80 and a collapse of the gross investment rate to under a quarter its 1963–70 level.[10] Coinciding with this, of course, was the second oil shock with the result that the purchasing power of Ugandan exports fell by 37.5 per cent from 1978–80. Military imports ballooned during this period. The resulting balance of payments deficit reached $250 million, much of it financed by payments arrears. As tax revenue collection difficulties mounted and military and other state expenditures grew rapidly, the budget deficit soared. In consequence the money supply doubled in these years further fuelling inflation. (See Table 3.3.) It was at this point, in December 1980, that the second Obote administration assumed power and turned to the international institutions and to bilateral donors for large scale assistance. It is to be noted that a detailed recovery plan had been drawn up by a Commonwealth team of experts in 1979 but had not been implemented by the three governments which had ruled in the interim.[11]

The reform package introduced in mid-1981 was to become, for a brief period at least, the IMF's model for adjustment in Africa and it attracted considerable donor support. The centrepiece of the programme was a massive, 90 per cent devaluation of the shilling from sh7.8 to sh78.00 to the dollar and to sh100 by July 1982, and less drastic but still huge increases in official producer prices, for example the robusta coffee price was raised from sh7.0 per kg to sh35.0 and cotton from sh6.0 to sh30.00. Many retail prices were decontrolled and the price of gasoline raised roughly in line with the devaluation. Utility rates were raised by between 125 and 700 per cent. The programme also provided for a reform of the tax system, replacing inflation-insensitive specific import duties by *ad valorem* duties, raising sales and excise tax rates and introducing ceilings on government spending, on deficits and, therefore, on credit expansion. Interest rates were also raised.

It was, however, the flexible exchange rate which was the key to the IMF programme and although the ratio of the black market to the official rate had fallen from 30:1 to 3.6:1 by July 1982, it was felt that further major adjustments were needed. In a bid to depoliticise exchange rate adjustment as much as possible, the IMF recommended a two window system and this began operations in August 1982. Under this system most key transactions took place through Window I at an official rate of exchange. Thus, exports of coffee, tea, tobacco and cotton, imports of petroleum and aid-financed products, official loan and grant inflows, and the servicing of debt and arrears were all initially Window I transactions. The balance of transactions, the amount depending on foreign exchange availability, were handled under an auction system under Window II. Gradually the range of items falling under Window II was widened so that by 1984 even major export crops and some World Bank credits were channelled through the second window at 'market rates' of exchange and the Window I rate was gradually adjusted upwards as the Window II rate depreciated.

The results of this dual exchange rate system, which can be seen in Table 3.2, were: (a) the Uganda shilling devalued significantly reaching over sh270 to the US$ in 1982–83; (b) the real effective exchange rate, that is adjusted for relative rates of inflation between Uganda and her trading partners, fell by 85 per cent between 1981 and 1984; (c) the Window II rate moved very close to the black market rate so that the differential in 1982–83 was between 2 and 26 per cent[12]; and (d) the Window I and Window II rates were gradually

TABLE 3.2 *Ugandan Exchange Rates 1979–84*

	Official rate/ Window I rate	Window II rate	Blackmarket rate	Real effective exchange rate 1979 = 100
1979	7.48	–	–	100.0
1980	17.42	–	80	174.8
1981	50.05	–	200	118.1
1982	94.52	270.8	300	34.9
1983	156.90	277.0	350	27.1
1984	271.32	362.5	650	17.2

SOURCE: World Bank 1985.

moving close together, the differential being reduced from 65 per cent in 1982 to only 25 per cent in 1984.

The object of exchange rate flexibility was to shift purchasing power to exporters and, in particular, to allow real returns to peasant farmers to rise at the expense of those who, under the control system, had been draining huge incomes in the form of rents from black marketeering and speculation. From 1982 to 1984 producer prices for major exports were raised more than fourfold and outpaced the increase both in general inflation, which stabilised at around 30 per cent, and in food prices. Supporters of this policy argue that it was successful and point to a 50 per cent increase in officially recorded exports from $246 million to $368 million between 1981 and 1983. Official purchases of coffee rose by 60 per cent during this period, cotton by 137 per cent.[13]

Recorded monetary GDP grew rapidly in 1982 and 1983, at 9.1 and 6.5 per cent respectively, growth in the overall budget deficit was reduced from 140 per cent in 1980–81 to 7 per cent in 1982–83 while money supply growth fell from 90 per cent to 46 per cent in those years. It was the combination of these factors which led to inflation falling from about 100 per cent in 1980–81[14] to around 30 per cent in 1982–83. (See Table 3.3.)

On the surface, therefore, the IMF programme appeared to be very successful but, by mid-1984, it had collapsed and the economy once again fell into deep crisis. Those sympathetic to the Fund would tend to argue that the collapse was not due to any weaknesses inherent in the programme but due, rather, to the deteriorating political situation in Uganda which led, eventually to the removal of

TABLE 3.3   *Ugandan Economic Indicators 1971–86*

	1971	1979	1981	1983	1984	1985	1986
Real GDP (monetary economy)	100.00	74	73	84	87	76	85
Real GDP per capita (monetary economy)	100.00	60	56	61	62	53	57
Inflation rate % p.a. (New Series 1981)	14.9	216.0	67.7	26.0	16.0	158.0	153.0
Budget deficit (Govt borrowing from banking system) as % GDP	0	-1.8	-2.1	-2.6	0.4	-4.2	-1.9
Balance of payments—current a/c deficit (-)$m	13.4	-141.5	-255.9	-157.4	-42.4	-39.6	30.2
External debt $USm	240	547	584	661	n.a	n.a.	1850
External debt servicing % exports	9.2	12.7	39.8	23.7	40.6	46.2	53.3
Net external reserves $m	64.8	16.8	17.2	129.9	95.0	63.0	64.0
Payments arrears $m	18.7	100.3	217.1	183.0	120.0	55.0	74.0
Real import volume	100.0	34.3	29.7	27.4	26.3	24.7	20.7
Coffee producer price sh per kilo (Robusta)	1.19	7.0	35	80	210	485	850
Real coffee producer price (index 1972 = 100)	97	20	48	72	133	115	80
Coffee exports (000 tonnes)	174.6	143.5	128.3	144.3	133.2	155.0	160.1
Minimum wage index-real terms	100	6.0	8.0	n.a.	15.0	n.a.	n.a.

SOURCE: World Bank and author's calculations.

the UPC/Obote II government by a military coup. There were, however, several aspects of the IMF programme that might have led to its unravelling, whatever the political situation and others which undoubtedly contributed to the political instability of the country. Furthermore, there are conflicting views in Uganda about the role played by the Fund programme in the recovery of the economy in 1982–84. These factors assumed importance in the initial reluctance of the NRM government to undertake policy measures demanded by the IMF and continue to shape the NRM's dealings with the Fund and the World Bank now that a new programme is in place.

To begin with, the 1981–84 programme was very hard on the urban working class or what remained of it after the ravages of the Amin and immediate post-Amin years. Massive increases in producer prices, well in excess of the resulting increases in production, implied huge shifts in the distribution of income. While some of these shifts might have taken the form of reduced rents to black marketeers and speculators, opponents of the UPC charge that racketeering and speculation continued to be rampant in these years. There are accusations of the foreign exchange auction being dominated by four or five large traders who could afford access to expensive and restricted bank credits for 'local cover'. Merchants are accused of making huge profits on lags between paying for imports and selling them on the local market during which time exchange rates had depreciated and local prices risen significantly. It is argued that speculation on the auction price of foreign exchange was widespread since the amount of foreign exchange available fluctuated greatly from week to week. Thus, the merchant class may simply have altered the form of its rents rather than their total. In addition, the monopolistic banking system made significant profits on foreign exchange transactions. Furthermore, while the market ostensibly had more influence during this period, most local companies could function only with the aid of the state apparatus for which bureaucrats demanded unofficial remuneration. Each of these redistribution mechanisms limited the impact of the market in reducing former levels of rents and helped push the burden of adjustment on the urban wage and salary earners.[15]

Apart from an early modest adjustment to the wages and salaries of state sector employees, the programme did not explicitly address the needs of the urban wage and salary earner whose real incomes fell steadily, yet again, from 1981–84.[16] Growing urban sector and military dissatisfaction over the erosion of living standards led the beleaguered UPC government to introduce a six-fold salary increase in 1984 on the heels of a major increase in coffee producer prices designed to buy the political loyalty of the coffee producing areas. The result was that the fiscal deficit and money supply growth ballooned, greatly exceeding IMF targets, by as much 17 times. These salary increases also increased the demand for imports at a time when foreign exchange was already scarce due to increased military expenditures and the alleged diversion for personal use of significant amounts of export proceeds by politicians, senior bureaucrats and military officers. As a result the auction system was abandoned and the IMF cancelled its agreement. In retrospect, the distributional implications of the programme seem to have been quite unmanageable and absolutely no provision was made for improving urban and public sector real income or productivity over the medium term. The sharp increase in inflation in 1984–85, to over 150 per cent per annum, reflects, in part, this weakness as urban groups reasserted their influence at the inevitable expense of real incomes of peasant export crop producers.

Another major shortcoming in the IMF programme was that it failed to lead to sustained recovery of the manufacturing sector. There are a number of factors explaining this but some of them, at least, point to contradictory and inadequate policies contained within the programme itself. For instance, high rates of exchange depreciation combined with tight domestic credit ceilings, led to many factories being denied the local cover they required to finance essential imports. Secondly, contrary to the advice of the 1979 Commonwealth Team of Experts, depreciation of the shilling was also accompanied by the virtual abolition of import rationing to key sectors of the economy. As a result, 40–60 per cent of imports under the auction system took the form of consumer goods,[17] both unnecessary luxury consumer goods and more basic ones which could be produced locally. Meanwhile, capacity utilisation of local industries averaged only 22 per cent. The auction system and import liberalisation deprived industry of raw materials, spare parts and machinery while permitting state functionaries and the merchant class not only to reap profits on imported consumer goods but also to export their capital gains. Not surprisingly, some Ugandans argue that IMF conditionality promoted deindustrialisation.[18] It is to be noted that the World Bank's reconstruction credits to Uganda during this time did not suffer from this weakness as they were carefully earmarked for priority imports.

Other impediments to industrial recovery, such as ambiguity over ownership of factories and shortages of managers and skilled technicians, cannot be laid at the IMF's door and it is difficult to say how significant these were relative to the programmatic weaknesses described above.

The external financing provisions of the IMF agreement also left much to be desired. In spite of large inflows of official aid and loans, the recovery programme relied heavily on expensive, short term IMF credits. By 1984, net flows of IMF assistance had become negative. There was, therefore, no provision for sustaining the real value of imports which fell steadily after the first year of the programme and sharply in 1984.

On the fiscal side, the programme underemphasised tax administration so that revenue collection was less than anticipated and reliance on coffee export duties greater than planned. Expenditure ceilings failed to take into account the fact that Uganda's state expenditures per head of the population had fallen to among the lowest in the world, with serious implications for the supply of basic social services. Moreover, these ceilings were untenable given the income distribution problems outlined earlier and the precarious political base of the ruling party. As the government met political opposition with a scale of military repression unprecedented in Uganda, making even Idi Amin's butchery pale by comparison, military expenditures skyrocketed. This state of affairs continued to be the case after the overthrow of the Obote II government.

Aside from these weaknesses in the concept and design of the IMF programme, there are legitimate questions to be raised about the relative weights to be assigned to different aspects of the programme in explaining the recovery which did take place in the official economy in 1981–84. For instance, how much of the increase in recorded output was due to exchange rate/producer pricing policies and how much to increased availability of foreign exchange which, in turn, improved transportation and peasant access to incentive goods? What role did the short-lived return to relative peace and security play in raising recorded production? What proportion of the recorded increase in production was a genuine increase in output and what proportion simply a transfer from the unofficial, unrecorded market to official, recorded, marketing channels? As we shall see, different answers to these questions, made possible by the lack of data on which to establish an unambiguous position on the issues, were to be crucial in the debates about policy formulation in the early years of the NRM government.

Economic Policy under the NRM Government

Eighteen months after the collapse of the IMF agreement, and after a military coup, further repression and economic chaos, the National Resistance Army marched triumphantly into Kampala (January, 1986). Their victory happened quickly. The army was a highly disciplined but very small guerilla force, about 10 000 strong, and though representing many tribes and regions of Uganda, was dominated for the first time in Uganda's history by the southern tribes. It included significant numbers of Baganda, many of them young orphans whose parents had been killed by previous regimes.

The political arm of the NRA, the National Resistance Movement, rapidly established a government of national reconciliation, the main platform of which was peace and security, national unity, honesty, political accountability, defending human and democratic rights, and economic reconstruction. The economic tasks facing it were daunting. Production was at a very low level, the transport system, after further warfare and looting, was in disarray, inflation was running at over 150 per cent per annum, the budget was completely out of control, there was little foreign exchange available, corruption and black marketeering were widespread, skilled personnel had left the country in droves and the social infrastructure had all but collapsed. Whole regions of the country in the fertile Luwero triangle, Mahdi and West Nile had been cleared of people and the physical and economic infrastructure devastated. The magnitude of the problems was simply staggering and the speed of the NRA victory meant that the NRM was totally unprepared in terms of a clearly spelled out programme of economic reform. Its long term programme, though, was quite unambiguous, emphasising 'an independent, integrated and self-sustaining national economy' [19] This would entail integrating agriculture and industry more systematically, diversifying production in both sectors, expanding import substitution, establishing basic industries, including machine tools, and building an independent research and technological development capacity.[20] The question was, how best to move in the short-term from a situation of economic chaos towards these long term goals.

There is no question that the NRA/NRM enjoyed widespread popularity when they assumed power. The population in general were tired of the violence, the arbitrariness and the insecurity which had characterised most of the previous fifteen years or more. They welcomed the discipline of the NRA, its honesty and civility and for the first time in years people felt able to move around freely after dark in most areas of the country. In spite of this, however, the NRM had a very fragile base of political support and relatively few cadres who could assume positions of responsibility throughout the economy. In consequence, and also in furtherance of the NRM's policy of national unity and national reconciliation, the movement drew heavily on personnel with former loyalties to the Democratic Party (DP) and the Uganda People's Congress (UPC).

The DP was the main opposition party to the UPC and was comprised largely of Baganda and Busoga members, many of whom were Catholic. The dominant social groups in the DP were traditionalist landlords and more recently, aspiring small-scale capitalists, and their economic programme was one of market oriented free enterprise. The essentially northern, Protestant based UPC which, in its first term of office had promoted petty bourgeois African interests through use of the state machinery to nationalise non-African owned ventures had, in its second-coming, adopted an economic programme quite similar to that of the DP. Mamdani's explanation for this switch is that Obote's political orientation changed from a contradictory one involving both anti-imperialism and anti-democracy to one in which he united with imperialism to fight the people.[21] One could argue, however, that this is a mere description, and a highly personalised one at that. A more plausible explanation is that the Obote II regime inherited a massive state sector and a pool of former Asian-owned assets, both of which offered the *prospect* of accumulation. IMF policies were necessary to attract the foreign exchange required to *realise* that potential. There was, therefore, no contradiction between state-assisted accumulation for the UPC petty-bourgeoisie and the pursuit of market oriented IMF policies.

After the overthrow of Obote II the DP had accepted participation in the Lutwa government which was at war with the NRA. Many of the senior personnel inherited by the NRM therefore, had preconceived views of appropriate economic policy and had served governments which had been discredited.

These elements were able to influence the NRM's economic policy in mid-1986 in the drawing up of the Interim Economic Measures, but the narrow and contradictory nature of this initiative indicates that the government, while unsure of which direction to take, was not altogether comfortable with the advice it was receiving. These measures introduced a dual exchange rate arrangement under which traditional exports, essential imports and debt servicing would be converted at an official rate of sh1200 to the US$, while, other transactions would exchange at a 'market' rate of sh5000. Producer prices and interest rates were raised significantly. Provision was made for selling of unclaimed Asian property to Ugandans and for establishing a committee to advise on the privatisation of some parastatals. Government spending was to be curtailed and more tightly controlled and a currency conversion was promised for the future.

The Interim Economic Measures were far from being adequate to deal with the economic crisis facing the country. They ignored entirely government tax revenue, immediate foreign exchange requirements, the rehabilitation needs of the major sectors of the economy and the issue of the pricing of consumer goods.[22]

What is more, the package further destabilised the budget by granting large price increases to farmers while converting the export proceeds of their production at the overvalued official rate of exchange. In addition, an imbalance was created between sales and purchases at the two rates so that more purchases took place at sh5000 to the US$ than did sales; the resulting losses on exchange adding further pressure on the deficit. The package was not, therefore, internally consistent and could not be sustained.

At this point the government invited a joint international/Ugandan team, sponsored by the International Development Research Centre, to recommend on the best course on economic policy given the NRM's long term objectives. In the process of this exercise it became apparent that even within the NRM there were quite conflicting views on how best to proceed which is not surprising given the complexity of the problems, the eclectic fragile base of the Movement and, the relative lack of expertise on economic matters.

At the other extreme from the UPC/DP policy spectrum were members of the NRM who advocated the use of direct controls to revive the economy. They saw the principal obstacles to recovery as supply bottlenecks in the form of inadequate transportation and the lack of incentive goods. They felt also that lawlessness, insecurity, corruption and black marketeering played an important role in reducing official transactions. If scarce resources were allocated sensibly to bottleneck areas of the economy, and if law and order were revived, production would increase and the unofficial market would be stamped out. Price incentives to farmers, in the form of a 'reasonable' proportion of the world price, at a given exchange rate, could be achieved by reducing corruption and marketing board incompetence. Devaluation and accompanying large increases in produce prices, it was argued, would simply generate further inflation necessitating a never-ending spiral of devaluation – price increases – devaluation, without the real effective exchange rate ever depreciating for any length of time. The only way to beat inflation was through a combination of supply expansion and, in the interim, price controls administered either centrally or through village and neighbourhood resistance committees. Exchange rate changes could play an anti-inflationary role but only through exchange *appreciations* which, it was argued would reduce the domestic currency costs of imports.

The inspiration for this 'control scenario' came apparently from two quite different political sources. On the one hand, and more importantly, it was informed by the dependency theory critique of IMF approaches to stabilisation and in particular, by the debates in Tanzania in the early 1980s. Indeed, it carried these debates to their logical conclusion in terms of the exchange rate by advocating *revaluation* as opposed to *devaluation*, a logic which the Tanzanian proponents of 'control' had always resisted. At the root of this position is a fear that the market-private sector oriented policies of the IMF would impede socialist and/or nationalist development strategies and a belief that the state in Africa is able to exercise extensive control over the economy in an efficient and democratic manner.

The other source of inspiration for this approach appears to have been a feudal/militaristic one. It originates in a belief that peasants do not react rationally to monetary incentives, that they can be forced to produce and market their crops once the crops are in the ground, whatever the producer price, and that attempts to avoid official marketing channels can be stamped out by police or military action. Feudal elements are still a force in Uganda and the broad alliances formed by the NRM allowed them a voice which, on this issue, happened to coincide in part at least with the more progressively inclined elements advocating greater use of direct controls.

It was this point of view which, despite strong opposition from the majority of the Uganda Study Team, prevailed in mid-1986 and it found expression in a unification of the exchange rate at the lower, official rate of exchange of sh1400 to the dollar. Since this rate was the same as that of a year earlier, in spite of the massive inflation, it was greatly overvalued. The consequences were exactly as predicted by the Study Team. The budget remained in serious deficit as export duties were eroded and money supply expanded at an alarming rate.

Producer prices fell in real terms as did official exports. The balance of payments moved into a crisis situation. With reserves dwindling and debt servicing falling into even greater arrears, donors were not prepared to support this programme with balance of payments assistance. The black market blossomed as the state was quite unable to keep it in check, inflation rose to over 200 per cent per annum and the parallel market exchange rate rose to several times the official one.

To the credit of the NRM it realised even before the end of 1986 that these policies were untenable and that a major change in direction was needed. By early 1987 it had agreed on a new policy package and started negotiations with the IMF and the World Bank for external assistance. It turned to the Fund only with great reluctance because Fund programmes were identified in the public eye with support for the brutally repressive UPC government and because it had genuine differences of opinion about the design and efficacy of IMF programmes.

The Economic Policy Package for Reconstruction and Development[23] followed much more closely the majority recommendations of the Uganda Study Team and sought to rehabilitate the economy with a combination of demand management and supply stimulation measures. It provided for a reform of the currency at a rate of one new Uganda shilling for 100 old ones. A conversion tax of 30 per cent across the board was also imposed on currency holdings, time and savings deposits and on treasury bills and government stock held by the public. One half of the anticipated sh250 billion net receipts from this tax (after conversion expenses) was used to retire public debt, which then fell by 36 per cent, while the other financed a Special Development Fund for priority infrastructural expenses. Tight monetary and fiscal policies were to reinforce these anti-inflationary initiatives.

On the supply stimulation side, the package was designed to attract very large foreign exchange inflows and was successful in doing so. The IMF provided an immediate $24 million under the Structural Adjustment Facility with an additional $32 million expected from this source over the next two years. A further $20 million was provided under the IMF Compensatory Financing Facility. The World Bank has agreed to a $100 million Economic Recovery Credit and a Consultative Group Meeting gave rise to commitments from bilateral donors of $160 million. On top of this, debt relief on a third of Uganda's outstanding foreign debt of $1.8 billion or so is expected which should immediately reduce debt servicing commitments from 50 to 33 per cent of exports. It appears, therefore, that the government has been successful in raising the $300 million it estimated it needed. to achieve industrial and agricultural rehabilitation in 1987–88.[24] Furthermore, government targets for increased imports in 1987–91 of between 40 to 70 per cent in dollar terms above their 1983–87 levels seem realisable. After 1991 repayments of the 1981–84 IMF credits will cease, enabling more breathing space in the balance of payments and overall debt servicing is anticipated to fall to no more than 16 per cent of exports by 1990.

The key to this foreign exchange inflow, which is expected to permit real GDP to grow at 5 per cent per annum in the foreseeable future, was the government's agreement to IMF/IBRD proposals on exchange rates and producer/consumer prices. In May 1987 a major devaluation of the shilling took place from sh1400 to sh6000 (in old currency units) per dollar. Producer prices were raised between three and five times and the prices of essential imports such as petroleum, salt and sugar were increased dramatically.

Though very similar in many respects to the 1981–84 IMF programme, the current one is considered by the NRM to be superior in a number of ways. To begin with, the terms of the IMF assistance are much easier. The loans are long term, repayable after five and a half years within ten years and carry only half per cent per annum interest. Almost all the balance of payments support commitments received are on even more concessional terms, so that the programme itself will not give rise, in the medium term, to the kind of debt servicing pressures experienced since 1984.

Secondly, the government has taken steps to ensure that the recovery will be more balanced than that of 1981–84. It has insisted on the direct allocation of foreign exchange to sectors most in need and will ensure, therefore, that the industrial sector and especially enterprises producing basic consumer goods and construction materials, receives sufficient resources to permit its revitalisation. A detailed listing of foreign exchange requirements by sector and industry has been drawn up. The auction system, which permitted misallocation of resources, has not been restored. Apparently, the government has agreed, however, that over the next three years, it will move gradually, as resources permit, to an open general license system for imports. By that time it is anticipated that industrial activity will have been restored to reasonable levels.

Steps are also being taken to ensure that industrial recovery is not frustrated by the difficulty of obtaining local credit for import needs. Revaluing company assets, clarifying ownership of factories and, where appropriate, divesting of enterprises to the private sector should help, but in addition, a foreign-financed revolving credit fund will be established, specifically to address the problem of local cover.

Budgetary weaknesses in the 1981–84 programme are being addressed by reducing sinecure and unproductive appointments in the civil service. To this end, a census of government employees was conducted in mid 1987. The tax system will be reformed to reduce dependence on coffee duty, to improve tax administration and collection, and to rationalise the tariff structure. Control over government spending will also be improved and subsidies to inefficient parastatals will be cut drastically. The relative size of the deficit will be reduced but, in recognition of the fact that Uganda's budget is among the smallest in the world as a percentage of GDP, the relative size of revenues will more than double from 4 per cent of GDP in 1986–87 to 9.2 per cent by 1989–90. This will enable a gradual improvement in the real salaries of the remaining public sector employees and a considerable strengthening of the basic needs services provided by the government. It will also facilitate restoration of the development budget from 4.7 per cent of GDP in 1986–87 to between 8 and 9 per cent, in accordance with a four year Rehabilitation and Development Plan issued in May 1987 as part of the reform package. The Plan lists priority projects for economic recovery and their sources of financing with external financing slated to account for 84 per cent of the total.[25]

Some progress towards strengthening and stabilising the fiscal base was made in the July 1987 budget. Equipment and facilities for tax collection were improved and monetary incentives introduced for tax collectors. The tax investigation function was reintroduced and steps taken to improve the quality of taxation staff and to appoint a Committee to review the whole taxation system.[26] The scope of income tax was widened to include some enterprises and individuals (including members of the Cabinet and of the National Resistance Council) not previously covered; customs duty on gasoline and diesel was raised as was excise duty and sales tax on beer and cigarettes and sales tax on soft drinks. A road user tax was also introduced.

The government moved quickly to raise civil servants' salaries, by 100 per cent in May and a further 50 per cent in the July budget.

Special allowances were paid to university professors and doctors and provision was made for transporting civil servants to and from work. The 1987 budget also provided for expenditure on trucks the object of which would be, specifically, to reduce urban food prices. Subsidies were introduced (or retained) on school fees and rates of sales tax, excise tax and customs duty on a wide range of basic necessities were reduced, while those on crucial intermediate or capital goods were abolished. Interest rates were also slashed to encourage investment. These measures were, apparently very popular with the public at large.[27]

Preliminary Assessment of the 1987 Reform Package

While it is far too early to say definitively how well the recent reform package will help meet the objectives of the NRM government, a number of preliminary observations are in order.

To begin with, it should be apparent that there is no necessary contradiction between the short term programme and the long term objectives of the NRM. The overwhelming requirement at this stage is one of economic recovery and rehabilitation, for without this there can be no progress towards self-reliance and national integration. True, the immediate impact of the programme will be to boost official coffee sales and the output of other export crops; but this is the logical source of surplus for future accumulation. At the same time, the 1987–91 investment plans of the government provide for strengthening food security, integrating rural development, raising agricultural production for industrial use, diversifying the export base and rehabilitating the industrial, mining and service sectors. Clearly, each of these would move the economy closer, in structural terms, to realising the NRM's long term goals.

Resort to even more foreign borrowing may also be questionable in terms of the NRM's long-run goals but the experience of the first year in power demonstrates that economic recovery *without* additional inflows of foreign exchange would be a long and painful process. Acute shortages of imported goods impeded both production and transport while large payments arrears undoubtedly gave rise to import surcharges. The current programme breaks the immediate import bottleneck, allows a large inflow of grant or concessional loan money, reduces the debt servicing burden, disposes of arrears and does not significantly increase the total debt of the country. While the NRM is seeking to diversify the sources of external assistance, an agreement with the IMF/IBRD was the only plausible way of unlocking the quantity of external resources required and of putting debt servicing on to a realistic and manageable footing. Any immediate move to de-link the economy would have worsened rather than weakened the balance of payment constraint on the recovery, and was not a realistic or a desired option.

The current programme is not without its dangers, however. The movement to an open general licensing system for imports must proceed cautiously so that local production is not replaced by imports where this is not warranted on *long term* economic grounds. The government must also ensure that sufficient resources, in terms of investment funds, foreign exchange and skilled personnel, are actually made available for projects which further its long term objectives. The danger with the investment plan is that it is so highly dependent on foreign donors that external interests could effectively shape the pace and pattern of accumulation in Uganda. This is not as important in the early stages of the plan, where the emphasis must be overwhelmingly on rehabilitation, as it might be later when incremental investments will present a clearer choice between the promotion of traditional primary exports and the realisation of economic integration and diversification goals; but this choice is a relevant one even at this stage and some balance must be ensured, until locally generated surplus and foreign exchange earnings are sufficient to reduce reliance on external assistance.

The distributional implications of the programme warrant closer scrutiny. Anticipated growth rates will permit a steady 2 per cent per annum or more, increase in per capita incomes and even with anticipated increases in the rate of investment, a 1 per cent per annum or more increase in per capita consumption. These goals are realisable and, if anything, the anticipated growth rates are very conservative given the base from which recovery will commence. The issue is really one of who will reap these benefits.

Given the steady decline in urban wage and salary income in past years there is little scope here for further cutbacks. Indeed, recovering urban productivity requires wage and salary increases at this point, and reducing unproductive public sector employment is one of the few methods available to achieve this. The government should, however, be prepared to put those laid-off workers to productive employment through public works projects if they are not absorbed in agriculture and other sectors. The very large increases in producer prices will only transfer real purchasing power to the rural sector, therefore, pending output increases, at the expense of some other, non-wage/salary section of society. In Uganda, this can only be the merchant class, and the black marketeers and racketeers. The coming to power of the NRM has undoubtedly reduced the possibility of using one's position in the government, parastatal sector or army to amass the vast fortunes that were appropriated in the recent past. If such large scale corruption can continue to be contained, this will assist in transferring income to the rural areas. Closing the gap between the official and the black market exchange rate will also reduce unofficial and/or illegal rents. Increasing the availability of transport and reducing parastatal inefficiency, both targets in the reform programme, will also enable real income transfers to farmers to increase by reducing cost margins.

There is some concern that promised foreign exchange inflows may be slow in coming and, therefore, in having an impact on resource availability. The Uganda programme is heavily front-end loaded in terms of large price increases but without prompt exchange inflows price-induced production responses may be frustrated. This lack of synchronisation, in the context of huge price increases, may lead to a resurgence of inflation and the failure to meet income redistribution objectives. The initial impact of the programme was to reduce the rate of inflation significantly thanks largely to the currency conversion tax, but continued control over inflation will require rapid inflows of foreign exchange.

Targets for increasing own-export earnings do not seem overly ambitious. Dependence on coffee is always problematic but coffee prices were falling in 1986 and assumptions about both quantity growth (5 per cent pa increase in exports) and price movement (minus 4 per cent 1987/88, plus 4 per cent for the balance of the programme) appear reasonable. Non-coffee export earnings are expected to grow more quickly, but obviously from a much lower base, so that overall dollar export growth is anticipated to reach 10 per cent pa which, again, seems realizable. Once more, it must be emphasised that growth of production for export will depend upon the government being successful in maintaining its short-run income redistribution objectives.

The programme is likely to have important distributional implications, and accompanying political ramifications, in other respects too. There is likely to be some expansion of small-scale private capitalism in the near future as the government reduces the parastatal sector to more manageable proportions and resolves the issue of the ownership of former Asian property. Neither of these two moves was imposed on the NRM which has always been committed on pragmatic grounds to a mixed economy. The question arises, however, of which group in society will take over this property. At the current time many owners of capital in Uganda owe their wealth to the property redistribution by past corrupt governments and a large proportion are said to be former supporters of Obote or Okello. Is the NRM to strengthen the hand of these groups simply because they are the ones with sufficient wealth to be able to afford the purchase price? Or, will the aspiring Buganda capitalist class of the DP be the beneficiary? Clearly, this is an issue of some importance to a movement which, as yet, has a very weak political base.

The NRM could seek to strengthen its base, as past governments have done, by transferring property to its own supporters. If it chose to do so, the nature of the recipient group would be indicative of the type of political direction the movement will follow in future. It could create its own group of state supported capitalists or it could transfer assets to groups of workers or tenants to be operated on a co-operative basis. The former would be consistent with past practice; the latter with the NRM's initiatives in establishing democratically based resistance committees in villages and work places. As yet there is no indication of how redistribution will be handled and no sign that property assigned by past governments will be re-assigned.

It is in the northern parts of the country that support for the government is weakest and where, in spite of initial overtures of peace and forgiveness by the NRM, military opposition continues. Pressure from this quarter continues to strain the budget and the Minister of Finance readily admits that the largest share of both recurrent *and* development expenditure in 1987–88 is accounted for by defence.[28] Control over defence spending, and hence speedy resolution of the conflict in the North, is crucial if the recovery programme is to be implemented smoothly and if NRM plans for salary increases and recovery of basic needs and infrastructural expenditures are to proceed as planned.

CONCLUSION

Given the severity of the problems facing Uganda, the NRM government had little option but to introduce far-reaching reforms and to seek foreign capital to support them. The programme adopted seeks to avoid the weaknesses of the 1981–84 approach and, if aid flows can be received and accommodated quickly, should prove constructive in rehabilitating the economy and in allowing the NRM leeway to gradually shift resources in support of a strategy of integration and self-reliance. Adjustment will, however, take time and will require that the government control those elements profiting from the past economic chaos. If the NRM tries to move too fast to satisfy all the various competing claims for resources, or if it fails to shift income away from the merchant class and racketeers the programme may come unravelled through the budget and/or through a resurgence of inflation. Likewise, military expenditures must be curtailed as soon as the northern situation permits. Above all, the Movement must begin to consolidate its political base, in a situation in which support for the two major parties is still strong, if it is to sustain reform. How it begins to do this and, in particular, how it handles the issue of property ownership, will determine the future path of economic reform and, especially, its impact on income and wealth distribution.

Notes

1. See Ricardo Parboni, *The Dollar and its Rivals* (London: Verso, 1981) and John Loxley, *Debt and Disorder: External Financing for Development* (Boulder, Colorado: Westview/Ottawa: North-South Institute, 1986).
2. See for example, Cheryl Payer, 'The Bretton Woods Twins', *Counterspy* (September–November 1982).
3. National Resistance Movement, *Ten Point Programme of NRM* (Kampala, Uganda: NRM Publications, 1985).
4. Quoted in *South* (October 1986) p. 51.
5. For details, see Jan Jelmert Jorgensen, 'The Crisis of the State Sector in Uganda, 1972–1978' (1979) mimeo.
6. See, Mahmood Mamdani, 'Background to January 25, 1986', paper read to Review of African Political Economy/Centre of African Studies Conference on 'Popular Struggles in Africa', Liverpool, England (September 1986).
7. World Bank, *Uganda: Country Economic Memorandum* (Washington, DC: 31 March 1982) p. 11, from which most figures in this section are drawn.
8. Commonwealth Secretariat, *The Rehabilitation of the Economy of Uganda*, a report by a Commonwealth team of experts, vol. 1 (London: 1979) p. 3.
9. World Bank (1982) p. 148.

10. Ibid. p. 11.
11. See note 8. The Report consists of two volumes.
12. See, Kathy L. Krumm, 'Exchange Auctions: A Review of Experiences', Country Programs Department Discussion Paper, (Washington, DC: IBRD, July 1985) no. 1985 – 22.
13. See World Bank, *Uganda: Progress Towards Recovery and Prospects for Development* (Washington, DC: June 1985) p. 149.
14. World Bank op. cit. (1982) p. 21.
15. 'A Critique of the IMF Programme in Uganda 1980–84' *Forward* vol. 7 (Kampala, Uganda: October 1985) nos. 2 and 3, pp. 4–12.
16. For an excellent discussion of rural/urban income differentials see Vali Jamal, 'Structural Adjustment and Food Security in Uganda', World Employment Programme Research Working Paper, WEP 10–6/WP 73 (Geneva: International Labour Office, October 1985).
17. Uganda Economic Study Team, *Economic Adjustment and Long Term Development in Uganda* Government of Uganda/International Development Research Centre (IDRC) (Ottawa: July 1986).
18. Op. cit. *Forward*.
19. National Resistance Movement, op. cit. (1985) p. 14.
20. Ibid. pp. 18–19.
21. See Mamdani, op. cit. (1986) pp. 5–6.
22. See Uganda Economic Study Team, op. cit. (1986) p. 49.
23. See President Yoweri K. Museveni, *An Address to the Nation on Uganda's Economic Policy Package for Reconstruction and Development* (Entebbe, Uganda: Government Printer, 15 May 1987).
24. Ibid. p. 6.
25. Ministry of Planning and Economic Development, *Rehabilitation and Development Plan 1987/88–1990/91*, vols I and II, (Kampala, Uganda: March 1987).
26. Hon. Dr C.W.C.B. Kiyonga, Minister of Finance, *Budget Speech* (Kampala, Uganda: 24 July 1987).
27. *Financial Times* 27 July 1987.
28. Kiyonga, op. cit. (1987) p. 11.

4 From 'Revolution' to Monetarism: The Economics and Politics of the Adjustment Programme in Ghana

EBOE HUTCHFUL

THE 1981 COUP AND THE ORIGINS OF THE IMF/WORLD BANK ADJUSTMENT PROGRAMME

The Rawlings coup that overthrew the Liman government in Ghana on 31 December 1981 was in several senses unique. It gave rise to a spectacular experiment in 'people's power' and a level of spontaneous mass mobilisation not seen since the early days of the independence struggle. Throughout the country 'defence committees' and other organs of 'popular power' sprang up. Students closed down schools in order to bring in the cocoa crop, artisans and mechanics salvaged abandoned and broken down vehicles and machinery, working people and unemployed, supported by patriotic soldiers and police, attacked 'kalabule' (profiteering) and formed price-control and anti-hoarding committees. Even more important the coup gave rise to a strong but unorganised syndicalist tendency among the Workers' Defence Committees. A number of state-owned factories were taken over, management was expelled, and 'interim management committees' of workers installed. These 'factory revolutions' culminated in the celebrated takeover of the Ghana Textile Printing (GTP), a joint-venture between the State and the United Africa Company, during 1982. In May that year the Provisional National Defence Council (PNDC) which had taken power after the coup, declared a 'National Democratic Revolution', the objectives of which were anti-imperialist struggle and the struggle for democracy on the basis of a broad progressive front.

How then did this revolutionary regime[1] become the vehicle of the most rigorously enforced IMF/World Bank adjustment programme in

Africa? This question must be answered before proceeding to an assessment of the current adjustment programme in Ghana, and to do so it is necessary to recall several key characteristics of the 1981 coup and its aftermath as well as the processes that produced the agreement with the IMF.

Firstly, 1981 was a coup (and a narrowly based one at that) that attempted to grow into a revolution.[2] Secondly, although the debilitation of state and economy that produced the coup was well advanced, it did not provoke a corresponding revolutionary consciousness or organisation – although it did effect the alienation of virtually every significant social sector. Ideologically and organisationally the political opposition, though popular and widespread, was heterogeneous, fragmented and predominantly urban, ranging in content and outlook from right-wing lawyers, professionals and clergy to nationalists and student and academic Marxists. Thirdly, and derived very much from this, one must insist on the complicated, multicentred character of the PNDC itself and its base(s). The PNDC did not possess a specific organisation, but was backed by a loose and spontaneous alliance of various left, workers, popular and soldiers groups, each of which retained a high degree of autonomy both from the PNDC and from each other and were linked tenuously through the person of Rawlings. In turn, each of these constituent groups tended (like the PNDC itself) to be further factionalised into opposing tendencies and interests. This unstable conjuncture of forces made it possible for Rawlings, with the backing of the majority of the other ranks, to hold the balance of power.

Finally, and most immediately important, this 'revolution' did not possess a concrete programme. Indeed its original socio-political objectives were quite vague, clearly intending to go beyond the previous 'accountability coup' of 1979 but, without ideology, programme, cadres or organisation, uncertain as to what route to take. The self-characterisation of the PNDC, in contradistinction with the left and the politicians, as 'simple Ghanaians dedicated to the salvation of the nation', must thus be accorded some credence.[3] Nevertheless both the PNDC and its supporters underwent a perceptible process of radicalisation in the first weeks after the coup. Much of this radicalisation however occurred *outside* the PNDC, without its sanction, and in several respects contrary to its wishes or those of key members. But in the furore and agitation of 1982 and early 1983 it was frequently difficult, if not impossible, to discern the true position of the PNDC with any certainty.

To this complicated political picture must be added the very limited options imposed on the PNDC by the state of the economy. Between 1975 and 1981 the Ghana economy entered a period of profound crisis. To an extent this reflected sudden adverse developments outside the immediate control of Ghanaian governments. Rain failures and drought after 1976 affected agricultural production at a time of substantial government commitment to and investment in food production. The rise in petroleum import costs badly affected overall import capacity; petroleum imports rose in value from 6.7 per cent of total export earnings in 1973 to almost 50 per cent of export earnings in 1981. In addition to this, generalised inflation on the world market led to severe import compressions. On the other hand the international climate for Ghana's main exports were on the whole much more favourable than in any period since the early fifties. Yet this coincided with a precipitous and continuing decline in Ghana's entire export structure. Cocoa exports fell from 397 300 metric tonnes in 1975 to 246 500 metric tonnes in 1981. Ghana's share of total world production dropped correspondingly from 24.4 per cent in 1974–75 to 15.4 per cent in 1980–81. Similar declines, of between 30 and 60 per cent, occurred for mineral and timber exports. It is noteworthy that lower export volumes were more than offset by higher export prices so that total export earnings actually rose. Nevertheless, current account deficits increased from C(cedis) 70 million in 1976 to c419 million in 1981 due at least partly to higher energy import costs.

This shrinkage in the export sector was only one aspect of a more comprehensive economic decline which also affected the domestic sectors. The local manufacturing index fell drastically, from 100 in 1977 to 69.0 in 1980 and 63.3 in 1981. Average capacity utilisation was estimated at only 24 per cent in 1981. The production of cereals and other agricultural staples also dropped sharply; between 1974 and 1982 the maize crop fell by 54 per cent, rice by 80 per cent, cassava by 50 per cent and yam by 55 per cent.

As alarming were the directions taken by state finances. Total public expenditures rose by 615 per cent in current terms between fiscal 1975–76 and 1981–82, while revenues appreciated by only 56 per cent. The total deficit rose by 690 per cent. This fiscal expansion occurred exclusively in the recurrent budget, with capital expenditures as a proportion of the budget shrinking from 35 per cent to 10 per cent. The state deficits were covered by heavy borrowing from the central bank with the result that money supply (money in circulation as well as demand deposits held by the banks) expanded by 933 per cent between 1975 and 1981. High levels of tax evasion – an indication of the increasing dominance of informal and parallel market transactions – and low tax effort on the part of governments intensified this fiscal crisis.

These developments raised serious questions about the domestic management of Ghana's economy. A number of general factors were responsible for this decline. Breakdown of the entire public infrastructure and transport sector interrupted haulage to the ports; an overvalued exchange rate lowered domestic prices to cocoa producers and other exporters, encouraging smuggling and deterioration of productive assets; balance of payments problems led to shortages of producer inputs and spare parts, and so on. To these must be added factors specific to particular sectors. In the case of cocoa, declining real producer prices and drastic changes in income relativities between cocoa and other crops encouraged a shift out of cocoa cultivation; for instance the 1977 price of C30 per load (30 kg) was estimated to be less than a third of prevailing producer prices in the 1950s in real terms. This was aggravated by protracted delays in making payments to farmers. The gold mining industry suffered from exhaustion of richer ores, complicated by obsolete machinery, liquidity problems and indifferent management. In addition to similar problems, the logging industry was affected by a fragmentation of existing concessions that made exploitation uneconomic; in this case however, higher domestic prices led to diversion from official export markets to the local market.

These factors should, however, be seen as only the immediate causes in an economic situation the remote origins of which lay in the attempts initiated during the early 1960s to transform a colonial economy characterised by structural 'fragility' and excessively dependent on a particular pattern of foreign trade and investment. These measures were precipitated by the emergence of fiscal and balance of payments problems in the economy, related partly to declining export prices.[4] They involved: domestic economic diversification and integration through rapid import-substitution industrialisation; emphasis on state-led accumulation channeled through a variety of mechanisms (taxation of cocoa surplus and foreign trade, use of accumulated reserves, reliance on short- and medium-term foreign credits, and deficit financing); expansion of the parastatal sector as the leading economic sector and nationalisation of key economic sectors wherever possible; and development of social and economic infrastructures. These objectives were supported by restrictive trade and foreign exchange controls and a range of fiscal, monetary and other regulatory instruments.

Although these measures had fallen short of transforming or even 'closing' the colonial-type economy, they did effect important sectoral changes in Ghana's economy, evident particularly in the growth of the public and parastatal sector, the relatively advanced socio-economic infrastructure and the large semi-industrial base. Yet, the overall effect of these measures was to redefine, rather than transcend, the morphology of underdevelopment in Ghana. The serious planning and implementational errors associated with this attempt at structural change (such as neglect of food, agriculture and exports, inappropriate capital and import-intensive industrialisation; excessive emphasis on social welfare and infrastructural projects; dependence on high-cost suppliers' credits, and extensive corruption) actually eroded the capacity of the local economy for self-reliance and triggered the supply shortages and inflation which came to characterise the economy. The crisis that subsequently emerged in the economy in the mid-1960s and which was to be accentuated in later years, should be seen as involving at least three inter-related elements.

First, a *structural crisis* characterised by a perverse combination of high domestic demand on the one hand and severe industrial and agricultural recession on the other. Failure to satisfy essential consumption needs existed side by side with deepening agricultural stagnation and underexploitation and chronic industrial excess capacity. Responsible for this was a malintegrated structure in which domestic productive sectors could respond to growth in domestic demand only via the mechanisms of foreign trade – a situation already inherent in the colonial economy, but with the specific new development that the collapse of the balance of payments made it impossible for it to fulfill its traditional function of bridging the gap between domestic consumption and production structures.

This structural imbalance should also be seen in terms of acceleration of economic and demographic trends already evident under colonialism: for example, structurally generated unemployment and underemployment (of labour as well as resources) and relative shrinkage of the agricultural population, proceeding in tandem with the absolute expansion of urban marginal and informal activities (petty trade and production, services), and non-productive large-scale administrative and other social infrastructures.

Second, a *fiscal crisis* of the state, expressed in external and domestic debt, mounting budgetary deficits, and uncontrolled growth of the recurrent budget. Debt in turn, eroded national sovereignty and state policy autonomy.[5] The basis of this fiscal crisis lay in the inability of the Ghanaian state to reproduce its traditional sources of export and agrarian (cocoa) surplus, or alternatively to diversify or develop new sources of surplus through semi-industrialisation or fiscal claims on the citizenry. Indeed, state dependence on cocoa revenues (42 per cent of total state revenue in 1972, as opposed to 17 per cent in 1964) became most pronounced at the precise time that the physical basis of the industry was dwindling rapidly under the impact of policies that discriminated against agriculture and exports. At the same time the state, impelled by its social base and by the structural crisis, continually expanded its social and bureaucratic infrastructures and scope of regulation and intervention and hence its current expenditures. To finance this, the state resorted to systematic debasement of the national currency.

Thirdly, an over-determining *political crisis*, following the overthrow of Nkrumah in 1966, of state instability, debilitation and increasingly delegitimation, evidenced by frequent regime changes and even more frequent policy revisions, increasing loss of policy control and effectiveness, and of popular confidence and support. Popular disillusionment crystallised at evidence of manipulation of the state and economic crisis for private ends, enhancing the divorce between successive regimes and the mass of ordinary Ghanaians.

What essentially occurred between 1975 and 1981 was the intensification of these structural, fiscal and political developments of the 1960s. While these elements operated together and at various levels to consolidate the crisis, it is nevertheless worth emphasising that the economic crisis was at its roots a *structural* one, although fiscal policies and bureaucratic allocation over time exacerbated this by grossly restructuring incentives away from production and toward exchange and rent-generating activities. It is principally by reference to such policy factors that the rapid deterioration of the mid-1970s should be explained. Bureaucratic allocation and engineered shortages were used by 'kalabule' (profiteering) alliances of bureaucrats, parastatal officials and traders to reap monopoly rents. With the connivance of state officials large areas of economic activity were diverted to the parallel market, out of the control and tax reach of the state; smuggling rings used illicit channels to transport large quantities of Ghanaian cocoa across the borders of neighbouring countries. Under the impact of economic stress, widespread venality and rapid regime changes, the Ghanaian state simply withered. By 1978 the administrative and policy structures had virtually collapsed, owing to decay of the public infrastructures, large-scale departure (in many cases migration) of critical personnel, diversion of the energies of the remaining public servants to personal subsistence and informal activities, and general widespread demoralisation among civil servants.[6]

The Policy 'Trap'

Yet to pose the case entirely in these terms (as is often done) would be to ignore the very real policy dilemmas confronting (politically weak) Ghanaian governments after 1966 with regard to how to approach Ghana's economic situation. Successive Ghanaian governments were trapped between two major but contradictory policy responses. The first, and the one preferred by governments for political and other reasons, relied on administrative management of the balance of payments: fixed exchange rates, administrative rationing of foreign currency, quantitative import restrictions, administrative determination of export prices, as well as domestic price and distribution controls. This was a regime of short-term crisis management rather than one concerned with structural transformation or freeing up new or existing sources of supply. However, it was politically appealing because of its theoretical emphasis on equity and artificially low official prices. Although this regime could be quite vigorous in its rationing of scarce foreign exchange, its disadvantages were numerous. It discouraged production (and thus perpetuated shortages) because of the disincentives imposed by price controls (however, this point should not be exaggerated since, with the exception of the export sector, official commodity prices were not always enforced). Exports could not respond to favourable world markets because of the overvalued currency and the intervention of official appropriating mechanisms. Inflation and decline in production were in turn reflected in a low national savings rate, low state revenue, resort to runaway deficit financing and overdependence on cocoa surpluses. A sharp drop in exports, overvaluation of the exchange rate and an inability to tackle inherited structural problems discouraged foreign investment and aid inflow. This policy approach thus ended in stagnation and ever narrowing policy options.

In reality, because of the limits of this administrative regime, no Ghanaian government persisted in it with any consistency, attempting to modify or counteract it with periods of relative liberalisation. Thus, private importers with their own access to foreign exchange were permitted to import under 'Special Unnumbered Licenses' (SUL) and, provided all taxes had been paid, could sell at free market prices. Such 'liberalisation phases' were introduced in various forms in 1969–71, 1978 and 1982–83, each time ending in suspension because of pressure on the parallel currency market rate and popular discontent at high prices.

A second policy alternative has adopted a diametrically opposed approach, advocating the abolition of direct controls and return to market mechanisms through: devaluation of the exchange rate; abolition of import licensing, price controls and subsidies; deflation of domestic demand (such as credit limits, wage/salary restraints) and stimulation of exports; and the reform of public expenditures and retrenchment of the state enterprise sector. This approach, associated with IMF stabilisation, was applied between 1966–68, 1978–79, and also attempted briefly (and unsuccessfully) at the end of 1971. Its most obvious advantages lay in balance of payments support, debt-relief and restraint of budgetary deficits. However, its negative effects were higher prices, controlled wages and retrenchment; these led to considerable popular resistance and made it a politically risky strategy – and after the January 1972 military coup, not one which a weak or elected government could contemplate with equanimity. But the policy considerations were not entirely political. The impact of this approach on the balance of payments and the overall behaviour of the economy were negligible or problematic, certainly in relation to the political costs.[7] Although extraneous factors were often cited, these limits were inherent in the approach itself, and included: (a) the emphasis on demand management and balance of payments concerns to the exclusion of structural issues and supply bottlenecks; (b) the attainment of balance of payments stability at the expense of severe domestic deflation; and (c) key assumptions, such as those regarding the nature of 'comparative advantage' and the effect of devaluation on primary export structures, that appeared open to considerable debate.[8] We shall return to some of these considerations below in our analysis of the current adjustment programme. The point to be noted is that for these reasons resistance to these programmes was not limited to the masses of Ghanaian wage and salary earners. Many Ghanaian politicians and economic-administrators considered them-

selves to be 'structuralists' (after a fashion) and accepted the monetarist assumptions of these programmes with great reservations.[9]

After 1966, successive Ghanaian governments, and sometimes the
same government, fluctuated uncertainly betweeen these 'administered', 'liberalisation' and 'monetarist' regimes. The weakness of these
governments and the rigid institutional dogma made IMF adjustment
politically unpalatable and economically uncertain in its results. A
dominant anti-IMF political coalition had emerged, even among
sectors of domestic business. On the other hand the governments
were constrained by the absence of an appropriate structuralist
formula for short-term adjustment[10] and after 1966 by the lack
of independent resources for a long-term structurally-oriented
adjustment.

Whatever factors are summoned to explain the situation, the
Ghanaian economy by the end of 1981 was undeniably in a critical
state, characterised by steep recession, serious shortages and inflation. GNP had stagnated, growing merely from C5241 million in 1975
to C5290 million in 1981 (1975 constant prices); per capita GNP
actually fell from C537 in 1975 to C467 in 1981. Prices moved up
sharply for both imports and domestic commodities; the price index
for consumer items escalated from a base of 100 in 1977 to 868.7 in
1981. The index of real wages fell correspondingly from 100 in 1976 to
54 in 1978 and 31 in 1980; by 1982 real wage levels approximated only
17 per cent of 1975 wage levels. The inflation and decline in
productive sectors were accelerated by a shift to speculative trading
activities that yielded vast returns, sucked liquidity from production
to short-term trade transactions and thus discouraged investment and
productive activity. Wholesale and retail trade increased their share
of GDP from 12 per cent in 1971 to nearly 30 per cent in 1981. The
severe shortages and inflation in the meantime wreaked havoc on
domestic industry, devastated the salaried middle class and imposed
drastic hardship and privation on the mass of wage workers. Malnutrition was widespread; hospitals had no beds or drugs, and most
schools operated without adequate books, desks or teachers. Public
transport had completely collapsed. Thousands of Ghanaians, many
of them skilled professionals and technicians, migrated to neighbouring countries and farther afield. It was into this scenario of immisera-
tion that the 'revolution' of 31 December 1981 suddenly exploded.

The PNDC initially attempted an independent and self-reliant
stabilisation policy. During 1982 a programme of financial reorganisation was begun. The budget deficit was cut (by 17 per cent); central

bank contribution to the remainder was reduced to 17 per cent, and the rate of growth in the money supply was slowed from 63.5 per cent in 1981 to 23.5 per cent. This was combined with several 'revolution-ary' initiatives: confiscation of C50 notes and their conversion into forced loans to the state redeemable over five to ten years; a freeze on all bank balances of C50 000 or over pending investigation of their owners by Citizens' Vetting Committees; a 'War' against tax evaders that led to a rise in taxes from the self-employed (a notorious source of tax evasion) from C128 million in 1981 to C307 million in 1982.

These limited initiatives did not disguise the increasingly obvious fact that the PNDC did not have an overall economic programme. Although the coalition of forces behind the PNDC held together, the limits of spontaneity and self-help became increasingly evident. 1982 and early 1983 were extremely difficult days: Nigeria imposed an oil embargo, and then expelled almost a million Ghanaian illegal immigrants; closure of the borders with neighbouring countries curtailed trade; there were attempted coups in October and No-vember 1982, and in February and June 1983 attacks by 'dissidents' based in neighbouring countries; and then there was the murder of four judges in which the PNDC was implicated. Although emergency shipments of oil from Libya kept the economy from complete devastation, in all sectors the economic crisis deepened.

The PNDC's Programme for Reconstruction and Development, introduced in December 1982, was the first statement of an economic recovery programme by the government. On the face of it, this 'Programme' was the initial phase in a nationalist and anti-imperialistic strategy of reconstruction corresponding to the NDR. In this programme, 1983 was designated as a period of preparation for launching a three-year recovery programme (1984–86) which would lay the foundations for a 'self-reliant and integrated national econo-my'. In this first year there was to be restructuring of the basic institutions of the economy – in the areas of import-export trade, internal distribution, tax and budgetary reform, banking and insu-rance – and the establishment of a 'sound macro-economic frame-work' which would cover fiscal and monetary policy, prices and incomes, with the objective of rationalising production incentives. A state monopoly was to be instituted in the import/export trade and internal distribution of essential commodities was to be taken over by 'People's Shops' under the control of the PDCs. These measures were meant to eradicate trading malpractices and attack the econo-mic base of the foreign commercial firms and of the indigenous comprador and commercial factions. The state share in Barclays Bank and Standard Bank was raised from 40 per cent to 80 per cent and foreign controlled banks were restricted to specialised banking. 'Rigorous adherence to financial discipline' was to be introduced to deal with problems of stagnation and inflation, income mal-distribution, and the foreign exchange crisis; the overvaluation of the cedi was to be tackled and a principle of 'repricing' introduced through a system of bonuses and surcharges on exports and imports. However, the recovery programme was not intended to be moneta-rist. What was required for recovery was 'proper complementarity between the restructuring of production relations and sound financial management'.

The 1982 Programme was in part a product of initial negotiations with the IMF, and also a compromise between two factions on the PNDC, one of which supported some form of agreement with the IMF, and the other – with strong support in the left and the workers' organisations – adamantly opposed to any collaboration with the IMF. This second faction proposed an anti-imperialist policy of self-reliance based on popular mobilisation and the principles of the NDR and supported by assistance from the socialist countries and other friendly states.[11] Because of this opposition and the political sensitivity of the question of devaluation in particular, the negotia-tions with the IMF were carried out in considerable secrecy. However, the position of the anti-IMF faction was weakened by the failure to obtain aid from alternative sources, beyond emergency fuel supplies from Libya.

Those who advocated an agreement with the IMF, principally the financial bureaucracy, saw it as the only realistic way of dealing with the critical constraints imposed by the state of the external balances and the severe shortage of foreign exchange. With the external reserves exhausted, a huge balance of payments deficit, no foreign exchange available for crucial industrial imports, and severe short-ages of every conceivable type of consumer and producers goods, it was felt that there was simply no alternative to an IMF facility. The need to establish an immediate life-line to hard currency resources was a decisive consideration. However it was also felt that an IMF facility would impose needed financial stabilisation and, from a longer point of view, prepare the ground for future rescheduling of debt service when the existing concessionary arrangements granted by the 1974 debt agreement came to an end around 1985.

Although such views were associated primarily with the traditionally pro-IMF financial bureaucracy, the general principle of an agreement with the IMF was also supported, for substantially different reasons, by a minority on the left identified with the New Democratic Movement (NDM) and principally its leading member, the PNDC Secretary for Finance. This element considered temporary collaboration, or at least a normalisation of relations with imperialism, as necessary for the long-term consolidation of the revolution. For this reason, agreement with the IMF was advocated as the tactical equivalent of the 'New Economic Policy' (NEP). In spite of its retrogressive features, the financial package of the IMF was also considered not totally inconsistent with the immediate objective of financial reform in Ghana, and would be particularly useful for squeezing out the 'kalabule' operators and other speculators. Although this position did not represent the views of the bulk of the left (or perhaps of even the NDM) it won the support of Rawlings.

To be sure the position of the bureaucracy and its allies was not devoid of political motives either. Alarmed by the 'anarchy' in state-owned factories, by 'people's power' and the attempts of the defence committees to undermine the foundations of the old state, the state and parastatal bureaucracy were looking for allies who could re-introduce 'discipline' and help arrest these developments. Confronted by the spectre of revolution on the factory floor, by the threat of 'People's Shops' on the one hand and further state intervention into banking and import/export trade on the other, the private sector as a whole was more than ready to embrace the IMF.

Negotiations with the IMF were thus supported by a strange 'coalition' of Marxists (albeit very much a minority) who hoped to use the IMF to consolidate the revolution, by bureaucrats and capitalists who hoped to use it to crush the workers' movement, and others who simply despaired of any other alternative. Nevertheless, it is important to state that none of these interests, diverse as were their motives, supported the conventional terms of IMF conditionality, which were considered to be doctrinaire and, on the basis of Ghana's past experience, unlikely to succeed. The Ghanaian negotiators therefore fought tenaciously for a greater structural emphasis and also for a more flexible programme which would be relevant to Ghana's situation. The multiple exchange rate system (import surcharges and export bonuses) was the result.[12]

THE STRUCTURE OF THE PROGRAMME

The adjustment programme negotiated with the IMF was presented in the budget in April 1983. The most important aspects of the budget were: (a) the introduction of a system of surcharges and bonuses which imposed surcharges ranging from 750 per cent to 990 on the face value of imports and conferred bonuses of the same magnitude on the face value of exports. This in effect established a dual exchange rate for the cedi and represented a massive devaluation of the cedi from US$1 to C2.75, to US$1 to C23.00 and US$1 to C30.00 respectively; (b) an increase in the basic wage from C12.00 to C21.19 a day; (c) increase in the cocoa producer price from C360 to C600 per load of 30kg; (d) increases of 100 per cent in the price of petrol, up to 1500 per cent in the cost of medical care, and up to 400 per cent in the prices of meat and some basic commodities. Unlike previous adjustment programmes, particular emphasis was placed on production. The centrepiece of the strategy to increase productivity was the 'mobilisation of all groups of people including professionals, students, workers and farmers'.

The 1983 budget represented a one-year economic stabilisation programme, to be followed by a three-year Economic Recovery Programme (ERP) covering the period 1984–86. The key to the recovery plan was an Export Rehabilitation Project covering the cocoa, timber, and mining sectors. This included World Bank assisted projects to rehabilitate two state-owned and 17 private sector timber firms; rehabilitate the Tarkwa and Prestea gold mines; as well as the on-going cocoa replanting projects in Ashanti and the Eastern Region. In the gold mining sector the IFC was involved in a proposed $120 million rehabilitation of the Ashanti Goldfields Corporation, and there was a plan for an international consortium to manage the state Gold Mining Corporation for three years. Under the rehabilitation projects cocoa exports were expected to rise from 210 000 metric tonnes in 1983–84 to 300 000 tonnes in 1985–86; capacity utilisation in the timber sector would rise from 20 per cent in 1983 to 60 per cent in 1985 and 80 per cent in 1986, with export earnings doubling within that period; and production was expected to increase by 125 per cent for the state gold mines and 30 per cent for the Ashanti Goldfields Corporation between 1984 and 1986. The recovery plan also hoped to attract foreign investment into petroleum exploration and production, mining and mineral processing, and a number of other industrial sectors. Under the rehabilitation plans for domestic industry, average capacity utilisation in the manufacturing sector was expected to rise from 30 per cent in 1983 to 50 per cent in 1984 and 75 per cent in 1986. Finally the transport sector was to be revived, particularly through assistance from the World Bank Rehabilitation Import Credit. The external financing requirements for the economic recovery programme were estimated as follows: 1983 – $651 million; 1984 – $452 million; 1986 – $408 million; 1990 – $247 million.

The adjustment programme commenced in Ghana in 1983 thus originated from three distinct sources: the IMF, the World Bank, and the PNDC's Programme for Reconstruction and Development, analysed above. The IMF has been responsible, in collaboration with Ghanaian officials, for evolving exchange rate and trade policy, fiscal issues and domestic resource mobilisation, and external debt management. World Bank staff have focused primarily on incentive policies and public sector reform policies. These include trade liberalisation and cocoa sector policy, public expenditure targets and public sector management, and reform of parastatals.

The overall programme objectives and sector policies have been developed by IMF and World Bank staff in collaboration with officials of the Ministry of Finance and Economic Planning, and are presented as consistent with the original objectives of the PNDC's Economic Recovery Programme announced at the end of 1982. As we saw earlier, this version of the ERP had also laid considerable emphasis on the need for reforms in fiscal and monetary policy, prices and incomes, and the structure of incentives. Nevertheless it does not take much insight to realise the considerable distance between the December 1982 'Programme' and the present ERP/SAP. Conspicuously missing from the structural adjustment programme are the references to the nationalisation of the banks, of import-export trade and the control of distribution through 'People's Shops'.

To understand the reasons for this difference one needs to refer to the process of 'rationalisation' of the ERP undertaken by the World Bank after the April 1983 budget, and in turn made a condition for securing donor finance. In October 1983 the system of multiple exchange rates (bonuses and surcharges), won after hard negotiations by the Ghanaian side in order to retain a degree of exchange rate flexibility while avoiding the politically suggestive word 'devaluation', was abolished as 'administratively cumbersome' and replaced by an across-the-board devaluation and unification of exchange rates. The World Bank insisted that the PNDC repudiate the freeze on bank deposits and publicly assure the sanctity and confidentiality of bank deposits.[13] The Standard Chartered Bank, which granted a pilot loan of £50 million in 1984 as an indication of its 'confidence' in the economic policies of the PNDC, also insisted that the PNDC publicly renounce its partial nationalisation of foreign banks. The World Bank also urged the PNDC to return properties seized under anti-corruption campaigns in 1979 to their owners, to commit itself openly to liberalisation, and to 'reassess the role of the People's Shops' as being inconsistent with efficient distribution.[14] But the concentrated fire of the World Bank was reserved for the workers defence committees and the 'propensity of workers to engage in disruptive tactics'.[15] The Bank criticised the 'unnecessary harassment of enterprises by WDCs and PDCs' [people's defence committees] and demanded 'clarification of the role, functions and limitations of the WDCs'. To put it vulgarly: having secured one foot in the door in the 1983 agreement, the Bank used the subsequent process of 'rationalisation' to push its whole body inside. On the other hand the Ghanaian officials, constrained by the need to win donor approval and by lack of domestic support for an unpopular agreement, were unable to resist this erosion of their political position.

The ERP thus finally emerged in the much more conventional form of market-oriented and supply-side reforms involving deficit and tax reduction, production incentives, trade liberalisation and exchange rate depreciation.[16] Its main elements have been the following:

Exchange Rate Reform

The 'establishment and maintenance of a realistic and market determined exchange rate is at the heart of Ghana's adjustment program'.[17] Between April 1983 and April 1988 Ghana's currency, the cedi, has been devalued by over 99 per cent in relation to the US$, from C2.75 to C260.00 to one US$. The objective has been to unify the official and free market exchange rates for the cedi. This has occurred in three stages. The first stage, commenced in September 1986, introduced a second-tier official market covering virtually all international transactions other than cocoa, petroleum, essential drugs and government debt-service payments on debts incurred prior to 1 January 1986. The second-tier rate was determined in weekly auctions at which only the public sector and private importers of non-consumables, but not importers of consumer items under the Special Import Licence (SIL), could compete. The second-tier rate depreciated by some 70 per cent in relation to the first-tier rate on its introduction. The second stage, initiated in February 1987, abolished the two-tier system and merged the two markets. The third stage, commenced in early 1988 merged the auction and SIL or parallel market rates to produce an exchange rate of about 250 or 260 cedis to the US$.

Price Decontrol and Reform

Changes in the exchange rate have been supported by upward revisions in import and export prices, and the abolition at the same time of state subsidies, and price and distribution controls. Unlike past practice the through-put of price increases has been immediate and except in very few cases has corresponded to the full extent of the devaluation. This has resulted in very severe revisions in official prices, both for traded goods and for government services. The list of essential consumer items subject to price control were reduced from 23 to 17 in 1984 and then phased out altogether; the requirement that 30 per cent of the production of these items by local firms be distributed through state organisations has also been abolished. The objective of the exchange rate and price reforms according to the World Bank is to 'shift incentives further from trading and rent-seeking activities to production . . . to permit producers to obtain a larger share of scarcity rents and to enable them to generate the liquidity necessary for expansion of production.'[18] Major increases in the nominal cedi prices of exports (particularly cocoa) following exchange rate adjustments, have been an important aspect of the export sector rehabilitation programme (see below).

Monetary and Fiscal Policies:

The third leg of the programme is a set of what even the World Bank[19] describes as 'very conservative monetary policies'. These include strict credit ceilings, and a rise in interest rates from 14 per cent in October 1983 to 22 per cent in December 1984 and 26 per cent in 1987, with the objective of reaching positive interest rates and encouraging a 'substantial increase' in the national savings rate. At the core of these policies is rigorous management of public sector finances, the main objective of which is a dramatic reduction in the budget deficit. This involves substantial reductions in current expenditures through a discontinuation of public subsidies, repricing of government services, massive public sector retrenchment; relative increase in development expenditure as a proportion of the total budget; the broadening of the tax and revenue base, with the intent of raising the ratio of public revenue to GDP to 14 per cent in 1986 and 17 per cent in 1989; and reduced reliance on the banking system. Government borrowing from the banking system is to be contained to no more than 0.5 per cent of GDP.

Export Sector Rehabilitation Programme

Unlike previous experience with Fund-Bank adjustment, comprehensive and systematic programmes have been put in place to rehabilitate the export sectors, concentrating initially on cocoa, gold mining, and timber and supported by several IDA credits and foreign grants. Two of the key ingredients in this programme are the improvement of producer incentives and an export earning retention scheme that permits certain exporters to retain a proportion of their foreign exchange proceeds (45 per cent in the case of the Ashanti Goldfields Corporation and 20 per cent for the state goldmines).

The producer price for cocoa has been raised successively since 1982–83, from C12 000 per tonne in that year to C56 600 in the 1985–86 season and C140 000 in the 1987–88 season. The objective in this is to improve the real returns to the producer, raise the domestic price as a proportion of the world market price, and reduce the share of the total price appropriated by the state. It is estimated that the latest price increase in 1987 would represent the first real improvement in returns to producers since 1975 (see Table 4.1). One of the objectives here is the reform of the state Cocoa Marketing Board (Cocobod) in order to reduce its operating costs as a share of total cocoa revenue from 32 per cent in 1985–86 to 15 per cent in the 1988–89 season. In the first phase of the ERP the Cocobod was turned into a statutory public corporation and reorganised into operating divisions and wholly owned subsidiaries. Other reforms involve the reduction of the labour force of Cocobod by 41 per cent or 41 000 workers (of which 25 000 were found to be 'ghost workers'), the divestment of 52 cocoa and coffee plantations, and the transfer of some of the board's present functions in production, marketing, transportation, research and extension to the private sector or to other state institutions.

TABLE 4.1 *Cocoa Producer Prices 1984–87*

	1984/85	*1985/86*	*1986/87*	*1987/88*
Production ('000MT):	174	219	230	243+
Producer price (C/tonne)	30 000	56 600	85 500	140 000
Real producer price (1970/71 =100)	38	62	80	124
Producer price as per cent of world price*	25	24	28	42

* At official exchange rate.

SOURCE: Adapted from World Bank/IDA (1987) p. 17.

Public Sector Investment Programme

A vital aspect of the effort to rehabilitate the productive (especially export) sectors of the economy is a public sector investment programme aimed primarily at rehabilitating economic and social infrastructure. The objective of this is to remove infrastructural bottlenecks that would 'impede the private sectors' supply response to the policy reforms', and it concentrates on repairs and improvements to the road, railway, ports and telecommunications systems, leaving the private sector with the responsibility for rehabilitating the productive base. Import credits made available by the IDA and foreign donors have therefore been channeled primarily to the private sector.

State Enterprise and Public Sector Reform

The objectives of the reform are said to be threefold: firstly to reduce state involvement in the productive sector and the financial and managerial burden of the state enterprises; secondly to improve the efficiency, profitability and productivity of state enterprises; and thirdly to increase the managerial autonomy and accountability of state enterprises. Thirty state enterprises are to be liquidated, sold outright, or converted into joint ventures in the initial phase of the reform programme; these include both loss-making as well as profitable enterprises considered potentially attractive to investors. The remaining enterprises are to be opened to increased competition and market discipline, including competition from foreign firms through trade liberalisation where no domestic competitors exist; preferential access to foreign exchange and credit for state enterprises is to be abolished. Ten per cent of parastatal staff are to be dismissed in an initial phase of retrenchment between 1987 and 1989. A Structural Adjustment Institutional Support Project aims to strengthen the planning, implementational, analytical and monitoring capabilities of the Ministry of Finance and Economic Planning and other key ministries and government agencies involved in structural adjustment work. A basic condition for assistance under this project is retrench- ment of 15 000 civil servants (or 5 per cent of the civil service) annually between 1986 and 1988 and improvement of working conditions for the remainder, particularly at the top of the system.

ACHIEVEMENTS OF THE ERP

The ERP can claim significant successes in a number of areas after being launched to a disastrous start in April 1983. Severe drought and bushfires devastated food and cocoa production and precipitated famine conditions; low water levels in the Volta forced rationing of electricity and disrupted industrial production, necessitating closure of two out of five potlines at the Valco aluminium factory; the 1983 budget precipitated a political crisis and severely eroded working- class confidence in the regime. Inflation reached an all-time high of 122.8 per cent as the effects of the April budget made themselves felt. From 1984 however gradual improvements in the economy became visible with key sectors recording modest positive growth for the first time in several years. The recovery has been led by food agriculture and exports. Although aggregate agricultural production has risen only modestly (9.7 per cent in 1984, 0.8 per cent and 4.6 per cent in 1985 and 1986 respectively), production of key food staples has improved significantly, beginning with the bounty harvest in 1984. In that year the maize crop increased by more than 300 per cent over 1983 (from 172 thousand to 574 thousand tonnes) while the cassava crop increased by almost 250 per cent (from 173 to 409 thousand tonnes). While 1983 was a disastrous agricultural year and thus tends to exaggerate the overall picture (the 1984 maize and cassava production were, by contrast, 55 per cent and 67 per cent over the 1982 production) the important observation is that in most areas food production since 1984 has outstripped any period since 1980, al- though it should be added that good rainfall, and return to sub-

TABLE 4.2 *Economic Indicators 1980–86*
(Average change)

	Inflation	Real GDP					Balance of payments*	
		Per capita	Total	Agriculture	Industry	Services	Exports	Imports
1980	50.1	-2.1	0.5	2.1	0.3	-2.3	3.6	12.5
1981	116.5	-6.0	-3.5	-2.6	16.0	3.3	35.6	5.1
1982	22.3	-9.3	-6.9	-5.5	-17.0	-3.6	-9.8	-32.2
1983	122.8	-7.2	-4.6	-7.0	-22.9	2.3	-31.5	-1.8
1984	39.6	6.0	8.6	9.7	8.5	6.9	28.9	10.0
1985	10.4	2.5	5.1	0.8	20.0	6.0	11.8	9.1
1986	25.0	2.6	5.3	4.6	6.4	5.4	22.0	17.0

* Based on dollar value of exports and imports.
SOURCE: Ghana: *PNDC Budget Statement and Economic Policy for 1987.*

sistence farming on a large scale, rather than official agricultural policies, are responsible for this outturn. In addition food prices remain high.

In the export sector improvements have also been marked, although falling well short of the initial optimistic projections of the ERP (Tables 4.2 and 4.3). The dollar value of exports rose sharply between 1984 and 1986 enabling a more modest but still strong recovery in imports. This has been reflected in some improvement in the balance of payments, with the gap in merchandise trade being virtually wiped out; nevertheless deficits in non-factor services and interest payments led to a negative current balance in both 1985 and 1986 ($283 million and $194 million respectively).

TABLE 4.3   *Production of Major Export Commodities 1982–86 ('000 units)*

	1982	1983	1984	1985	1986
Cocoa (tonnes)	179	158	175	186	200
Gold (troy oz.)	331	281	289	310	369
Diamonds (carat)	684	347	346	630	800
Manganese (long tonnes)	160	191	287	300	350
Bauxite (tonnes)	64	70	49	130	250
Logs (cu. meters)	410	560	578	600	700
Sawn wood (tonnes)	150	189	180	223	232

SOURCE: Ghana, *PNDC Budget Statement and Economic Policy for 1987*, p.4.

However, the most important aspect of the ERP (at least in the view of the IMF) is the extremely rigorous monetary, fiscal and external debt management. As our previous analysis suggested, budgetary deficits have been contained in spite of very strong pressures. This has been done primarily by keeping a strong lid on government expenditures and in particular at the cost of critically needed injections of public investment capital. Subventions to state organisations have suffered severe contraction (particularly in 1985, when transfers were contracted by 40 per cent to help balance the budget). Although government revenue has increased substantially in nominal terms it has lagged behind upward growth in public recurrent expenditures, chiefly because of pressures for increased wages and salaries in response to increased prices and the massive depreciation of the cedi. In 1985 salaries and wages were 27 per cent over budget; in 1986 salaries and wages composed 36 per cent of current expenditures as opposed to 30 per cent in 1985 and 18 per cent in 1984; and a 25 per cent across the board increase in civil service salaries and wages from January 1987, as well as additional increases in allowances and reduced income tax levels, have exerted further pressure on state finances. In spite of these increases, however, real wage levels in the public sector have depreciated consistently in dollar terms, in line with the objectives of the ERP. Not surprisingly, inflation fell from the record high of 123 per cent in 1983 to 40 per cent in 1984, and 10.4 in 1985 before rising again to 25 per cent in 1986 owing to the large currency depreciation that year.

External debt management has been similarly rigorous. Arrears on short-term debt fell from US$601 million at the end of April 1983 to about US$257 million at the end of 1984. While debt servicing between 1983 and 1987 amounted to US$0.75 million above 1982 levels. This was made possible by foreign capital infusion of an additional US$1 billion over that period. Unlike previous Ghanaian governments, therefore, the PNDC has been relatively successful in attracting foreign assistance.

The current structural adjustment programme in Ghana therefore has a number of new elements which differentiate it from previous adjustment programmes imposed by the IMF. The first is obviously the much greater rigour in domestic management. Both in terms of its technical management and co-ordination, and its political consistency and ruthlessness, the ERP appears to be an outstanding example of neo-classical economic management. It is, in particular, the ability to discount the political limits usually associated with Fund programmes that distinguishes the PNDC both from its Ghanaian predecessors and from other regimes in Africa. This is supported by a new level of technical sophistication and political commitment among state managers evident in the relative coherence of the ERP. A second element is the much more serious attention to structural and supply problems and to the attainment of 'stabilization with growth'. As I have argued elsewhere, previous programmes were almost entirely monetarist and focused on monetary aspects of balance of payments disequilibria and reform of public expenditure and fiscal regimes.[20] What has emerged in the present programme, in contrast, is a new sensitivity (more evident on the side of the World Bank than the IMF) to the structural aspects of inflation and balance of payments crises and the inadequacy of fiscal, monetary and trade (liberalisation) instruments. To that extent the 1987–89 programme represents evidence of a learning process within the two institutions, although this is constrained very much by the strict theoretical limits which the institutions have imposed on themselves. A final factor is the mobilisation on a much larger scale than previously of balance of payments support and concessional financing, even though the practical impact of this remains constrained, as in the past, by disbursement difficulties. In terms of the standard economic aggregates there is no doubt that the ERP has been successful in achieving many of its immediate objectives – that of 'improving the working of the economy as presently constituted'[21] – and that these new elements have much to do with this success.

PROBLEMS OF THE ERP

Nevertheless, it is also clear that the Ghana SAP/ERP remains fragile and subject to considerable pressure. This is inevitable given the background from which it commenced, but it is also due to several other factors. These issue partly from the internal contradictions of the SAP itself, which suggest that in spite of the observations above the SAP has not moved much beyond its previous conceptual limits. The first problem concerns the *limitations of the demand management approach*, which attempts to tackle inflation and balance of payments disequilibrium by relying heavily on restrictive fiscal and monetary instruments. In practice this approach does not differentiate between excess liquidity and excess demand/consumption; the presence of excess liquidity is taken *ipso facto* to imply excess consumption. The result is that in trying to control monetary expansion it also typically depresses consumption for many groups in society, often severely, and frequently below already unacceptable levels. Although the Ghana situation demanded monetary contraction it obviously did not justify further falls in popular consumption. A related problem is that in its classic form this approach does not tackle supply constraints, which may be at least as important as the money supply in generating domestic inflation and balance of payments difficulties. For this reason it does not address the basic problem, which is that the external balances cannot be brought into sustainable equilibrium without changes in the *composition* and *function* of the balance of payments – in other words without attacking the underlying structural causes of balance of payments disequilibrium. Killick and others express a similar point when they argue that 'restoration of a healthy balance of payments requires longer-term changes in the [domestic] structures of production and demand'.[22] For this reason they stress the 'importance of designing a balance of payments programme to stimulate output and productivity' and to tackle 'key bottlenecks and constraints within the productive system'.[23] Demand-management measures would form a supporting ingredient rather than being the centrepiece of such a strategy.

While the Ghana programme has, fortunately, moved beyond the rigid position described above, problems associated with a demand-management emphasis remain. Excessive credit restrictions have militated against the very structural and supply changes required and precipitated domestic recession, particularly in the industrial sector. Massive depreciation of the cedi, major price changes, tight limits on credit and high interest rates have produced a liquidity crisis for importers and the industrial sector and depressed the domestic market. Following the devaluations, the mobilisation of local funds to meet import costs and the production objectives of the ERP has been a serious problem; banks have refused to lend to importing firms because the costs of imports in the depreciated currency often exceed their total equity. This has limited the utilisation of the Reconstruction Import Credits (RIC) for the export sector. For instance, of $25 million 'quick-disbursing credit' advanced in 1984 by the IDA for reviving logging and sawmilling operations, only three of 38 participant firms were able to secure cedi guarantees from local banks. This covered only 10 per cent of the total available credit.[24] The inconsistency in the SAP described here is obviously the result of the failure to rationalise the separate World Bank and IMF inputs into the SAP; hence the IMF has been emphasising deflationary demand-management and balance of payments concerns while the World Bank has laid greater stress on supply and growth objectives. Although officials of the two institutions have been attempting to negotiate a compromise,[25] no satisfactory solution has emerged.

Second the *export emphasis* at the centre of the ERP is emerging as the Achilles' heel of the programme. The attempt to expand cocoa exports over the short term through very large price increases to producers has coincided with large market surpluses and a major slump in world prices. World prices have fallen to their lowest prices in six years, descending well below the floor price set by the International Cocoa Organisation (ICCO); the May 1988 New York delivery price of some $1 550 per tonne (before the return to the market of the Ivory Coast further depressed prices) was less than 30 per cent of the peak price of $5 347 per tonne obtained during the 1970s. Market surpluses for 1988 have been estimated variously at 122 000 tonnes (Gill and Duffus) and 150 000 tonnes (ICCO), producing a situation aptly described as a 'chocolate lover's dream and a cocoa-producing country's nightmare'.[26] In 1987, following the failure of the ICCO to defend prices, Ghana and the Ivory Coast initiated an unsuccessful attempt to withhold supplies from the market.

The causes of these record surpluses are hardly accidental. While they reflect improved technology, expanded production in response to favourable prices in the seventies and so on, they are also the result of similar export-based adjustment policies adopted by other cocoa producers like Brazil, the Ivory Coast and Indonesia, again with the encouragement and support of the World Bank. In justifying this pressure for primary export expansion among African countries the Bank has argued that 'the lack of major alternative foreign exchange earning opportunities reinforces the need for Africa to recognise its comparative advantage in most of these agricultural exports and to regain a much larger share of the international market for them'.[27] The result of this policy advice, pursued simultaneously in a large number of individual producing countries, is now becoming evident. The current surpluses are expected to worsen when new plantings begin to yield in Malaysia, where production is being undertaken utilising sophisticated new techniques, at a fraction of the cost of older producers like Ghana and the Ivory Coast. Malaysian production has increased from virtually nothing in 1980 to 100 000 tonnes currently and an anticipated 200 000 tonnes in 1990. Since Ghana is diverting considerable domestic resources into export expansion and also predicating its present borrowing strategies on the outcome of its export drive, the world market situation is a source of serious concern and potential threat to the adjustment process as a whole.

While primary export expansion is proving a shaky basis for adjustment, it is at the same time undermining the domestic productive sectors (food agriculture and manufacturing) and the establishment of viable inter-sectoral linkages. This is likely to magnify the threat to successful adjustment posed by possible export collapse. While massive depreciation of the cedi has conferred windfall benefits on the cocoa sector (particularly given its low import content) it has created additional problems for *food production* and industrial activity. Repeated large increases in cocoa produce prices have led to substantial shifts in relative prices and turned the terms of trade sharply in favour of cocoa and against food producers.[28] This situation may force a diversion into cocoa from food production, (particularly if, as expected, inflation is stimulated by the resulting large cash infusions into the rural economy) thus further prejudicing the possibility of local food sufficiency. Food agriculture has not received nearly the same degree of support, either in terms of inputs or credible price supports; indeed the ERP has yet to develop a domestic agricultural programme, beyond the assumption that market liberalisation and prices incentives will trigger appropriate supply responses.[29] The maize 'boom' of 1984 for instance bankrupted many of the larger farmers when the market price fell below official indicated prices, with little effort by the government to defend prices. In spite of some increases in output as a result of improved weather conditions the overall situation of food agriculture remains precarious, predicated on small scale or backyard farming and primitive methods, and exposed to the vagaries of the weather. Food prices have remained extremely high although subject to considerable seasonal variations, and, in relative terms, well below those of cocoa.

The situation of the *manufacturing sector* is no less problematic. Struggling under the liquidity squeeze, high input and labour costs, and a depressed domestic market, the industry faces competition from a flood of consumer imports from liberalisation and the legalisation of SIL. The decision to admit consumer goods imports into the currency auction also has important repercussions on the ability of manufacturers to bid successfully for limited foreign exchange resources against importers with much more rapid turnover and probably higher profit margins. The requirement for a 100 per cent deposit against foreign exchange bids is also said to be creating difficulties for this sector, given the tight liquidity situation. Nevertheless, the IMF refuses to liberalise liquidity levels on the grounds that this may prove inflationary.[30] Manufacturers are thus caught in a *Catch-22* situation. It is already evident that, at least for the moment, the ERP has benefited the industrialists less than the very 'kalabule' stratum whose operations have now been legitimised and rationalised by the ERP. On the whole, domestic industry has been penalised by its import-dependent structure, as well as by rapid increases in the minimum wage to compensate for higher prices. (Although local employers who cannot afford the latest wage rates have been granted the option of a waiver.)

The planned objective is to re-orient domestic manufacturing toward exports – a virtual necessity since the domestic market is constrained by high prices and tight liquidity. However export competitiveness clearly cannot occur without major restructuring of the industrial sector. Although the World Bank sees this happening (in the area of local raw materials sourcing) in practice action in this area has been non-existent. Support has been meagre and confined to improving supplies of foreign inputs, the bulk of it channeled to the private sector to ensure, in the words of the Bank, that 'the public sector would not pre-empt the private sector'.[31] This helps to account for the persistence of large industrial spare capacity (estimated at between 40–60 per cent). In any case, developing the local raw material base is not in itself enough; some development of local technology and basic industry is also required. These are areas not seriously addressed by the ERP. Because of the scale of investment and the degree of co-ordination and timespan involved, development of these sectors cannot occur solely through the 'market' but must involve purposive state intervention. Without this it is unlikely that Ghanaian industry will survive the twin assault of high input prices and liberalisation.

The lack of policy in these areas and the emphasis on 'comparative advantage' suggests that domestic economic integration is not a priority of the World Bank, particularly if it hints at 'autarky' in any form. By excluding this element ERP strategy is liable, as it stands, to restore the precise structure that lay at the basis of Ghana's crisis in the early 1960s – the divorce between domestic production and demand structures, the high export coefficient of economic activity and high commodity concentration of exports, and the criticality of the balance of payments. In designing a viable balance of payments a strong export drive and domestic economic integration are complementary, not alternatives. In this light a strong argument may be made for resuming within a redefined and carefully regulated framework the domestic economic restructuring commenced in the early sixties. A return to a commodity-driven open economy is decidedly not the solution.

Another area of concern lies in the *external debt implications* of the ERP/SAP. Ghana's external debt service ratio (DSR) was estimated at only 10.7 per cent of exports (goods and non-factor services) in 1982, rising, however, to 34.2 per cent in 1984 with the expiration of the 1974 debt rescheduling grace period and further projected decline in export earnings. With new borrowing, much of it in the form of expensive short-term IMF credits the DSR was expected to rise sharply to 48 per cent in 1986 and 61 per cent in 1987 before falling again to 40 per cent by 1990. Concessional new financing has only deferred the problem; new capital inflows have been offset almost dollar for dollar by outflows for debt servicing and repayment of arrears.[32] An increasingly large proportion of Ghana's debt is assumed by the IMF and the World Bank and constitutes non-renegotiable debt. Service on World Bank/IDA credits (disbursed since the end of 1983) makes up 25 per cent of total debt service, while IMF repayments (and reduction of outstanding arrears) constitute another 40 per cent.

Ability to maintain repayment schedules on IMF stand-by resources advanced as part of SAP has emerged as a serious problem among a number of countries. At least eight countries (including Sierra Leone, Liberia, Zambia and the Sudan) have recently been declared ineligible for further funds after defaulting on IMF repayments. This is not surprising given the vicious circle inherent in the structure and financing of these programmes. New loans are contracted by an already indebted nation to finance export-oriented schemes; saturation of export markets and falling commodity prices cause financial shortfalls; new and old loans combine to aggravate existing debt and balance of payments problems. A fresh and more intense round of adjustment is thus required, incorporating fresh borrowing, deferred repayment of already existing debts, and the same assumptions of the desirability of primary export-led growth. This goes on and on, with the crisis being reproduced on an ever intensifying scale.

Finally this export strategy is likely to exacerbate the high *ecological* costs, associated in the past with Ghana's export orientation, with further destruction of tropical rain forests. It is estimated that the high forest zone (HFZ), from which hardwood timber is extracted and which also supports cocoa farming, is being destroyed at the rate of 4.5 per cent annually. In 1962 the total HFZ outside the forest reserves was estimated at 9 283 sq. km and twenty years later (1982) this had been reduced to 3 740 sq. km.[33] Forest reserves are estimated at less than 19 per cent of the HFZ as a whole. Forest management and conservation are non-existent outside the reserves because the staff of the Forestry Department are said to be underpaid and critically stretched; replanting has been minimal and confined largely to quick growing species rather than the prime hardwoods which may require over a century to mature. In 1979 the export of 14 species in log form was banned, not as a conservation measure but in order to gain more value from local processing.

The method of logging has been very selective and wasteful; marginal operators abandon large trunks unprocessed after sawing off contract sizes and minor species are often felled and ignored. The devastation initiated by logging companies is only the first in a cycle of destruction, with fuelwood processors, and then slash-and-burn farmers, penetrating the forest zone behind them. In spite of the rapid disappearance of Ghana's once extensive HFZ, rehabilitating and expanding the logging and cocoa industries is a major objective of the ERP. Export volumes of wood products are expected to increase from 126 565 cu. cm. in 1983–84 to 210 000 cu. cm in 1986–87. Erosion, soil impoverishment and adverse climatic change are the likely outcome of this strategy.

The ERP/SAP has been beset by other difficulties. Disbursement of foreign aid remains low (34 per cent in 1984, 21 per cent in 1985) and has actually deteriorated over time because of an increase in project aid, which is slow-disbursing, as opposed to the quicker disbursing programme and commodity aid. Liberalisation and price decontrol have led to a flood of non-essential and luxury consumer imports while shortages of productive inputs persist. Termination benefits for large numbers of retrenched public workers (estimated conservatively at cedi 4.8 billion in 1985) has increased the strain on the recurrent budget, making it necessary to either slow down the pace of retrenchment or forego workers' benefits. After a succession of spectacular price increases, public utilities are encountering diffi- culty collecting payment from hard-pressed businesses and con- sumers. Now, after subsiding for a while, inflationary tendencies have begun to re-emerge in the economy since 1986. Perhaps partly for this reason the differential between the official and parallel market currency rates began to widen again after progressive closure through successive devaluations – reportedly the first such case in which exchange rates on the two markets have begun to diverge after a period of convergence.[34] To counter this development and move toward full integration of exchange rates (a requirement for the release of the second tranche of the Bank's Structural Adjustment Loan) the government has recently authorised the opening of li- censed bureaux de change to offer free market rates in competition with the underground currency market.

Social and Political Costs of Adjustment

The social impact of adjustment, though obviously substantial, is difficult to calculate with any precision because of the lack of data. However the impact appears to differ significantly according to sector. There are indications that real wage rates have risen in the public and large and medium-scale industrial sectors where strong unions exist.[35] However, the fact that the TUC has emerged as the most determined opponent of the ERP may suggest that the actual situation is more complex. For one thing a declared objective of the programme is to widen income differentials between the top and lower levels of the public sector, so that aggregate income figures may not be altogether meaningful; in pursuance of this the income gap has been enlarged from 2:1 at the beginning of the programme to about 6:1 currently. Secondly, income improvements have occurred at the expense of considerable retrenchment, particularly in the public sector. In addition to job losses, massive currency adjustments and very stiff increases in charges for public utilities and basic services have drastically affected the living standards of poor and marginal groups who have no way of defending their income levels. The position of the informal sector celebrated by the World Bank as an instance of resistance to statisation and at the same time condemned as a source of 'leakage' from rationally organised markets – may also be expected to be eroded as activity in the formal sector picks up. This large and potentially thriving sector is almost completely ignored by the ERP, in spite of evidence of its role in absorbing excess labour and relieving the pressure on the formal sector and its work force.

The usual response by the Bank to criticisms of the social impact of the programme is that price levels did not reflect the full rigour of devaluations and that there is no guarantee that living standards of marginal groups would not have declined even further without the ERP. While it is true that the initial devaluations squeezed rentier incomes and prevented free market prices from rising proportionately this was no longer the case with subsequent devaluations, such as those in 1986, where prices did rise substantially. Secondly, this argument does not hold for one major area in which the purchasing power of workers and marginal groups has obviously deteriorated drastically. This is in the area of government services (hospital care, water, electricity and now education), where price controls had been effective in the past, although at the cost of deteriorating service. While there is much justification for it, the extension of 'cost recovery' to basic government services – involving tariff increases on the magnitude of 500–1000 per cent for power and 1500 per cent for hospital care in 1983 alone and regular and proportionate increases since then – has threatened to cut off the poorer strata from these services. An attempt to 'reprice' education, which would have the effect of at least doubling educational costs to students, led to campus protests and closure of all three universities. In many ways it is in the area of access to basic services – the pride and joy of Ghana's past development – that the real social impact of the ERP may be felt.

The PNDC had on the whole been slow to act to counteract this impact, especially since 1984 when attempts to minimise retrenchment were abandoned. However largely in response to local and international criticism the World Bank has shown (at least rhetorically) an unusual level of concern with the 'social impact' of the Ghana programme.[36] A 'Living Standards Survey' was devised during 1987 to monitor the impact of the programme on the poor and marginal groups. A 'Programme of Action and Measures to Address the Social Costs of Adjustment' (PAMSCAD), has since been adopted, involving the expenditure of some $70 million, primarily on public works job programmes and health (drugs) and education facilities.

The *political* costs of adjustment, in terms of the erosion of national sovereignty and the autonomy and popular direction of the regime is by contrast more readily perceived. What has emerged in Accra is a parallel government controlled (if not created) by the international lender agencies. The level of influence exercised by the World Bank over the policy process in Ghana is by all accounts very high indeed.[37] This outcome is the result partly of debilitation of the state machinery and the serious shortages of Ghanaian technical personnel, and partly of the tomes of detailed statistical and sector studies and the abstruse, technical jargon that attends World Bank policy intervention, and which are likely to prove overwhelming, if not impenetrable, to all but the most determined technocrats. Attending this emergence of parallel governments are two conflicting perceptions of the future of the ERP. While the IMF and the World Bank extol the return to market rationality, some in the PNDC continue to insist that the ERP is a tactical step on the way to the 'revolution'.[38] The agreement with the IMF was the 'political price' to be paid for securing 'as much space as possible' for the revolutionary manoeuvre.

While the nature of the ERP revolution awaits clarification, the extent of the 'political price' is already clear enough. The other side to the external appropriation of policy-making powers is the deliberate de-politicalisation that has occurred under the ERP, and the displacement of popular participation and mobilisation by a narrowly-based, bureaucratic management. One by one the organs of 'people's power' – the defence committees and the worker's self-management committees – have either been dismantled or emasculated. The militant cadres of 1982 and 1983 have, by and large, been absorbed into safe bureaucratic posts; there have been arrests of left militants who persist in their criticism of the ERP and the PNDC. The politics of the PNDC has taken a decidedly right-wing direction, and 'true democracy' has replaced 'popular democracy' as the political objective of the regime. Although much of this is to be explained in terms of the politics of the PNDC itself, it is clear that there is a fundamental inconsistency between the market ideologies of the ERP/SAP mass mobilisation, and between the highly secretive conditions of the programme's negotiation and the exercise of democratic participation.[39] Ghana has been turned into a laboratory for extensive neo-classical experimentation, unencumbered by the distractions of popular democracy. It is this political direction that above all undermines any comparison between the ERP and the NEP. In the latter, compromises could be made and justified politically because the Bolsheviks were firmly in control of state power. In Ghana few on the left persist in the illusion that 'the revolution' is in control of state power. Popular enthusiasm, the greatest asset of the regime, has once more been replaced by what Rawlings bemoans as the 'culture of silence'.

CONCLUSION: TAKING A BROADER PERSPECTIVE

A consistent theme in the Ghanaian experience has been the conflict between the 'political rationality' of the political cadres and the 'technocratic rationality' of the specialist planners and administrators which has often proved decisive in determining the policy directions of the Ghanaian state. This conflict is in part ideological (for example, the extent to which rational accumulation should take precedence over immediate satisfaction of social needs) but also relates to the different bases of power of the two state groups and the conditions for reproducing their power. The political brokers and

their patronage interactions were responsible for the strong instru-
mentalist and welfarist ethos, the emphasis on large social infrastructures and the tendency to fiscal expansionism which came to characterise the Ghanaian state and political process. The technocrats
resisted this by advocating less spending on social welfare and
infrastructure, and more on directly productive sectors.[40] In the
'socialist' phase they insisted on the priority of accumulation over
redistribution. The overthrow of politicians and the subsequent
political demobilisation that occurred in 1966, 1972 and – as has now
become apparent – 1981 were designed to install this 'technocratic
rationality', specifically in response to the decay in the productive
structure precipitated (at least in part) by the bureaucratisation of the
national economy.

In addition to the urgent function of reorganising the productive
structure these military coups – the principal mechanism of recent
political change in Ghana – may be seen more broadly as a situation
in which rival elements based in the state have attempted to gain the
ascendancy required to organise society (or specific social strata)
behind their own projects. A principal component therefore is the
reordering (alongside state-society relations) of the internal relations
of the state apparatus and of the index of dominance and precedence
among state institutions and functionaries while preserving the state
as such as the basic collective resource and the dominant instance in
production and allocation. For this reason coups do not lead to
permanent integration of the masses into political life. What requires
further explanation however is the increasing violence and radicalism
assumed by this process.

Those who by contrast see the Ghanaian state as appropriated or
excessively permeated by society usually see this as occurring through
the influence of patronage structures. While it is true that such
structures have played an important role in linking state and society
in the past, Ghanaian political history since the 1960s has nevertheless been marked by the progressive decline and collapse of the
broad-based patronage structures characteristic of electoral mobilisation, the victim of economic crisis, of increasing political closure, and
of the intrinsic limits and excesses of such structures. Gaining ground
concurrently was an altogether different type of political and economic interaction, involving reciprocal, corrupt ties between individual
state functionaries (politicians as well as administrators) and 'entrepreneurs' of a particular type (rent-seeking importers, informal
'businessmen'). The logic and reality of these networks, constructed

(or reconstituted) by every regime on coming to power, had consisted in the manipulation of the restrictive conditions of state economy and administrative allocation and pricing to derive quick speculative gain. State nationalisation, intervention into trading circuits, and regulationism in conditions of economic scarcity provided the basis for the rise and persistence of these networks. The short-term rent-seeking activities of these networks, by nature opposed to conditions of economic predictability and calculation, led to major distortions in the pricing, allocation and investment decisions of the state sector and also seriously impaired the ability of the private productive sector to operate successfully.

These networks functioned as the dominant core of successive Ghanaian regimes, reproducing and extending the crisis through their activities. In other words: a combination of inflation and of the state's fiscal difficulties, in particular the inability to reconstruct or expand the fiscal basis of the state, led to the increasing resort by state functionaries to irregular means of raising personal income, in the process exacerbating the foundations of the crisis. Although acknowledged under various names – the 'party corporation' of the 1950s and 1960s, 'kalabule' in the 1970s – the noteworthy aspect of these networks over time was their increasingly restrictive and politically irresponsible character, best exemplified by the Acheampong regime, when senior military officers emerged as the dominant faction within the 'kalabule' stratum. It was precisely this that precluded their being seen as a form of 'clan politics' or patronage linkage, if by this is implied some form of articulation with broader community interests. Indeed the very virulence of Rawlings' coup would suggest the emergence of new ideological and political alignments clearly inconsistent with patronage or similar forms of political accommodation.

While it is easy to see why 'kalabule' exchanges would alienate most of Ghanaian society and provoke a crisis of both accumulation and legitimation, what requires to be included in the account, and in the final analysis proved determinative, were their effects on the internal relations of the state apparatus itself. Politically the most important immediate impact of the crisis was the impoverishment of the subaltern strata in the state institutions (most critically the army) and of the middle classes with their fixed, politically determined incomes. This process of growing material contradiction *within* the state apparatuses (the military in particular), combined with the institutional crisis of the army,[41] proved decisive in triggering the

1979 and 1981 coups. What these coups demonstrated was the fact that the existing Ghanaian state – as a particular, concrete mode of distribution of power and privilege – was losing legitimacy not only in relation to 'society' but also *within* the state structure itself, as an organisation of apparatuses and of living, functioning officialdom differentiated according to access to and leverage over the fruits of office. This notwithstanding the fact that officialdom had not itself been innocent of the crisis, since the state apparatuses as a whole had constituted a primary line of resistance to internal economic reforms designed to improve public sector efficiency and restrain state fiscal expansion. Nevertheless these contradictions within the state itself, as well as between 'state' and 'society', were responsible for the meshing in Rawlings' rhetoric of themes both of societal protest and of state revitalisation (in which, by the way, increasing the tax revenues of the state by ruthlessly punishing the tax evaders was a major ingredient). Nevertheless for all its eruptive populism and its suggestion of radically new political and ideological realignments, Rawlings' coup followed the recent practice whereby political and economic reorganisations were launched from within the state apparatus, and involved, relative to the state apparatus, the re-appropriation of the state as the collective resource of officialdom in general. The fact that neither the populist nor statist projects have been sustained is a commentary as much on the inherent contradictions of the projects as of the diminished autonomy available to internal forces in Ghana.

To conclude: while the emphasis on the state in theorising the economic crisis is justified, it is incorrect to see a specific 'class logic' behind the Ghanaian state, if by this one means a logic derived from the interests of one or other of the fundamental classes. State interest in Ghana has been conceived and elaborated to a large degree autonomously of and in conflict with not only the popular interests of labour and the peasantry but also with those of external and domestic capital, to which developmentalist rhetoric (and formal investment laws) otherwise pay lip-service.[42] Even less satisfactory, on theoretical and other grounds, is the attempt to reduce the state to the actions of a single 'personal ruler'[43] to see it as appropriated by a 'peasant mode of production'[44] or as 'excessively permeated' by 'society' in the abstract,[45] positions which render mysterious and incomprehensible the erosion of popular legitimacy and Rawlings' coup – twice – to restore public 'accountability'. While these elements are undoubtedly implicated in various degrees, it is only by grasping the state as both autonomous and – in certain historical conjunctures – causally prior (that is, as a decisive scene of struggles in its own right) able (at least over the short haul) to determine through the outcome of these struggles the general direction of broader social and political processes, that we can more adequately understand the nature of events in Ghana. The politically ruptural process of decolonisation in Ghana further produced conditions conducive to this autonomisation of the state: while making it impossible for imperialism to continue directly as a politically dominant force or seen as a faction in a ruling coalition of class forces (as in the Ivory Coast or Kenya), it did not guarantee that the weakly developed local classes could supply the alternative basis for political class rule. The result is a complex parallelogram of internal and external political forces, each of which is capable of impinging on the state in particular ways but none capable of effective or long-term dominance. The state in Ghana has thus become the object of endless and inconclusive contestation among rival political and class forces – the only permanence being provided by the (albeit increasingly weakened) state mechanism itself.

This still leaves us with the central question suggested by this analysis: the absence of an effective structural and ideological domination capable of assigning a rational role to the Ghanaian state, particularly with respect to the accumulation process. The constant 'revolutions' and 'liberations' demonstrate the unset character of power and at the same time the inability of any of the contending forces to impose a particular social project. 'Statolatry'[46] has been demonstrably unable to fill the vacuum. The result has been a paralysis conducive to neither socialist nor capitalist development.

The fundamental problem that then has to be faced is: from whence is this domination, and the productive discipline associated with it, to be derived? There are two ways in which this paralysis may be terminated: either a hegemony constituted around an alliance of domestic and foreign capital and a capitalistic project capable of the rational subordination of productive labour and resources; or a hegemony, organised around a socialist project, capable of harmonising the multiple contradictions in Ghanaian society and led by the working classes. For the moment it is clear that the IMF intervention has altered drastically the balance between political forces and the alignment between the two ideological projects. Yet it is in precisely this result that the 'progressive' effects of the IMF intervention may well consist: in consolidating a new class rule and class politics out of the decay of agrarian communalism, a dominant class rooted in production, whose politics is the politics of production. The IMF may introduce from outside the discipline which the formation is incapable of generating internally. Once interpreted from this standpoint, the IMF intervention may no longer be seen to be aimed exclusively at the working class, and may even prove beneficial to it. Rather its primary victims – and this is a job for which monetarism is particularly well suited – may be the corrupt networks and the large and unproductive intermediary layers – of military officers, bureaucrats, magistrates, traders and so on – which have sloughed off the social surplus under various statist and welfarist formulae. In the absence of properly constituted class rule these have dominated and manipulated the state apparatus, endowing it with its ideological fuzziness and destructive autonomy from production. In pre-Rawlings' Ghana politically the most alienated forces were precisely those rooted in production, and in this respect it was immaterial whether they were domestic capitalists, MNCs, workers or export peasants. In this sense all productive classes have a joint if obviously unequal interest in the theoretical vision of the ERP. At the least, by abolishing these strata or subordinating them to the imperatives of value, the IMF would have clarified the conditions of class struggle by, as it were, clearing the undergrowth of peripheral society, a development which can only be favourable to the working class in the long run.

Notes

1. Emmanuel Hansen, 'The Military and Revolution in Ghana', *Journal of African Marxists*, 2 (1982); Victoria Brittain, 'Ghana's Precarious Revolution', *New Left Review* (1983) 140; and Donald Ray, *Ghana: Politics, Economics and Society* (London: Frances Pinter, 1986). For a more pessimistic analysis, Chris Atim and Ahmed Gariba, 'Ghana: Revolution or Counter-Revolution?', *Journal of African Marxists* (1986) 10.
2. Or as Hansen, op. cit (1982), terms it, 'a coup with a revolutionary import'. See my 'New Elements in Militarism: Ethiopia, Ghana, and Burkina' *International Journal* vol. XLI (Autumn 1986).
3. Speech by Flight-Lt Rawlings, Chairman of the Provisional National Defence Council (PNDC), on 31 December 1986, *West Africa* (12 January 1987) p. 61.
4. See, R. Genoud, *Nationalism and Economic Development in Ghana* (New York: Praeger, 1969).
5. E. Hutchful, 'International Debt Renegotiation: Ghana's Experiences', *Africa Development*, vol. 9 (1984) no. 2.

6. N. Chazan, *An Anatomy of Ghanaian Politics: Managing Political Recession 1969–1982* (Boulder, Colorado: Westview, 1983).
7. See E. Hutchful, *The IMF and Ghana* (London: Zed Press, 1987).
8. Ibid.
9. See for example, J.H. Mensah, Minister of Finance and Economic Planning in the Busia Government, *The State of the Economy and the External Debt Problem* (Accra: 1970) pp. 3–4.
10. On this see M. Sutton, 'Structuralism: the Latin American Record and the New Critique', in Killick, T. (ed.), *The IMF and Stabilisation: Developing Country Experiences* (London: Heinemann, 1984).
11. A third option proposed was the possibility of some form of adjustment policy under national management and excluding the IMF but supported by foreign credits. This would have included devaluation and other fiscal and monetary measures.
12. Much was made of the allegedly novel 'concession' of the multiple exchange rates by the government media, undoubtedly to make the negotiations and impending agreement more palatable to an extremely sceptical public. This 'soft sell' was largely responsible for the shock and surprise with which the harsh budget of April 1983 was received.
13. World Bank, *Ghana: Managing the Transition* (2 vols) (Washington: 7 November 1984) p. 88.
14. Ibid. p. 33.
15. Ibid. pp. 37, 86 and 90.
16. See the instructive recent study by John Loxley, *Ghana: Economic Crisis and the Long Road to Recovery* (Ottawa: North-South Institute, 1988). Also Reginald H. Green, 'Ghana: Progress, Problematics, and Limitations of the Success Story', in Christopher Colclough and R.H. Green, 'Stabilisation – for Growth or Decay?', *IDS Bulletin*, vol. 19 (January 1988) no. 1.
17. World Bank/IDA, 'Report and Recommendation of the President of the International Development Association . . . on a Proposed Development Credit . . . to the Republic of Ghana for a Structural Adjustment Program', report no. P–4403–GH (Washington: 23 March 1987) p. 14.
18. *West Africa* (13 January 1986) p. 78.
19. World Bank, 'Report and Recommendation of the President of the International Development Association . . . on a Proposed Credit to the Republic of Ghana for a Second Reconstruction Imports Credit', report no. P–3987–GH (Washington: 5 March 1985) p. 17.
20. See Hutchful, op. cit (1987) pp. 9–39.
21. Dr Botchwey, PNDC Secretary for Finance and Ghana's chief negotiator with the IMF, in *West Africa* (13 January 1986) p. 69. The present analysis may be contrasted with my critique of earlier IMF stabilisation programmes in Ghana, Hutchful, op. cit. (1987) pp. 1–39.
22. T. Killick, G. Bird, S. Sharpley and M. Sutton, 'The IMF: Case for Change in Emphasis', in Richard E. Feinberg and Valeriana Kallab (eds), *Adjustment Crisis in The Third World*, (London: Transaction Books, 1984) p. 59.
23. Ibid. p. 64.

24. *West Africa* (13 January 1986) p. 80.
25. See World Bank, op. cit. (1987) p. 49.
26. 'Cocoa Surpluses a bitter blow to producers', *The Globe and Mail* (Toronto: 11 April 1988).
27. World Bank, *Sub-Saharan Africa: Progress Report on Development Prospects and Programs* (Washington: 1983).
28. Loxley, John, *Ghana: Economic Crisis and the Long Road to Recovery* (Ottawa: North-South Institute, 1988) pp. 28–30.
29. This lack of planning for the domestic food sector is a traditional source of difficulty with IMF programmes in Ghana. See Hutchful, op. cit. (1987).
30. See Loxley, op. cit. (1988) p. 32.
31. World Bank, op. cit. (1985) p. 14.
32. Loxley, op. cit. (1988) p.73.
33. Ghana Commercial Bank, *Quarterly Economic Review*, vol. 8 (1985) no. 1 p. 8.
34. Loxley, op. cit. (1988) p. 34.
35. Ibid. p. 26.
36. World Bank, op. cit. (1987) pp. 46–48
37. See Loxley, op. cit. (1988) p. 49.
38. Botchwey in *West Africa,* 13 Jan 1986, p. 69. This is the interpretation also put forward by Ray, *Ghana.* For a critical review of Ray's position see Hutchful, 'Ghana and the Ghanaian Revolution', *Canadian Journal of African Studies*, vol. 21 (1987) no. 2.
39. For an attempt to argue the authoritarian implications of IMF programmes, see Hutchful, 'The Modern State and Violence: the Peripheral Situation' in *International Journal of the Sociology of Law*, 14 (1986).
40. Ghana, *Economic Survey 1961*, pp. 128–9, and Seven-Year Plan, pp. 3–4. See also Genoud, op. cit. (1969) pp. 76–77, who argues that this difference between the planners and the politicians on where to concentrate state investment 'might be seen to contain all the explanation that is required for the Coup which ousted Nkrumah and the CPP'.
41. Internal problems featured prominently in the justifications given by Rawlings for both the 1979 and 1981 coups. Old institutional problems of the military, aired during the period of the AFRC (Armed Forces Revolutionary Council) in 1979 and made the subject of a commission of inquiry during the civilian government of Dr Limann, remained unresolved. An insight into the background of some of those problems is provided in Hutchful, 'Organisational Instability in African Military Forces: the case of the Ghana Army', *International Social Science Journal*, vol. XXXI, (1979) no. 4.
42. It should be stated clearly that this analysis is specific to the Ghanaian state. It cannot be extended without substantial qualifications to states such as the Ivory Coast and Kenya, where a much greater degree of ruling class control arguably does exist over the state, without however eliminating the state apparatus as a major player in its own right. The tendency to see the Ghanaian state as unproblematically subordinated

to an exploiting imperialism, a position propagated in my own earlier work, is limited and naive, and the critique by Price is, in spite of its difficulties, a useful corrective. (See R. Price 'Neo Colonialism and Ghana's Economic Decline: A Reassessment', *Canadian Journal of African Studies* 18.3, 1984.) What is being stressed here by contrast is that the ever increasing demands of the state for short-term revenue, the inattention of bureaucratic production to the requirements of value, 'middle-class' welfarism and plain corruption contradicted the interests of both labour and capital and were responsible for the sharp contraction in the productive base of the economy.

43.   R. Sandbrook, *The Politics of Africa's Economic Stagnation* (London: Cambridge University Press, 1985).

44.   G. Hyden, *No Shortcuts to Progress: African Development Management in Perspective* (Los Angeles: University of California Press, 1983).

45.   See Price op. cit. (1984).

46.   A. Gramsci, *Selections from the Prison Notebooks*, translated and edited by Q. Hoare and G.N. Smith (New York: International Publishers, 1971).

5 Structural Disequilibria and Adjustment Policies in the Ivory Coast[1]

GILLES DURUFLÉ

THE GENESIS OF STRUCTURAL DISEQUILIBRIA

The severe economic crisis which the Ivory Coast has experienced since 1980, and of which the first symptom was the deterioration in the balance of payments position after 1978, is frequently presented as the consequence of the deterioration of the international economic environment (the second petroleum price hike and the decline in world market prices for primary resources), and in particular, the declining terms of trade. These phenomena, and specifically the downward turn of coffee and cocoa world market prices, after the peak reached in 1976 through 1978, may be regarded as catalysts in setting off the crisis, but do not constitute the deep and fundamental causes.[2] Rather, from a macroeconomic point of view, the origins of disequilibria are embedded in a certain number of long standing divergent tendencies, intensified throughout the 1970s, which constitute the counterpart of the model of growth and redistribution which had ensured the sustained growth of the Ivorian economy from 1960 to 1980. These phenomena can be identified at a number of levels and systematised in the following manner:

Foreign Trade

From 1960 to 1980, economic growth in the Ivory Coast was achieved through increasing reliance on foreign inputs to production (including imports, technical assistance, direct investments and loans) and growing foreign transfers of savings (expatriate and Ivorian). Increasing recourse to foreign factors was not accompanied by a significant diversification of export capacities (particularly with respect to the industrial sector). Consequently, despite the strong growth of exports (composed for over 80 per cent by agricultural and forest products) and the constant improvement in the terms of trade until 1978, export earnings were less and less able to cover the foreign exchange costs of growth. The deficit in the current balance of payments accounts increased regularly as of 1970 and surpassed 10 per cent of the Gross Domestic Product after 1978.

Agriculture

A principal source of foreign currency, an essential component of agricultural monetary income and an important source of state revenues, agricultural exports (in particular, coffee and cocoa) constitute one of the central elements of Ivorian economic growth. Agricultural exports have slipped from a growth rate of 10 per cent a year between 1950 and 1964 (parallel to the global growth rate) to a growth rate of 2 per cent between 1972 and 1978, before regaining a rate of 5 per cent a year since that time. The drop in the rate of growth of agricultural exports is tied to the limits encountered by efforts to diversify and to the decline in real prices paid to agricultural producers between 1965 and 1973. The renewal of growth after 1978, owing principally to cocoa and cotton, did not permit the re-establishment of the growth rates of the 1950s. In addition, this new phase has been confronted with unfavourable prospects for export prices and progressively (with respect to cocoa) the limits of 'extensive' agriculture cultivation. Since the beginning of the 1970s, export agriculture no longer constitutes the driving force behind the Ivorian economy as it once did in the 1960s.

Industry

The industrial sector may have appeared to certain observers to constitute a substitute for the engine of growth which agriculture had represented in the 1960s. However, after the rapid upsurge of import substitution industries whose share of the Gross Domestic Product grew from 4 per cent to 10 per cent between 1960 and 1972, these industries levelled off and their share of the Gross Domestic Product returned to less than 7 per cent in 1978. From the position of a leading sector, they fell back to becoming one pulled by internal demand. More specifically, they failed to achieve any real export activity and failed to produce any backward integration which might have involved intermediary products or capital equipment.

Public Expenditures

The real shift from export agriculture as the motor of Ivorian growth since the end of the 1960s has been that to public expenditure and in particular to investment expenditures which increased from 10 per cent of the Gross Domestic Product during the period 1965 to 1970 to 15 per cent in 1975 and 23 per cent in 1978. The multiplier effect of these investments (the expansion of demand) was the central determinant in sustaining the level of economic activity in the 1970s. On the other hand, these expenditures exercised a minimal effect in increasing the capacities of production (the accelerator effect) and in overcoming the 'blockages' which confronted the development of industry as of the beginning of the 1970s. When public spending progressively dried up (after 1980), the general level of activity in the modern sector was severely affected. Moreover, increasing public expenditures and rates of investment had been necessary to maintain the overall growth rate of the economy throughout the 1970s, a situation which reflected the decreasing efficacy of investments and the exhaustion of the endogenous nature of the economy's growth. This public spending was partly financed by the levies on agricultural exports[3] and, increasingly, by external borrowing. Public sector foreign borrowing increased from 3 per cent of Gross Domestic Product in the period 1965–67 to 12 per cent of GDP in 1976–77, at the peak of market prices of coffee and cocoa, fuelling the disequilibrium in external finances from the period of prosperity onwards.

State Commitments

Apart from the role of sustaining growth through public spending, the Ivorian state assumes other roles entailing expenditures whose rate of increase has been structurally more rapid than that of state resources. The principal roles have included the provision of educational facilities and training at all levels. (The share of current state expenditure allocated to education grew from 6.2 per cent in 1965 to 32 per cent in 1975). There was also a major role which resulted from the mode of political and economic regulation which was established after independence. This pattern implicitly assumed that the large majority of those leaving secondary and higher institutions of learning would have access to 'modern life' (meaning jobs, incomes, housing and public services). Demographic factors and the external standards upon which this lifestyle was to be achieved meant that this pattern entailed costs (direct or parallel) which increased relatively more rapidly than the national wealth, and generated increasing foreign indebtedness. Rising costs were highest in sectors such as subsidised housing, of which the principal beneficiaries were the newly salaried urban-dwellers (middle and high level cadres). Rising costs were also provoked by massive transfers to the public sector which can be explained by the role of this sector in the creation of regular and parallel incomes.

The roots of the disequilibria in both public and external finances, as well as the exhaustion of growth, were, therefore, in place well before the turning point in 1978. Favourable price trends in coffee and cocoa and the ease with which financing could be procured through the international debt economy, aided in hiding the effects during the 1970s at the price of intensifying the disequilibria, making the aftermath all the more onerous.

If a macroeconomic analysis over a long historical period allows us to show the progressive exhaustion of the country's economic dynamism, the rise of disequilibria and their inter-relations, the explanatory power of such an analysis nevertheless remains limited. The blockages in agriculture and in industry should each be analysed at the sectoral level: the contradictions in which the state happens to be the focal point should be analysed from a political-economic perspective as well as centring on the mode of regulation. These types of analysis cannot be adequately elaborated upon within the confines of such limited space. Nevertheless, in order to clarify the origins of the disequilibria, two basic elements of the Ivorian model of growth, which are the focal point for an analysis of its exhaustion, merit consideration: the place of foreign interests and the role of the state.

It has been argued widely and correctly that the substantial role of foreign resources (capital, technical knowledge and personnel) integral to the Ivorian model of growth has been one of the pillars of sustained growth in that country until 1978: the beginning of industrial development, the quality of the infrastructure, and the proper functioning of basic services (all the more essential to the smooth functioning of the economy and in particular, for the plantation sector) are largely a result of this foreign presence. Nevertheless, the resulting costs of these developments constitute one of the prime and deep-rooted reasons for the model's collapse, and the emergence of fundamental disequilibria. Furthermore, the strong foreign presence, in addition to the direct costs of remuneration (man-power, technical knowledge, capital) which it engenders, has contributed to the following:

(a)   The choice of production and infrastructural norms, life style and consumer standards which were not in keeping with the economic potential of the country from which developed a source of disequilibrium in public finances and public services and pressures for increasing costs for the entire economy. Further, these standards induced a high and increasing level of imports which bore the seeds of disequilibrium in external finances.

(b)   The institutionalisation of an industrial structure and more generally a 'modern' sector whose cost structure requires strong protection. This aspect constitutes one of its central limitations, as well as disadvantaging other sectors of the economy. More specifically, the industrial salary structure in the Ivory Coast (differences from one to 20 and one to 30 between unskilled labour and technicians) has mortgaged the country's future development. In the course of time, this 'modern' sector in which the foreign presence plays a decisive role, has become an important consumer of foreign exchange to which it barely contributes, while necessitating increasing investments, to shore up its waning economic dynamism.

(c)   The hampering of the emergence of a dynamic Ivorian modern sector in view of the fact that the majority of Ivorian cadres found refuge in the public sector (administration and public corporations) where income distribution is not linked to criteria of efficiency or economic dynamism.

The state is seen as the privileged site for enrichment and as guarantor to access to 'modern life' (encouraged by the presence of foreign interests) by the majority of those who were educated in secondary and higher level institutions. This role corresponds to the objectives of a particular political project and reflects the method of tension management, which has accompanied a foreign dominated extraverted pattern of growth. Such a mode of regulation implies increasing costs, and in so doing generates increasing disequilibria. Furthermore, part of the blockages in the modern sector (notably the lack of endogenous dynamism and the levels at which prices are set) result from the modes of income redistribution which have developed around the state and which are not based on criteria of economic efficiency.[4]

PROGRAMMES FOR ECONOMIC AND FINANCIAL CORRECTIVE MEASURES AND INTERNATIONAL FINANCIAL ORGANISATIONS

At the beginning of 1978, in the face of the rapid deterioration of the public accounts deficit, the government adopted an initial financial programme covering the period of April 1978 to March 1979. Then in recognition that the necessary adjustments could only be accomplished in a middle-term time frame, the government called the IMF to endorse the carrying out of its adjustment programme. An extended facility agreement was signed in January of 1981 which was supplemented with renewed stand-by agreements.

The Ivory Coast received assistance from the World Bank and the CCCE (Caisse Centrale de Coopération Economique) for its adjustment programme along with the support of the IMF. Three structural adjustment loans (SAL) were signed between 1981 and 1986. The World Bank financed as well a loan for technical assistance and more than ten new projects.

The CCCE does not have a programme of structural adjustment as such in the Ivory Coast. In 1980 however, it issued complementary financing for development projects which constituted direct aid to public financing in order to enable the Ivory Coast to provide its share of the funding for projects which benefited from external aid. From 1982–84 it financed a loan for the restructuring of the rural extension agencies and two loans for the restructuring of public sector corporations. These funds constituted non-project aid and are similar to structural adjustment loans.

The following data give some indication of the size and scope of these contributions. In May 1985, credit assistance from the IMF to the Ivory Coast totalled close to 600 million in Special Drawing Rights. However, net capital flows from the IMF, excluding interest payments, have been negative since the last trimester of 1984. The new commitments from the World Bank group in the period 1980–84 rose to $800 million. By 30 September 1985, the total amount outstanding increasing to $1352 million of which 916 million had been disbursed. From 1980–84, the CCCE's new commitments increased to fr2662 million.

The programmes concerning financial and economic corrective measures adopted since 1980 have resulted from regular and frequent discussions and negotiations with the international financial institutions (IMF, World Bank, CCCE). Moreover, these organisations frequently operated in close concert; the World Bank and the IMF in the area of macroeconomic policies; the World Bank and the CCCE in the area of state corporations. Therefore, we can neither separate government programmes from the recommendations of these institutions nor view them as in opposition. Nevertheless, in conformity with its mandate which is to assist governments in dealing with the short-term balance of payments deficits, the IMF has in fact concentrated both its analyses and strategies on deficits of the public accounts, on monetary policy and credit while the World Bank and the Caisse Centrale have focused largely on strategies of re-organisation and restructuring the economy, with particular emphasis on public enterprises. Consequently, the interventions of the IMF can be distinguished from those of other institutions on these grounds.

In the area of the public accounts, money and credit, the programmes implemented, principally at the instigation of the IMF, have entailed the adaptation to the Ivorian situation of the usual panoply of measures designed to reduce deficits by means of compressing demand. They include control of the money supply and of credit, limiting public operating expenditures (with specific emphasis on salaries in the public sector), drastic reduction in investment spending, reduction or suppression of subsidies (price of rice, public services, agricultural inputs), and the increasing of certain taxes. Moreover, particular emphasis was placed on restoring order in public and para-public accounts with respect to debt inventory, auditing and clearing of arrears, more stringent controls and better follow-up.

The sectoral policies proposed by the World Bank merit more in-depth discussion because they are more differentiated and individualised when compared with macroeconomic policies. But more importantly, they merit careful consideration because the package recommended for the Ivory Coast represents the most elaborate and thorough programme proposed by the World Bank for sub-Saharan Africa, and designed to profoundly alter the country's internal economic environment.[5]

As early as the 1970s the World Bank had undertaken an extensive analysis of the structural difficulties it perceived were emerging in the

Ivory Coast. In its 1978 country economic report, *The Challenge of Success*, it highlighted these developing constraints:

(a)   increasing vulnerability and responsibility *vis-à-vis* coffee and cocoa prices as a result of the increasing share of Ivorian production in world supply;
(b)   limits to forestry exploitation;
(c)   problems of relatively weak comparative advantage encountered in efforts aimed at economic diversification;
(d)   decreasing opportunities for import-substitution industries and more generally, declining rates of return on capital;
(e)   persistence of rural-urban inequalities as well as between zones (forest vis-à-vis savannah);
(f)   rapid growth in urbanisation and in unemployment in the cities;
(g)   tensions which can arise as a result of the emergence of strong foreign cultural communities: non-Ivorian African, Lebanese, French and the problems encountered in Ivorisation;
(h)   finally, the uncontrolled growth in public spending and the rising debt.

The report came to the conclusion that the limits had been reached by this model of growth in which rapid but costly development of industrial activities, initiated and controlled by foreigners and based on foreign standards and factors of production, were financed by agricultural surpluses. It insisted on the immediate Ivorisation of the economy in the full meaning of the term: jobs, factors of production, and the necessity of orienting initiatives towards types of industrialisation in which costs were lower.

The World Bank's analysis of the Ivorian financial crisis at the beginning of the 1980s takes up and extends the analyses formulated in *The Challenge of Success*. The Bank not only attributes the financial disequilibria to the external shocks as the immediate cause, but also to more profound reasons which are seen to have contributed to a more costly and unsustainable growth pattern in the Ivory Coast. According to the same source, the causes are situated at two levels:

(a)   an uncontrolled, often inefficient over-developed public sector;
(b)   a system of incentives which has engendered strong price distortions in favour of an over-protected and inefficient consumer goods import substitution sector, to the detriment of export industries, intermediate goods and agriculture, simulta-

neously advantaging certain groups, specifically certain urban sectors, who benefit from strongly subsidised services (housing, transport, education), to the detriment of the public accounts and savings, other sectors of the economy and in particular investments in agriculture.

These are certainly the central elements of the analysis underlying the policies negotiated with the Ivorian government with the introduction of the structural adjustment loans.

The principal characteristics of these policies can be summarised in the following manner:

(a)　Macroeconomic and financial management. Paralleling the efforts undertaken by the government and the IMF to introduce greater control over spending in the public sector, measures are being studied or have been implemented with the technical help of the World Bank: (i)　to improve the evaluation, programming, administration, follow-up and control of investment projects; (ii) to recover the costs of investment and recurrent expenses in education, housing and urban transport; (iii) to initiate reforms in the civil service; (iv) to strengthen the personnel and the tools available for macroeconomic forecasting and financial management of the economy.

(b)　Reorganisation of the public sector. Simultaneously with the introduction of tools and procedures permitting better financial control, auditing of the major state corporations is undertaken with a view to their reform, to the introduction of 'contrats-plans' (the signing of medium-term contractual agreements between firms and the state) or the transfer of certain activities to the private sector.

(c)　Industrial policy. This is one of the strong areas of the structural adjustment policies. It aims to reform the system of incentives in order to restore the competitiveness of business and to promote integration of the industrial matrix. The principal objective is to harmonise the rates of effective protection characteristic of each industrial branch to the level of 40 per cent. Half of this level of protection is justified by the over-valuation of the CFA franc and the other half as a supplementary measure to promote nascent industries. The principal measures adopted to achieve this goal (custom tariffs, export subsidies, an investment code) are outlined below and will be discussed with respect to the consequences of their implementation.

(d) Agricultural policy. This constitutes another major aspect of the programmes of structural adjustment lending. The specific details are also outlined below and examined with respect to their effects. They are essentially designed to establish profitable terms of trade for agriculture, to generalise the principal of market prices and create an environment which is favourable to the modernisation of agriculture and investment in this sector.

(e) Housing policy. The central objective is to reduce the burden which this sector represents for the public accounts. The principal measures which have been adopted are: (i) the establishing of the principle of shifting the largest part of the cost on to the user; (ii) the reorientation of public investment so as to favour a large number of prepared lots according to lower standards than previously, leaving construction the responsibility of the private sector; (iii) the reform of the financial mechanisms concerning housing; (iv) the reform of public sector enterprises; (v) the progressive freeing of rents on housing owned by public enterprises and the transfer of a part of this housing to the private sector; (vi) the reduction of the expenses resulting from the housing for civil servants: the reduction of potential claimants, of indemnities and cost sharing.

The first SAL (1981) largely centered on macroeconomic and financial management, administrative reforms, and the restructuring of public enterprises. The second SAL (1983) focused in greater depth on the restructuring of public enterprises and the introduction of industrial policy, while the third SAL (1986) aimed at perfecting industrial policy, pursuing the restructuring of public enterprises and development banks and implementing agricultural policy (prices, incentives, restructuring, modernisation and privatisation).

THE CONSEQUENCES OF MACROECONOMIC POLICIES

The Ivory Coast may be considered a model student of the IMF. The entire gamut of measures for compressing demand envisioned by the Fund has been applied and at times surpassed. However, until 1983, the Ivorian macroeconomic situation continued to deteriorate and that year performance criteria clearly could not be met. Much of the unfavourable turn of events and weak performance must be attributed to the deterioration in the international economic environment (the contraction of international commerce, high interest rates, the exchange rate of the dollar and the prices of primary resources), to climatic factors (the drought in 1983 resulted in bad harvests and a decline of hydro-electric resources), a less favourable re-evaluation of the prospects for petroleum exploitation and a recognition of an initial underestimation of the disorders and resistances within the public sector. The Ivory Coast intensified its austerity programme in 1984 and 1985 at a time when it benefited from good climatic conditions and favourable market prices for exports. As a result, the public and external accounts improved notably, which incited many to cry victory a little too prematurely.

At the level of appearances, recovery seemed to be remarkable. In the period of 1980 to 1985, the public accounts improved from a deficit before the debt service of CFA fr200 billion to a surplus of 367 billion and from a state of net indebtedness totalling CFA fr272 billion to one which showed a reduction of indebtedness of 89 billion. At the same time, the external current account balance was transformed from a deficit of CFA fr386 billion to a surplus of 90 billion.

The extent of reorganisation and the nature of reform in public accounts, somewhat hidden by macroeconomic indicators but certainly more enduring, merit particular attention. Prior to the reforms, the Ivory Coast was characterised by a financial administration in which a host of public organisations took it upon themselves to accrue debts which entailed state endorsement, and which were contracted without the approval of the central government. There existed a multitude of accounts, held in a more or less orthodox manner, and a multitude of financial decision takers, so that it was impossible to draw up a consolidated account for the public sector. The answer to this situation was to return to a more centralised financial administration which has permitted that most accounts be verified, that debts be inventoried and consolidated, that procedures be improved and in which the minister of finance has at his disposal tools permitting relatively effective follow up and control over transactions for the better part of the enlarged public sector (development banks excepted). However, it should be pointed out that the achievements resulting from the macroeconomic reforms are of a costly, fragile and limited nature.

The cost of the above reforms was to be deflation-orchestrated adjustment. From 1980–85, total investment dropped by nearly half in constant francs and public investment by 70 per cent. Per capita consumption declined more than 30 per cent, as was the case of employment in the modern sector.

From an economic standpoint, such a deflationist environment is detrimental to the emergence of renewed dynamism in the modern sector, capable of acting as the impetus for growth. Moreover, if investments remain at their depressed 1985 levels for several years, economic potential, the quality of the infrastructure and basic services (education, health) will find themselves mortgaged.

As a result of the weaknesses of the statistical tools and indicators, the socio-political dimensions such as the consequences of the drop in employment, incomes, consumption indices and the contraction of public spending are difficult to measure precisely. However, many indicators strongly suggest that the consequences have been particularly severe in urban areas. Overall calculations based on the national accounts show a net drop in urban per capita income of 45 per cent from 1978–85. These statistics raise numerous unresolved questions concerning how to account for income in the informal sector and concerning current demographic trends. However, the statistics do indicate a very real net level of impoverishment as substantiated by the drop in the overall consumption of basic necessities such as meat, fish and cotton cloth from 1980–85, and a general trend toward less expensive products. The rise in cost of public services (transport, electricity and less directly, education and health) has equally contributed to deteriorating conditions of urban life.[6]

The fragility of these reforms can be seen clearly by examining Table 5.1. The re-establishment of more balanced public accounts can be attributed entirely to the increase in the funds of the state marketing agency (owing to good harvests in 1984 and 1985, as well as good market prices for exports) and to the decline in investment spending. On the other hand, current savings did not increase as a share of GDP. This means that all the efforts to reduce current spending and to increase public revenues were wiped out by the impact of deflation on state revenues. Under these conditions, and in view of the fact that the country has used up its foreign sources of borrowing, the public accounts (and the external accounts) remain extremely vulnerable to any climatic variation and to any drop in export prices. This was clearly demonstrated with the deterioration of

TABLE 5.1 *Central Government Financial Transactions 1976–86 as a percentage of GDP*

	1976	1977	1978	1979	1980	1981	1982	1983	1984	1985	1986
Current revenue excluding Stabilisation Fund	24.0	22.5	23.9	25.0	24.7	26.2	24.3	25.6	22.6	26.5	25.8
Of which tax revenue	20.3	20.1	20.1	20.8	21.4	22.9	22.0	21.0	19.9	19.4	19.5
Current expenditure excluding interest on debt	−16.2	−13.5	−17.4	−18.9	−19.3	−19.1	−18.4	−18.5	−17.9	−18.2	−19.3
Current saving excluding Stabilisation Fund and interest on debt	7.8	9.0	6.5	6.1	5.4	7.1	5.9	7.1	4.7	8.3	6.6
Revenue from Stabilisation Fund	4.9	15.5	10.0	7.9	4.0	1.3	2.7	3.7	8.8	8.8	4.3
Current saving excluding interest on debt	12.7	24.5	16.5	14.0	9.4	8.4	8.6	10.8	13.5	17.1	10.9
Capital expenditure and loans	−14.8	−22.1	−23.2	−21.6	−18.7	−14.9	−14.5	−13.0	−7.3	−5.4	−6.0
Surplus or deficit	−2.1	2.4	−6.7	−7.6	−9.3	−6.5	−5.9	−2.2	6.2	11.7	4.9
Debt service (interest and principal)	−4.1	−4.3	−5.0	−6.0	−8.3	−10.4	−13.5	−17.8	−17.3	−16.8	−14.1
Of which interest	−1.5	−1.5	−2.0	−2.8	−3.3	−4.8	−7.4	−8.7	−9.9	−8.9	−7.6
Of which principal	−2.7	−2.8	−3.0	−3.2	−5.0	−5.6	−6.1	−9.1	−7.4	−7.9	−6.5
Gross financing needs	−6.2	−1.9	−11.7	−13.6	−17.6	−16.9	−19.4	−20.0	−11.1	−5.0	−9.2

SOURCE: IMF Reports on the Ivory Coast and Ivory Coast Ministry of the Economy and Finance.

the situation in 1986, which led to the country's refusal to continue interest payments as a result of the decline in coffee and cocoa prices.

According to the initial estimates of the Ministry of the Economy and Finance in the Ivory Coast, in 1987 the Caisse de Stabilisation or State Stabilisation Fund was to show a deficit of CFA fr60 billion and the balance of public accounts, before debt-servicing (see Table 5.1) was almost nil, indicating the need for financing, before rescheduling, in the neighbourhood of CFA fr450 billion or almost 15 per cent of the GDP. The 1988 forecast was not much better. In addition, as has already been emphasised, there is a risk of mortgaging the economic potential of the country if the trend of low public investment continues over a long period of time.

With respect to the balance of payments, the relative decline in import content and foreign transfers suggests a positive development. Initially, this was principally due to the decline in the level of activity. The real question then is to what extent can this trend evolve into an enduring structural modification, compatible with the renewal of growth, which of necessity would entail the implementation of a different model than the one analysed above. The strategy of increasing exports is, on the other hand, extremely vulnerable to climatic disturbances and to the fluctuations of international commodity prices. In 1987, the current balance of payments was once again heavily negative, in part owing to the drop in world prices for coffee and cocoa, and despite the drop in import prices (particularly energy).

The limited, not to say insignificant, nature of the results is revealed by an examination of these statistics. It was with the help of extremely favourable climatic and prices conditions and an austerity programme of which we have outlined the extreme severity, that the state was able to achieve a reduction of indebtedness of the public accounts of CFA fr89 billion, and 90 billion in the case of the external accounts, at a time when the external public debt climbed to 2600 billion. From a technical standpoint, the conclusions are obvious: the external public debt service which in 1985 absorbed 16.8 per cent of the GDP could not be borne without strangling the country's economy. Inversely, the only way to progressively absorb this burden and to reduce its weighty effect is to restore regular growth. However, government deflationist measures, adopted to fulfil obligations to the international institutions, run directly contrary to such an objective. The international financial institutions, in principle, and contrary to the officially held position prior to the weak overtures of

TABLE 5.2 *Evolution of the balance of payments as a % of GDP 1979–85*

	1979	1980	1981	1982	1983	1984	1985*
Exports f.o.b	29.8	29.6	32.4	32.4	30.6	41.1	43.0
Imports f.o.b.	−24.4	−25.7	−24.4	−24.4	−22.0	−18.8	−19.8
Trade balance	5.4	3.9	8.0	8.0	8.6	22.3	23.2
Service balance net of interest on public debt	−11.6	−11.7	−11.1	−9.4	−9.1	−8.3	−8.3
Current transfers	−6.2	−7.0	−5.9	−5.9	−5.1	−4.3	−3.8
Interest on public debt	−2.7	−3.2	−4.5	−6.2	−8.0	−8.5	−8.2
Current account balance	−15.1	−17.9	−13.5	−13.5	−13.6	1.2	2.9
Principal on public debt	−3.4	−5.3	−5.9	−6.1	−7.9	−7.8	−8.6
Gross financing needs	−18.5	−23.2	−19.4	−19.6	−21.5	−6.6	−5.7

*Estimates

SOURCE: Banque Centrale des Etats de l'Afrique de l'Ouest (BCEAO), 'Rapports sur la balance des paiements' and IMF Reports.

the Baker plan, no longer systematically reject these conclusions. On the other hand, financial consolidation and refinancing plans of the Paris and London Clubs are based on overly optimistic projections, and remain too constricting to permit a successful, non-deflationist strategy out of the country's financial strait-jacket.

THE EFFECTS OF SECTORAL POLICIES

We shall focus our analysis on industrial and agricultural policies which constitute two pivotal aspects of structural adjustment programmes negotiated by the World Bank. The implementation of these policies is carefully studied and scrutinised by Bank teams. Moreover, these two areas of policy are, and continue to be, the most likely to be instituted elsewhere in Africa. In addition, they constitute a configuration of policies designed to alter the system of internal and external relative prices in a situation where devaluation is excluded a priori as a strategy, due to the Ivory Coast's participation in the Franc zone. Bearing this in mind, the case of the Ivory Coast represents a prototype, with respect to adjustment policies proposed in a situation characterised by a fixed exchange rate.

Industrial Policies

The central measures were decided upon between June 1984 and March 1985 and their implementation took place over the following years. The investment code became effective in November 1984. The new customs tariff which replaced the former quotas by a declining system of surtaxes, was instituted as of March 1985. The export subsidy began to be implemented in January of 1986. The modifications in the general taxation code which introduced accelerated amortisation was implemented in 1984-85, and consequently applied to statements deposited from 1 January 1986. Therefore, it is still too early to properly assess the overall effects of these measures. However, a number of preliminary comments can be made.[7]

The New Customs Tariff and System of Surtaxes

The World Bank's initial intention was to apply rates of nominal protection of 40 per cent on all products (equipment, semi-finished and finished goods) in order to establish a uniform rate of effective protection of 40 per cent while not discouraging the establishment of new concerns in the equipment and semi-finished goods sector.

After negotiations with the Ivory Coast, it was decided not to alter protective tariffs on capital equipment in view of the fact that new industrial plants in this area were not very likely in the near future. The decision was taken to limit tariffs on semi-finished goods to 25 per cent, and in some cases to 20 per cent and to bring tariffs on finished products closer in line to 40 per cent. These changes translate into an increase of about 10 per cent for semi-finished goods which moved from a rate of protection of 5 to 15 per cent to 15 to 25 per cent. With respect to finished goods, in some cases there were increases and in others, there was a lowering of rates, as was the case of the assembling industries. Finally, the quota system was replaced by a system of surtaxes which are to decrease over time.

As might be expected, industry was extremely critical of this aspect of the reforms. Automobile assembling plants felt their futures were threatened, and announced their intention to close down. The chemical sector, electrical and mechanical equipment and certain textile sectors were hard-pressed to adapt as a result of the increase in duties on their intermediate imports. Other sectors such as chemicals again and textiles found themselves in difficulty as a result of the abolishing of quotas and restrictions on imports. The World Bank teams estimated that in 1980 the tariff equivalent of fixed quotas was 36 per cent for textiles and 6 per cent for chemicals.[8]

Moreover, in sectors such as textiles, the prevailing concern was that the doing away of the system of import licences would encourage the resurgence of customs under-billing. Such fears were not allayed by the fact that the new agency designed to limit such abuses was in fact very slow in becoming operational. It is very possible that these measures will modify the basic principles of the modus vivendi established between official circuits and fraudulent practices. On the other hand, by opening up the market, they force industrial enterprises to increasingly adapt to their markets and concentrate on less costly products.

Nevertheless, the reforming of the protective system is but one mechanism in a configuration of policies that are designed to profoundly alter a situation of over-protection for weak performing sectors which, because of its consequences on the system of prices is seen to have blocked in the past the development of more promising industries (upstream integration, export-oriented industries). The above reforms must be complemented by a system of export subsidies. Obviously, in the short-term certain negative effects of these reforms will become evident particularly with respect to their impact on over-protected sectors. However, in order to be able to evaluate the overall effects of these policies in the long run, it will be important to consider the following points: what proportion of industries, principally oriented to the internal market, have succeeded in adjusting? and whether other sectors have in fact profited from these changes, in particular from the export subsidy and from changes in the investment code?

Export Subsidies

As originally conceived, these were to be subsidies to the value added, with the objective of also providing effective protection of 40 per cent to export industries. Practical and administrative implementation of this measure, as well as the actual determining of the amount of the subsidy, proved to be relatively complex operations, for example, with respect to the conception and design of forms to be filled out in order to establish the nominal rate for each product; problems in evaluating the use of local primary resources, obtained at a price lower than world market prices; and difficulties in evaluating world prices for products which were not traded internationally.

The initial major beneficiaries will be the agro-food industry (tuna, instant coffee, canned pineapple, chocolates, confectionery, food concentrates), textiles (threads, printed cotton cloth, dress-making) and the wood industry. The subsidy is expected, with time, to apply to other sectors.

During the first two years, the subsidy could be financed by surtaxes on imports.[9] Afterwards, in view of the expected increase in exports and the reduction of the surtaxes, the cost of the subsidy will be greater than the amount obtained through surtaxes on imports.

What will be the consequences of these measures on the increase of exports? It is too early to judge. The reactions of industries in the second semester of 1985 were divided between a favourable reception in the hope of a strong increase in exports, and a certain scepticism in the face of the complex nature of the procedures. The first estimates made by the Ministry of Industry point to a pronounced positive effect for the wood industries (wood peelings, moulding, planes, floor planks) and in confectionery (chocolates, biscuits).

The Investment Code

The principal aspects of the reform in the investment code entail the doing-away of exemptions of tariff duties on imported primary materials, the prolongation of tax exemptions (eleven years of decreasing exemptions instead of five), the institutionalisation of a subsidy to the value added, calculated on the basis of the total salaries disbursed to Ivorian personnel, decreasing over five years and weighted in order to favour the establishment of enterprises in regions outside Abidjan. Finally, small and medium enterprises can apply under the new code.

Several developments linked to the changes in the economic environment and to new reforms can be identified. The majority of projects submitted since the introduction of the reforms have been implemented in the wood and agro-food industry, with two-thirds in regions outside Abidjan, as opposed to one-third in the period 1959–84. Finally, of the 24 projects, 16 have been initiated by new firms, more than half of which (nine to be exact) are small-or medium-sized firms.

One can conclude from this cursory examination that the new industrial policy has in fact been progressively implemented and that it has had various consequences. The most immediate of these consequences have been negative for those previously over-protected and relatively weak sectors, such as automobile assembling. Certain positive consequences may be observed with regards to the wood and agro-food industries.

The criticism levelled at these measures suggest that they may very well have a negative impact on the public accounts which are already very constrained. This critique appears to be relatively weak because it does not appear that, at least in the short term, their impact has been negative. Moreover, in the longer term, if the mechanisms are efficient and stimulate more rapid growth in the industrial sector, based at least in part on export activities, fiscal revenues will increase as a result of this growth.

The real issue is whether these reforms can effectively re-invigorate the waning process of industrialisation, which since 1970 has been one of the central causes in the disequilibrium in the growth pattern of the Ivory Coast, while at the same time, contributing to a healthier balance of payments situation.

If one accepts the results of simulations established by the World Bank teams by means of a model of general equilibrium,[10] the answer is affirmative. The introduction of a uniform customs tariff of 36 per cent and an export subsidy of 42 per cent (which is similar to the reform implemented with a slightly higher export subsidy) in the context of heavily reduced public investment (in order to reduce the deficit of the current accounts) will, according to this source, provoke an increase in industrial exports of 32 per cent and, in spite of the drop in investments, an increase of GDP in the secondary sector of 7 per cent, while industrial imports may be expected to decline significantly. Moreover, these gains in the secondary sector are expected to limit the deflationary pressures set off by the severe cuts in investments.

These results assume a relatively high capacity to substitute local and foreign products (in imports and exports) and in particular, a relatively high elasticity of exports in relation to prices. Sensitivity analyses have shown, moreover, that the results are not sensitive to variations in price elasticities of imports, but very sensitive to price elasticity variations of exports. In other words, and the results come as no surprise, the efficacy of these reforms depends on the capacity of the industrial sector to respond positively to incentives to export, to abandon over-protected weak sectors in favour of sectors which are export competitive, with the help of subsidies. A short term response as positive as that outlined by World Bank forecasts, is both problematic and highly unlikely. On the other hand, these reforms will stimulate the industrial sector and perhaps eventually provide new avenues and prospects for change, both of which were singularly absent in the past.

In order to evaluate the consequences of this policy for the industrial sector as a whole and for the balance of payments, it is important to ascertain whether enterprises which respond to the incentives will do so with less recourse than in the past to foreign factors of production, (import content, expatriate personnel, transfers at the level of value added) and in such a way which reinforces the cumulative effects for the national economy. The new measures (export subsidies based on the local value added, aid to establishment calculated on the total salaries disbursed to Ivorians) encourage this. However, one will only be able to appreciate the concrete results in the middle term.

Although macroeconomic analysis allows us to establish economic interconnections, it nevertheless impoverishes reality by presenting a homogenous picture. The determinants of the reaction of the industrial sector rest in the differing responses of diverse types of industry and entrepreneurship in the Ivory Coast: multinationals, small and medium business started by expatriates, Lebanese entrepreneurs, Ivorian entrepreneurs. The principal characteristics are:

(a)   The growing place occupied by a few large multinationals. First of all, Unilever which, with the purchase of Blohorn (palm and cotton oil) controls the greater part of the oil processing industry. Unilever is also heavily involved in textiles (Uniwax, CFCI and with the recent creation of Woodin); in general commercial transactions (Trading) and in importing of materials (Matelec, Matforce). Nestlé has also expanded (Capral, Novalim). With the privatisation of the management of certain state corporations, other large corporations have established themselves in the Ivory Coast (for example the consortium 'Terres rouges' which has assumed the administration of Palmindustrie). Others are candidates, specifically should Sodesucre be partially or wholly privatised, an option which seems for the present to have been put on hold. These large corporations have a particularly important place in the agro-food sector which should be the principal beneficiary of adjustment policies.

(b)   The relative decline of the medium business sector, largely French in origin, long active in the Ivory Coast in such sectors as consumer goods, in light materials, in repairs and services, and distribution companies. The majority have experienced difficulties in adapting to the crisis. Overtly high costs, tight links with expensive foreign suppliers, ingrained customs of the past, and aging directors, all contributed to the fact that many would not or could not adapt to the compression of local demand and the trend toward less expensive products. These businesses had a difficult time particularly in 1983 and 1984. A trend towards disengagement and selling off of assets could be observed. The most solid companies proceeded to tighten and rationalise their assets, withdrawing somewhat in order to adopt a low profile. In some cases, the head office did invest some new capital to consolidate their financial position, but in general most strategies of investment were reduced to their bare bones.

(c)   The growing place occupied by Lebanese entrepreneurs. Often more flexible and quicker to respond to demand, to find new suppliers, having lighter, more adaptable fixed costs, these businesses have been the principal beneficiaries of the withdrawal of French enterprises in the distribution sector, where they strongly increased their share of the market. This has also been true to a lesser extent in light industry. The purchase of Monoprix and the CFAO building by a Lebanese entrepreneur is very symbolic in this respect. Lebanese entrepreneurs are also involved in hosiery which they have dominated for the last ten years and more recently, in plastics and household articles.[11] In general, they do not have problems in financing, given their reliance on financial circles in the local Lebanese community.

(d)   Developments in the Ivorian business sector. Since the beginning of the crisis, there have been numerous bankruptcies of small and medium businesses which had been started up in the years when the economy was booming, often under hazardous conditions and without a valid professional base. A large number of these have been liquidated and the arrears erased either by the state, the banks or other creditors. As a result banks are increasingly wary of lending money to new small and medium business. In spite of this over the last few years, there has been a tendency towards the emergence of a new generation of Ivorian entrepreneurs. They are mostly located in distribution, installation and maintenance services to business or services linked to export-import activities to which there is easier access than exists to the directly productive sectors, where Ivorian controlled firms are more rare.[12] There are several to be found however, in the building and public works sector. These entrepreneurs managed to get their start from their original enterprises sometimes with the help of that enterprise (this was the case of sub-contracting from the Energie Electrique de la Côte d'Ivoire, EECI), or profit from their experience in order to start up business in a specific sector of their choice. While still on a limited scale, this trend to create new firms is original to the extent that these firms are not the creation of well-placed personalities or notables, that they are not developed in the shadow of the state, and that they rarely have foreign partners even if their initiators have usually received their training in foreign firms.

The new orientation of economic policy, notably its strategy to favour export-oriented activities and the privatisation of state corporations, will have the result of reinforcing the place of large multinationals, particularly in the agro-food processing sector. International trade of agro-food products is dominated by these firms and no local enterprise is in a position to compete with them. The foreign business sector, which is principally oriented towards the internal or the regional market, where costs are frequently high and which often benefited from protective tariffs, finds itself confronted with the necessity to undertake far reaching changes or redeployment. It is possible that the importance of this sector will decline.

In conclusion, while one may affirm that the new industrial policy in the Ivory Coast will most likely successfully encourage the development of large groups oriented towards export activity, particularly in the agro-food processing sector, the effects on the rest of the industrial fabric remain unclear. A number of promising signs have appeared in the textile and wood industrial sectors. Nevertheless, the level of investment in the industrial sector in 1985, if one sets aside large projects, remained weak. The development of a matrix of small and medium businesses depends on developments which are not solely economic such as developments in business practices and the performance of professional organisations. The role played by Lebanese enterprises, in due time, needs also to be clarified. Finally, there needs to be a strengthening of efforts directed at channelling private savings for investment into productive sectors, for up until now an important portion have been invested in real estate or transferred outside the country.

In the longer term and in the event that the strategy of export-oriented industries based on agro-food processing is confirmed (textiles, wood, industries using unskilled labour), this will require that the Ivory Coast protect itself against the risks inherent in this strategy. These are well-known and include:

(a) the 'de-industrialisation' of industries oriented toward the internal market as a result of the opening up of the market;

(b) the severe drop in salaries of unskilled labour to the exclusive profit of a few enterprises, often foreign owned, involved in the first stages of transformation of the primary resources of the country, without a long term perspective with respect to the appropriation of technical knowledge, and without the prospects of further integration of activities to include those of greater value added and more generally greater integration of the industrial sector;

(c) vulnerability vis-à-vis world demand, all the more so, given that this policy has already been recommended to a large number of countries in the periphery and the Ivory Coast is one of the last to attempt such a strategy;

(d) vulnerability vis-à-vis the strategies of multinationals which control the greater part of the export networks and which determine their strategies on a world scale as opposed to the level of a given country.

Remedies for these risks can be identified in the following areas:

(a) the reinforcing of industries oriented to the internal market; the articulation of the internal market with export-oriented activities, which presupposes assisting industries in adapting (a loan for restructuring and industrial development from the World Bank totalling $30 million has been earmarked to this effect) and as we have outlined, the encouraging of the cumulative effects of the activities of large export-oriented companies on those of local small and medium enterprises;

(b) the strengthening of the internal market depends as well on the structure of demand and income distribution. The greater the concentration of income, the greater the tendency towards transfers outside the country, and towards the consumption of imported luxury goods at the expense of mass consumption;

(c) the reduction of salary scales in such a manner as to allow for competitive production costs, without pauperisation of un- or semi-skilled labour;

(d) attempting to maintain a certain margin of manoeuvre with respect to foreign investments, in order to retain the capacity to act autonomously in the face of changes in the international environment[13] and to be in a position to encourage firms to increase the degree of transformation carried out locally.

Agricultural Policy

Agricultural Policy is formulated around the following principles:

(a) the redefining of the terms of exchange between agriculture and the other sectors in such a manner as to favour agricultural producers; the elimination of negative rates of effective protection for products other than coffee and cocoa (by the doing-away with export levies; the refunding of the tax on value added in the agricultural sector, and the introduction of export subsidies); increases in producer prices for coffee and cocoa in order to re-direct a greater part of the surplus to agricultural producers allowing them to invest in and modernise their farms;

(b)   the alignment of producer prices with world prices (except for coffee and cocoa) through an automatic system of price revision. The re-establishment of a price differential for coffee for which world market prices are more favourable.

(c)   the doing-away with the entire gamut of subsidies for inputs;

(d)   the improvement and more wide-spread application of agricultural extension work through greater access to and utilisation of the BENOR method (training and visit system), and strengthening of research, in particular with respect to food production;

(e)   the continuation of the policy to privatise state corporations engaged in production and in particular Sodesucre.

It is obviously too early to adequately evaluate the impact of these measures which for the most part will make themselves felt in the middle term. Not all of these have been adopted. The Ivorian government has refused to raise coffee prices in relation to those of cocoa, as well as to adopt measures for the reorganisation of Sodesucre in preparation for the privatisation of the most profitable of the four sugar complexes.[14]

As had been the case for exports subsidies, these strategies were criticised and encountered opposition on the basis of their negative impact on public finances. One can object that these measures constitute a totality and that one must evaluate the impact of this totality on growth and on the public finances.

Similarly, it is only after a new balance of the entire economy has been achieved that one will be able to evaluate the impact for non-agricultural sectors of the redefining of the terms of exchange in favour of agricultural producers and the impact of the doing-away with subsidies. There is no doubt however, that initially these measures should give rise to a contraction or the reduced growth of real urban incomes, whether it is through food prices (rice in particular) which will be raised, or through the transfer of a lesser portion of agricultural surplus to other sectors through the intermediary of the state.

One last point deserves to be emphasised: the measure which transfers directly on to producers (although with certain slight adjustment procedures), world price fluctuations of export products, places producers in an extremely vulnerable position. This is particularly the case in view of the fact that Ivorian producers do not presently have systems of organisation or information which exist in certain industrialised countries and which might ensure them a minimum of flexibility in the face of the fluctuations of world market prices. In the majority of industrialised countries, the harmonious development of agriculture was accompanied by more or less sophisticated systems of protection, insurance and compensation. The vulnerability of producers directly exposed to the vagaries of world market prices is proportionally greater in view of the fact that many countries protect their producers, at least in the short term. Directly exposed producers will be the first victims of the necessity to adjust supply to demand. Recently, had the drop in world prices of cotton been transferred directly on to producers, the impact on the development of agriculture in the savannah region would have been extremely negative.

The central issue then is whether the reforms instituted are capable of stimulating the growth of Ivorian agriculture, of bringing about its diversification, of lessening its vulnerability relative to the world market prices of coffee and especially cocoa, and setting in motion a trend toward intensification, before the current constraints of land (in the forest zone) and labour (in the savannah zone) impact more profoundly on the situation.

Despite substantial increases in producer prices of cotton and rice, the system of relative prices gives a very net advantage to the valorisation of the work day in the forest zone. In the savannah zone, cotton remains privileged if we take into account the initial investment necessary for irrigated rice cultivation and the greater security of income which results from cotton production. In the forest zone, the comparative advantage of cocoa remains unchanged. Consequently, the price system remains favourable to the already privileged development of cotton and cocoa cultivation which have been the two most dynamic crops in the recent past, but whose prices are also the most fragile.

On the other hand, increases in the consumer price of rice, the efforts directed at favouring the production and commercialisation of local food crops (rice and other products), and good climatic conditions have permitted a decrease in imports of rice and the substitution of locally grown products.

The transition to a more intensive form of agriculture is a long term undertaking. The restructuring of agricultural extension agencies is proceeding and giving results which are unequal and which vary depending on the agency concerned. The auditing procedures undertaken at the request of the World Bank and the adoption of 'contrats-plans' (medium-term contractual agreements between firms and the state) have taken longer than initially anticipated. It has been suggested by several sources that the good management of the latter could be threatened by the policy of aligning the salaries of their personnel. The restructuring of credit practices is also on the agenda, as is the adoption of new methods of extension work and training.

The assumption made is that given an improved technical-economic environment (training, credit), an improved system of price incentives (the alignment of the price of inputs on market prices, and a greater part of agricultural surplus attributed to producers through higher producer prices), there will emerge a new strata of 'model farmers' more likely to invest in their land, more likely to intensify production and to increase the productivity of their land and labour.

This development presupposes certain profound changes. Studies undertaken at the end of the 1970s on savings in rural areas showed that up until then, peasants who extracted a surplus used it to expand their crops or their plantations (extensive and not intensive techniques), to invest in real estate or in commerce in the city, to pay for education or for conspicuous consumption, but very little for the intensification and modernisation of their farms.[15] Several observers have also emphasised that undertaking of investments for intensification presupposes that the issue of land tenure has been addressed. To date this explosive problem has not been satisfactorily resolved.[16]

Considerable work is therefore in progress in order to improve the efficiency of interventions in the rural sector. Given the scope of the changes planned, the full effects will only be felt in due time and on the condition that too rigid an application of the measures–the effect of the alignment of salaries but also too brutal a decrease in subsidies for inputs, for the preparation of land, or for the purchase of equipment–does not counter these efforts. In the agricultural industrial sector and notably the second palm-tree plan, the results will only be felt in due time so that one may not anticipate major structural changes in Ivorian agriculture for several years to come, whether these concern the rate of growth or the relative place of coffee and cacao. The only significant change may be the possibility of a levelling off of rice and wheat imports.

CONCLUSIONS

Before addressing the direct effects of adjustment policies, three conclusions can be drawn from the preceding analysis.

The first observation from the analysis of disequilibria over a long period of time is that of the limits of the model of growth which was instituted before independence and over the following two decades. The macroeconomic signs of its exhaustion can be enumerated as follows: the slowing down of growth in agriculture; blockages in industry; the growing costs of maintaining growth through public expenditures; and finally and consequently, growing extraversion and indebtedness. At a deeper level, hidden behind the rise of structural disequilibria, are the limits of the mode of political and economic regulation which had been the basis of the Ivorian experience during the 1960s and 1970s.

The second conclusion which can be drawn from the analysis of macroeconomic performance since 1981, is that there is the need to lessen the financial constraints which have resulted from the country's debt burden. This conclusion is strongly reinforced by the fact that the government has indeed accepted to administer the austerity of the structural adjustment programmes prescribed by the Ivory Coast's creditors. The disproportionate nature of the results obtained with regards to the costs which have resulted from deflation, disinvestment and the deterioration of social services, provide ample evidence to justify this conclusion. Moreover, and in spite of what may be claimed by optimistic projections of scenarios for resolving the crisis by a non-deflationist strategy, one need not be a high priest, in view of the preceding analysis, to realise that barring the unlikely appearance of new sources of revenue (a new take-off in coffee and cocoa prices or the discovery of easily exploitable oil resources), the Ivory Coast will experience the greatest difficulty in meeting these deadlines for a long time to come. Also, since the Ivory Coast does not possess the same capacity to negotiate as do the Latin-American countries, there is a very real risk of witnessing the administration of economic regression, in which the government is forced to negotiate refinancing after refinancing, while austerity increases, the social costs of adjustment mount and a process of disinvestment sets in. Should such a process be set in motion, the country's productive and organisational capacity would be undermined and, as a result of the excessive reduction of educational and health budgets, so would the country's future human resources.

It is therefore necessary in the Ivory Coast, as in other over-indebted countries, to find, one way or another, means to limit in relative terms and in a lasting manner, the debt-service payments (for example through the consolidation of debts at very low interest rates, or the writing-off of certain loans), in order to generate new investment levels, both social and productive, compatible with the adoption of development strategies.

The third conclusion stems from the preceding two. It centres on the necessity of according priority to development and a renewal of growth which is premised on foundations very different from those of the 1960s and 1970s. The need to renew sustained growth is first and foremost an internal requirement, dictated by demographic factors (natural growth, immigration, urbanisation, education), but it is also financial since no matter what solutions are chosen to limit the amount of reimbursements, only strong growth will permit the progressive decrease in the relative weight of the debt burden. The need to re-orient policies towards new mechanisms of growth, also results from the exhaustion of the past model as well as from the financial constraints with which the country is currently confronted. Agriculture alone cannot be responsible for strong economic growth and given the country's financial constraints, public spending cannot, as in the past, constitute the motor of development.

It is obvious and easy to call for a renewal of the basis on which growth has been founded; it is necessary however, to evaluate the implications of such concrete changes. From a technical point of view, sustained growth which respects the limits of current constraints, implies the following:

(a) a strong resumption of local private investment in order to replace public investment which, even if the current financial constraints are lessened, will not be able to reassume the role it played during the 1970s. Up until now, private investment has been weak and located in those sectors which were being pulled by the rest of the economy. In addition, a substantial part of private savings has been drained off either externally or to non-productive sectors as, for example, into real estate;

(b)   a spectacular increase in the productivity of investment. From a macroeconomic perspective, the situation has deteriorated from 1960 to 1980. This therefore presupposes the emergence of dynamic processes other than those engendered so far by the public and para-public sectors in the 1970s and whose economic efficacy declined as a result of a number of highly economically questionable investment decisions, often characterised by abnormally high fixed costs, as well as, in many cases, very high administrative costs;

(c)   a positive balance in foreign trade which assumes on the one hand, a significant increase in non-agricultural exports (at the beginning of the 1980s, industrial exports excluding processed agricultural products and re-exporting, constituted only 6 per cent of total exports) and above all, on the other hand, a lasting recentring of the economy so as to decrease the costs of imports, which implies a change in consumption patterns, investment norms and an accelerated and durable trend in favour of Ivorisation.

Each of these profound modifications presupposes radical changes in behaviour. The policies of structural adjustment had as their explicit objective instituting structural changes of this nature. From the standpoint of a purely economic evaluation, the questions to be asked are what kind of changes these policies will effectively manage to bring about, and whether these changes are truly capable of creating the conditions for the resumption of growth on a more balanced basis. In response to these queries, the preceding analysis provides a number of elements, as well as showing the limits of a strictly economic approach.

A first aspect of the answer which has already been suggested is negative. It is unreasonable to imagine that a new dynamic process will emerge in the forseeable future, given current financial constraints imposed on the country. In the present situation, the expectation that economic forces can be generated through private investment (given that it is not at all obvious as to where this investment might come from) appears more as a means to mask the fact of the disinvestment of the public sector which up until now has been the principal motor of development. It is equally unrealistic to think that in the short or middle term, an increase in exports could somehow compensate for the slackening off of depressed internal demand which has resulted from structural adjustment policies. The scenario for resolving the crisis by a non-deflationist strategy which rests on responses of high elasticity of exports in the short term to measures taken in the industrial sector (without concretely analysing the mechanisms of response underlying this strong elasticity) is based on illusion. Having said this, while the loosening of financial constraints constitutes a necessary condition for resolving the crisis, it is not a sufficient condition. Moreover, what is of concern in the present situation and despite the very real reform of the public and para-public sectors, is that any loosening of the constraints may encourage the same economic mechanisms which were so prevalent before, in particular the undertaking of large building and public works projects which have turned out to be unproductive and heavily dependent on foreign suppliers.

A second element of the answer, even if it is based on more positive observations, raises nevertheless a number of important questions. It would seem that, at an economic level, the adjustment policies have attempted to attack the principal causes of the disequilibria which have been identified in the analysis over a long period of time: the disorder of the public accounts; excessive draining of agricultural surplus to the benefit of the modern urban sectors (and incomes), which are protected and not economically productive; blockages in the process of industrialisation, partly due to the system of protection and incentives which are inappropriate and economically unsound; and excessive costs of the para-public sector, non-sustainable increases in the size of public spending on education, and subsidised housing; obstacles placed in the way of the process of Ivorisation. When taken as a whole, the World Bank's diagnosis, which was in part articulated before the crisis, identifies the essential points. With respect to each of these points, the measures recommended by the Bank, to its credit, have forced action to be taken in the face of a tacit coalition of Ivorian and expatriate interests which favoured a standstill. Initial results are apparent in the re-organisation and reform of the public accounts, in the restructuring and reform of the public sector and the trends emerging with respect to the re-organisation of the industrial sector. As a result of the crisis, a reorientation of the economy has begun to take place, and its progressive Ivorisation is underway. It is not possible as yet however, to evaluate to what extent these changes will give rise to the emergence of new structures above and beyond the adjustments caused by deflation.

Nevertheless, even if a large part of the World Bank's diagnosis is well founded, and in spite of certain positive results, its interventions, when taken as a whole, raise a major political problem. The problem revolves around the fact that under the cover of technical assistance, an international agency in which the Ivory Coast has almost no voice has come to intervene directly in order to reshape national choices in sectors as crucial as education, the country's insertion into the international economic environment and the role of the state, and does this in line with its own view of what is appropriate. This type of intervention raises obvious problems of political legitimacy: how does one legitimate internally, painful choices in the area for example of reorientation of the educational system, which have in effect been dictated from the outside? The question is doubly difficult, given that the external agency prescribing these policies also plays the role of guarantor of solvency *vis-à-vis* the country's foreign creditors and, as a result of this, is in a good position to insure that the argument of solvency has precedence over all other policy considerations. As we have seen, given the present state of affairs, such an approach is incompatible with the formulation of a new development strategy. One may also question how an entire set of fundamental choices which, for the most part, have been drawn up abroad, may succeed in winning sufficient local support so that there emerges at the national level, a set of new local initiatives which are the pre-condition for the setting in motion of a new dynamic within the national economy.

Finally, and returning to a more explicitly economic level of analysis, a number of key points of the World Bank's proposals which constitute the formal expression of the liberal credo, need to be examined seriously; for, it is highly debatable that liberal policies as presently formulated permit the Ivory Coast to assemble the conditions necessary for stable, balanced and sustained growth. One of these revolves around the direct linking of internal agricultural prices to world market prices. As we have emphasised, this strategy has every chance, if it is applied on a large scale, of making more fragile and destabilising agriculture. A wide range of experiences (including the Ivorian experience not only of cocoa, but also of rice and cotton) demonstrate that in order to flourish, agricultural production requires prices which are profitable and guaranteed.[17] The Ivorian policy of agricultural pricing did in fact require a certain degree of rationalisation (particularly in order to encourage the development of food crops). However, the use of world prices, which adjustment policies seem to have chosen as the sole reference point surely does not constitute a desirable rationality for encouraging the development and progressive intensification of Ivorian agriculture.

The second point centres on the position taken with respect to the opening up of the industrial sector to international markets and capital, without simultaneously reinforcing national capacities for integration and initiatives in economic activity. There is an active and on-going debate about the merits of export-oriented strategies. If a few lessons can be drawn from it, it is amongst other things, that countries which have profited from these types of strategies had adopted them before the disequilibria of the 1970s had set in. Also, these countries managed to retain a strong capacity to intervene in the national economy which was precisely what allowed them to adjust without delay to the changes in the international environment. The four 'Asian dragons', so often mentioned as cases in point, continually provide evidence of this capacity for intervention and adaptation. Moreover, brutal opening imposed from the outside as a remedy for the crisis in industrial sectors, which up until now had been heavily protected, has frequently ended with poor economic results and engendered a highly repressive situation (Argentina, Chile, the Philippines).[18] In the Ivorian case, a redefinition of the country's position with respect to the international environment is necessary (and the initial adjustment measures have permitted some positive steps). However, a simple opening to foreign markets and capital, without other more interventionist strategies at the national level may very well lead to the dismantling of the over-protected import-substitution sectors, to the increase in control by large multinational corporations of the country's principal branches of production and transformation of its primary resources, with all the risks we have already emphasised, in the absence of other prospects for development and integration of the industrial sector.

Finally, the absolute priority given to market forces and almost exclusive attention given to an economic environment as defined by prices and fiscal policy, presupposes a homogenous economic fabric which is determined mainly by these variables. Although a good number of the criticisms levelled by the World Bank at the past price and incentive systems are justified, its own policy which gives absolute priority to market prices, to the exclusion of any other form of regulation or incentive, cannot be said to be appropriate, for such a policy minimises the weight of strategies, constraints and distortions which are of a non-market nature. The land-tenure question for agricultural development, the heterogeneity of the industrial sector, and the specific problems facing Ivorian entrepreneurs, are but a few examples of this point. If one ignores or remains silent on these issues, there is a real danger of under-estimating the problems and over-estimating the effectiveness of the 'answer' provided by adjustment policies. The scenarios for resolving the crisis through the introduction of such overly optimistic strategies are premised on the under-estimation of these factors. The first step in order to account for these factors would be the provision of means for observing and analysing concrete and *different* responses of agricultural producers and entrepreneurs to changes in their economic environment. But this would assume, as a logical consequence, that one could envisage voluntarist strategies or corrective measures aimed at particular target groups, which would be contrary to the philosophy of the World Bank.

In conclusion, and in the light of analysis undertaken over the long period, one can only emphasise the scope and breadth of the changes in economic and social behaviour implicit in all the scenarios put forward to solve the crisis. The importance of these changes helps account for and explain the resistance encountered to adjustment policies, as well as the difficulties in evaluating the scope of the changes in fact taking place. Since Independence, and especially during the 1970s, the 'modern' Ivory Coast (which had sprung up from the secondary and higher education system) had found its cohesion in a project of wealth creation and enrichment which took place in the shadow of the state, and which was to provide its participants with a standard of living, consumption patterns and public services at par with those of European societies. This project contributed heavily to the emergence of a particular pattern of salary and income distribution. It was reflected in urbanisation, roads and auto-route networks, universities and institutions of higher learning. The catchword was 'non au rabais' (no urbanisation, no housing, no roads, no Ivorisation at a discount). The project was to be relatively inclusive in view of the fact that schools and universities were fairly open. Foreigners were closely associated with its conception, institutionalisation and financing, and also profited from it.

The crisis has revealed that the project was impossible to realise: the enrichment of the 'modern sector' considerably surpassed the increase in production and productivity which it procured. The pattern could not continue, therefore, without ever-increasing transfers of surplus from agriculture and from foreign sources, revealing by this, its own limits.

By the same token, the standards for urbanisation, housing, teaching, the level and mode of salary and income formation in the 'modern' sector were thrown open to question. Consequently, there is a pressing need for the training of nationals and for the emergence of efficient national entrepreneurs in order to replace the over-costly expatriates who have been so closely linked to inappropriate choices and standards of investment and consumption.

In order for such a dramatic change in the rules of the game to take place, in particular under the present conditions of austerity, and in such a way that it can spark fresh economic processes, implies that the majority be convinced that things must change and that they are in the process of changing *for all concerned*. Otherwise, it is unlikely that they adhere to such a process and give it the backing it will require.

Despite the pertinence of some of the economic analyses of the World Bank and those measures which have acted as a stimulus for change, and even if one assumes that current financial constraints are loosened so that all development prospects are not totally wiped out, there is still room for considerable scepticism. For it is highly improbable that a strategy, largely imposed from the outside, based on diluting the national economy into the international economic environment, will be capable, given current international conditions which are unfavourable to African countries, of encouraging the putting forward of a new national, economically viable project, founded on a wide consensus integral to its success.

NOTES

1.   It is impossible to adequately demonstrate the validity of these contentions within the confines of this text. For a more complete analysis see G. Duruflé *et al.*, *Déséquilibres structurels et programmes d'ajustement en Côte-d'Ivoire* (Paris: Ministry of Co-operation, 1986) pp. 1–45 and pp 119–146, and G. Duruflé, *L'ajustement structurel en Afrique*. (*Sénégal, Côte-d'Ivoire, Madagascar*) (Paris: Karthala, 1988) pp. 89–148.
2.   The low level reached by the terms of trade in 1981–83 was equivalent to that of the early 1960s. Subsequently, it improved to a level higher than that of the early 1970s.
3.   Although the share of the volume of agricultural exports in overall growth declined after 1965, the same cannot be said for its value. The

regular increases in the terms of trade permitted the state to appropriate a growing levy which contributed to the financing of public spending and helped in procuring foreign loans.

4.   To be very brief, these costs increase proportionally with the number of 'cadres' who could aspire to this level of 'modern' life and standard of living. During the 1970s, the rate of increase of these costs was greater than the rate of increase of national wealth produced. The above theme is extensively developed by L. Gouffern, 'Les limites d'un modèle? A propos d'etat et bourgeoisie en Côte-d'Ivoire', *Politique Africaine* (May 1982) no. 6, pp. 19–34.

5.   The size of the teams mobilised in Washington and in the new Abidjan office, as well as the level of loans disbursed constitute indications of the particular attention accorded by the World Bank to the Ivory Coast.

6.   Ministry of Rural Development statistics show a 20 percent drop in per capita consumption of fish and meat between 1980 and 1984. Nevertheless these statistics do not provide any information on the breakdown of this drop in consumption. As far as we are aware, there are no comprehensive statistics dealing with malnutrition for the Ivory Coast. These cursory remarks bring to our attention the fact that both the social consequences of adjustment and the survival strategies of disadvantaged groups are largely neglected and consequently unexplored dimensions of present economic analysis.

7.   The data in the following paragraphs are from Duruflé op. cit. (1986) annex III: 'Les nouvelles mesures d'incitation du développement industriel en Côte-d'Ivoire'.

8.   G. Michel and M. Noël, ' The Ivorian Economy and Alternative Trade Regimes', in *The Political Economy of the Ivory Coast* (New York: Praeger, 1984) p. 100.

9.   From March 1985 on, these surtaxes provided revenues of about a billion CFA francs a month.

10.   See G. Michel and M. Noël, op. cit. (1984).

11.   The Lebanese business sector is relatively uncovered by the Ivorian Central Statistical Agency which deals with firms (the Centrale des Bilans). Consequently, it is difficult to quantify the growth in importance of the place occupied by these enterprises.

12.   On the importance of the tertiary sector, as the initial stage and springboard for the creation of national, small and medium industries, see 'Analyse ex-post de la promotion des PME et de l'artisanat en Côte-d'Ivoire' (Ministry of Foreign Relations, Cooperation and Development Paris: SEDES, CECOF, December 1985).

13.   South Korea is often cited as the model of a country which has successfully achieved an export-oriented industrialisation strategy. This country is equally remarkable because of the degree to which it has been able to formulate interventionist policies in response to changes in the international environment.

14.   Ex-post evaluation of the Borotou complex demonstrated that the administration of Sodesucre was in fact satisfactory and was not one of the causes of its disastrous economic performance. Rather, its perfor-

mance was linked to mistaken economic choices, at the very beginning which were based on biased studies endorsed by foreign lenders. At least for this complex, there is no obvious economic justification for privatisation. See 'Evaluation ex-post du complexe de Borouto-Koro' (Paris: Ministry of Cooperation, 1984).

15. See 'Epargne et financement en milieu rural'(Ministry of the Plan and Industry of Ivory Coast Paris: SEDES, 1981–1982).

16. In most regions according to customary law, land use may be granted to someone else, but ownership may not be transferred. Moreover, usufruct rights can be challenged with each new cultivation cycle. Hence the importance of perennial crops is a crucial issue in the scramble for land. On the other hand, complete clearing of all trees in order to replant could be an issue which might engender a challenge to usufruct rights. See F. Ruf 'Quelle intensification en économie de plantation ivoirienne?' *L'agronomie tropicale* (1985) no. 40–1, pp. 44–53.

17. This assertion does not exclude the fact that policies for agricultural prices may take into account the comparative advantage of the country. Also, in the case where a country is a net exporter, measures may be taken in order to progressively adjust production to a down turn in world prices. But it does exclude immediate adjustments to short term fluctuations and a systematic opening up of the internal market to a world surplus.

18. See M-F. l'Hériteau, 'Le Fonds monétaire international et les pays du Tiers-Monde' (IEDES, PUF, Paris: 1986) p. 195, 252.

6 Structural Disequilibria and Adjustment Programmes in Madagascar[1]

GILLES DURUFLÉ

THE ORIGINS OF STRUCTURAL DISEQUILIBRIA

In contrast to the other former French colonies of Sub-Saharan Africa and the Indian Ocean, Madagascar is characterised by a very particular configuration of characteristics which are a reflection of its situation as an island, its pre-colonial history and the political and economic choices it has made especially since the beginning of the 1970s.

Despite the specificity of Madagascar, it should be pointed out that the origins of the economic and financial crisis there, which began in the early 1980s, share many commonalities with those of other non-oil exporting countries in the Franc zone. These countries inherited relatively similar economic structures at independence and have had to operate within the same international environment. Nevertheless, it is the specific character of development in Madagascar which sheds light on the particular difficulties which the country is currently facing.

The Common Characteristics of the Origins of Disequilibria in the Non-Oil Exporting Countries of the Franc Zone

The common origins of the disequilibria in the non-oil exporting countries of the Franc zone may be periodised in the following manner:

(a) At independence, the economy was structured around an *'économie de traite'* (colonial trading economy) based on the production and export of primary resources, which were

169

essentially agricultural. Activities concerning agricultural production, commercialisation, exporting and the recycling of agricultural revenues constituted the principal motor for the other sectors of the economy. The 'modern sector' was largely dominated and controlled by foreign interests.

(b) Then came the policies implemented immediately after independence aimed at the strengthening of agriculture through large rural development schemes and the creation of an industrial sector based on import substitution. The nascent industrial sector benefited from a very favourable investment code and heavy tariff protection. The institutionalisation of a variety of new state functions (administration, education, social services) led to the relatively sustained growth of the public sector. The growth of the state and the emphasis given to industry and urbanisation contributed to the growth of a relative price system which worked to the detriment of the agricultural sector. The balance of payments showed a slight deficit. This deficit was to a large degree offset by foreign grants (in particular from the former metropolitan power), with the result that indebtedness remained at a low level.

(c) The vigour of the trading economy was sustained with only a few short falls, until the end of the 1960s but it began to show serious signs of exhaustion at the beginning of the 1970s: (i) the exhaustion of agricultural growth largely due to the drop in real prices paid to producers (which is one of the principal causes of the disorganisation of rural development schemes during this period) and in some cases, the saturation of the soil; (ii) the deterioration of the terms of trade due to declining market prices for agricultural primary resources and the growth of world inflation; (iii) blockages in the process of import-substitution; (iv) the increase in imports as a result of industrialisation and modernisation; (v) the rapid growth in state expenditures (infrastructure, sustaining economic growth, education, social needs, jobs). In most of the countries, the beginning of the 1970s was characterised by a slowing down of growth, increasing pressures concerning internal economic equilibria and rising social tensions. However, the political events in Madagascar in 1972 gave rise to a strategy of radical change, unknown in the other countries of the Franc zone.

(d) The soaring of prices for primary resources between 1974 and 1977 and the policy of international indebtedness promoted by industrialised countries had the effect of momentarily easing tensions. This was made possible however, because of a strategy of flight before the storm through a rapid increase in the rate of investment of the public and semi-public sectors and further indebtedness. Nevertheless, these investments did not culminate in the removal of the blockages in the productive system. The downturn in market prices, the second oil shock, the rise in the dollar and in interest rates sparked off the crisis.

In spite of the fact that Madagascar sought an alternative course in 1972 and in particular in 1975, it experienced, although with a certain delay, a phase of over-investment and over-indebtedness which, as a result of the deterioration in the international environment, was the immediate cause of the financial crisis of the 1980s.

With respect to this general pattern, Madagascar's uniqueness resides in the strategy of deep-rooted change which the country implemented from 1972 to 1975, designed to profoundly modify the structures inherited from the colonial past. Nevertheless, prior to this period of radical change, although the country seemed to be endowed with abundant physical and human resources, Madagascar experienced particularly weak economic growth over a long period of time. Over the same period, from 1945 to the end of the 1960s, the other French colonies were experiencing for the most part, relatively sustained growth and on the whole more rapid growth than demographic trends. This weak dynamism is both the cause and the consequence of a certain number of structural characteristics which the country must still confront today.

The Specific Characteristics of Madagascar

Geographic and Historical Factors

These factors can only be cited in the most cursory manner in view of the predominantly economic nature of the synthesis presented here. Nevertheless, three traits reveal themselves to be particularly important with respect to the object of this study:

(a) A geography which impedes transportation. This is the case for internal transportation (the island is vast and mountainous). It is the case as well for external transportation. Madagascar is not close to any major markets, and given its weak economic power, it has always been the victim of unfavourable shipping costs.

(b) A long history and tradition of resistance of rural societies to centralised power which maifested itself regularly in revolts (the latest of which were those of 1947 and 1971) and a long-standing and vigorous tradition of nationalism.

(c) An ancient and solid system of social stratification in both rural and urban areas which accords considerable amounts of power to certain upper echelons of the population, a phenomenon which does not exist in most of the other countries of the Franc zone.

The Weak Internal Dynamics of the Trading Economy

Unlike Senegal where groundnut production increased regularly by 4 per cent a year, between 1945–65, or even more so, the Ivory Coast where during the same period the plantation economy (coffee and cocoa) experienced growth rates which were greater than 10 per cent a year, Madagascar did not experience a very sustained rate of expansion of export-oriented agriculture after the Second World War. On the contrary, it is commonplace to see studies contrast the impressive potentiality of Malgache agriculture and its possibilities for diversification on the one hand, with the country's weak economic growth on the other. Over the long term the economy did not grow faster than its population.

In Senegal, although groundnut production was introduced by the colonial power and although the groundnut economy remained dominated by foreign capital, the development of this crop took place from the 1930s under the impulse of the development of internal processes which affected the social organisation and gradually provided a stimulus for the entire groundnut basin (transportation services, commercialisation, monetisation of the economy). The situation of the plantation economy in the Ivory Coast was similar.[2]

In Madagascar no such process occurred. One cannot really speak of an internal development of such scope in export-oriented agriculture that it might have given rise to a transportation network, commercialisation, and growing monetisation of the rural economy. One of the central causes was without a doubt the predominance of large European plantations which lasted up until the 1970s. Transportation problems and the rigid structure of traditional society contributed as well to this situation.

Irrespective of the hierarchical ordering of causes, the weakness of the endogenous process generated by the trading economy is very much interrelated to two other factors which characterised the Malgache economy over the long time period: the weak role which exports have played and the lack of internal linkages in the economy (in particular concerning transportation, commercial networks, monetisation).

The Economy's Weak Capacity for Externally-Oriented Growth

This aspect constitutes a counter-part to the weakness of export agriculture. Historically, exports comprised well under 20 per cent of the GDP, whereas in Senegal or in the Ivory Coast, they made up roughly 30 per cent of the GDP. As a consequence, import levels were also lower in Madagascar.

This weak potential for externally-oriented growth, which one might have seen as an important element contributing to greater autonomy, constituted in fact a big handicap. The weak structure and articulation of the extroverted economy (in particular the lack of impact on the development of the transportation network or modification of the economic environment) have not been compensated for by alternative structures springing from the development of the internal market. Rather, on the contrary, the weak growth of exports has made Madagascar particularly vulnerable to external shocks, limiting its capacity to respond and reinforcing external constraints.

Low Rates of Investment and the Weak Impact of Foreign Capital

Another feature which has been characteristic over long periods of the history of the Malgache economy is its low level of investment, which constitutes less than 15 per cent of GDP and often closer to 10 per cent. In an economy which has been dominated by foreign capital, at least up until 1972, the low level of investment reflects the former's weak impact and is linked as well to the weakness of the trading economy. Since the end of the 1960s, the state has attempted to compensate in order to improve the low level of accumulation and the ageing productive capacity but its efforts have been in vain.

The Weak Articulation of the Internal Economy

Madagascar was a settler colony, albeit a small one, where foreigners dominated not only industry, the modern tertiary sector, commercial trade, banking and education, but also large sections of agriculture and activities in less important urban centres. Consequently, foreign interests and the economic discontinuities which they engender (inconsistencies between the modes of production and consumption, income inequalities, segmentation of the labour market, urban/rural disarticulation) have had a profound impact, while at the same time the economic linkages resulting from the activities in the important sectors controlled by foreigners have remained weak.

In addition to the above, one must add the following factors: the weakness of the trading economy, the underdeveloped state of the transportation and commercial networks, the weakness of productive investments, and the relatively low level of integration of the rural population to the market economy. Furthermore, the narrowness of the fiscal base of the state reduced its capacity to intervene in an effort to restructure the economy.

The Importance of Intermediaries

Many studies and reports on Madagascar have pointed out that the sphere of production is often hampered by the price system in comparison with the sphere of distribution, and that speculative activities or situations of rent collection impede all efforts to stimulate production. The burdensome place which intermediaries occupy is a reflection of the weakness of the linkages within the economy, the difficulties and the cost of transportation, the low elasticity of production and the rigidities arising from a social organisation in which certain social groups are able to maintain their privileged positions over the distribution networks of basic goods such as the import-export trade and the sale of rice and, in this way, exert important pressures on prices.

The Radical Break

Apart from these structural characteristics which explain the weakness of the Malgache economy historically, Madagascar further distinguishes itself from the other countries of the Franc zone by the strategy of radical change initiated in 1972 and largely achieved after 1975.

The adoption of this strategy may be explained by a variety of factors which include the importance of foreign interests in Madagascar, the vigour of Malgache nationalism, the intensification of certain contradictions (in particular the drop in rural revenues which normally financed other sectors of the economy, and the limited opportunities opened to those formed by an expanding education system) and, more generally, to the inability of the economy to reabsorb the tensions engendered by these processes.

The Strategy of Radical Change and its Economic Failure

The Strategy of Radical Change

The major choices made after 1972 were those in favour of national independence-Malgachisation, a strategy of internal accumulation and industrialisation and the meeting of a number of social objectives (providing jobs and a minimum wage). The principle measures for achieving these objectives were nationalisations (of the banking system, trading companies, energy and mines, plantations); restrictions on foreign exchange (withdrawal from the Franc zone, controls over currency, institution of stringent protection); priority given by the taxation system, by protection and allocation of currency to support the construction of the state, industrialisation by import-substitution and accumulation (the building up of a stock of capital equipment).

This type of strategy which rejects market mechanisms, disconnects the structure of internal relative prices from the structure of world prices, and refuses to accept the principle of comparative advantage in the short term, and which favours import-substitution industrialisation rather than agricultural exports, has been analysed by the international financial institutions in terms of 'distortions' with respect to the supposedly optimal functioning of an externally open market economy. The latter analysis overlooks the rationality of the strategy chosen which, beyond being an expression of nationalist affirmation, was aimed at overcoming the weakness and the low rate of accumulation of an economy which, up until then, had been propelled by the foreign sector. Moreover, the relatively small degree of extroversion of the Malgache economy, appeared to be an advantage for the implementation of a strategy based on local accumulation and the development of foreign markets.

The Tightening of Constraints

Rather than unleashing new economic processes, the strategy of radical change quite rapidly provoked the tightening of constraints and a deterioration in the economic situation which was aggravated by the fluctuations of the international environment.

The break with France, along with the measures taken to curtail foreign capital resulted in a drop in public and private capital inflows, and very probably as well, the flight of capital from the country. The departure of a number of expatriates, the disorganisation resulting from the implementation of certain measures to nationalise trade and commerce, led ultimately to a drop in exports, which was intensified by the deterioration in the terms of trade throughout the 1970s. As a result of efforts to maintain a balance in external finances, contractions of imports occurred particularly in the area of equipment. This was in direct contradiction to the goals of investment, local accumulation and industrialisation.

The departure of a sizeable number of foreigners as well as foreign military bases and the contraction of foreign trade, resulted in a drop in state revenues, a decline in public investment and a rise in taxes imposed on agriculture (which meant a drop in real prices), all of which hindered production. This tightening up of constraints on public finances was in clear contradiction with the objectives of the construction of the state and state initiated restructuring of the economy, as well as constituting the source of initial disequilibria in the public finances.

As a result of the strategy of radical change and the fluctuations in the international environment, economic performance deteriorated and the structural blockages inherent in the Malgache economy intensified. Previous low levels of growth were transformed into a situation of stagnation and, in some instances, for certain agricultural products (sisal, tobacco, bananas, cotton) and industrial products (construction materials, wood industries, transportation equipment), the situation actually regressed. The first signs of serious back-sliding appeared as problems of inflation and public finances. Private and public investment which were already low to begin with, slackened even further. As a result of the lack of upkeep of capacity and the more general disorganisation, the country's productive structure deteriorated and became increasingly antiquated and obsolete, particularly in the industrial sector. The disarticulation of the economy was accentuated; transportation and commercial networks deteriorated. Peasants withdrew from the money economy, and their mistrust in the central power increased. The slackening of external trade undermined efforts aimed at internal restructuring which were linked to external markets (the basis of the trading economy) while the advocates of the new policy were unable to create new foundations on which to base a more integrated and better articulated local economy.

The Policy of Investment and Indebtedness (1979–80)

In an effort to counter this deteriorating situation, the Malgache government decided to undertake a massive investment programme in 1978–79 based on external debt financing. This initiative was undertaken in the most unfavourable conditions, and the economic and financial consequences were to be disastrous.

The rate of investment which was only 12 per cent over the period from 1974–77, increased to 15 per cent in 1978, to 24 per cent in 1979 and to 23 per cent in 1980. However, last minute decisions taken with respect to investments and encouraged by foreign suppliers of materials and financing, introduced highly capital intensive techniques which induced imports far more than it stimulated local production. At the end of 1980, as soon as external constraints made themselves felt, these investments penalised local production even further (investments for renovation and inputs were the first to be curtailed, even before new investments).

Moreover, because they were often badly conceived and uncontrolled, these investments proved to be largely inefficient and did not contribute to unblocking the bottlenecks of the Malgache economy (transportation, weak integration, disarticulation). On the contrary, because of the rationing of which they were the immediate cause, they contributed to intensifying these bottlenecks.

From a financial standpoint, they were the cause of an extremely onerous debt burden (private borrowing, loans, suppliers' credits) contracted at a very inopportune moment, that of the downturn in prices for agricultural primary resources, the second oil shock, the rise in the dollar and in interest rates, together with the withdrawal from the Franc zone which deprived Madagascar of an important means of absorbing the crisis. During the period from 1980–85, the deficit of the current account balance, or the burden of the country's debt as a percentage of the Gross Domestic Product were of a magnitude similar to that of other African countries as for example Senegal and the Ivory Coast. However, the consequences were far more disastrous for Madagascar, on the one hand, given its lower levels of exports (the debt service ratio was proportionately higher) and, on the other hand, given the country's currency shortages and rationing.

The Crisis and its Consequences

The financial crisis, resulting from the policy of over-investment and over-indebtedness (the increasing deficit of the current account balance, the debt and the debt service) had the direct consequence of rationing imports which immediately affected both capital equipment and inputs. As a result: (i) industrial production declined by more than 25 per cent between 1980–82; (ii) the deterioration of the transportation system increased (equipment, spare parts, maintenance of infrastructure); (iii) the internal economy's disarticulation was exacerbated (deterioration of transportation and commercial networks, increasing speculation and the increase in parallel markets, greater insecurity and the withdrawal of the peasantry from the market); (iv) the place of intermediaries increased to the detriment of production (difficulties and cost of transportation and marketing, development of parallel markets and increased speculation); (v) the poor administration of the economy shattered the last remaining element of the economic strategy which had been attempted at the beginning of the 1970s, and contributed as well to the delegitimisation of the latter.

The country found itself embroiled in a two-fold vicious cycle; economic and financial: the rationing of imports led to a deterioration and disorganisation in productive structures, and the diminished export capacity exacerbated external constraints. The increasing burden of debt service had a cumulative effect in absolute terms and even more so in relative terms, given the simultaneous decline in both production and export levels.

Finally, the increasing constraints forced the state to arbitrate in the manner it set prices, clearly in favour of the public finances and urban consumers, and to the detriment of agricultural producers. This only had the effect of eroding production, reducing exports, and encouraging peasants to withdraw from the money economy.

Industry

After a period of sustained expansion in the 1960s, in the 1970s, industry ceased to be a key sector stimulating the economy. In this respect, the situation in Madagascar bore striking similarities with the situation in Senegal and in the Ivory Coast when in the 1960s (Senegal) and at the beginning of the 1970s (the Ivory Coast) import substitution industrialisation strategies began to lose steam.[3] From 1972 onwards Malgache industry progressively experienced a marked deterioration as the productive structure became outdated and productivity declined. The 1979–80 investment period barely benefited industry, while the rationing of inputs and spare parts represented a very severe blow to the sector. Although as of 1982 the structural adjustment loans from the Caisse Centrale de Coopération Economique, and World Bank's credit assistance to industry (CASI) did permit a slight lessening of constraints, most firms found themselves with an ageing and delapidated productive structure, increasing costs (due to buffer stocks, delays and the cost of supplies and the cost of transportation) and a deteriorating financial structure. For many, supply outstripped demand as a result of the deterioration in the standard of living of the population and the squeeze placed on family budgets, as a result of the growing place occupied by foodstuffs.

THE ROLE OF INTERNATIONAL FINANCIAL INSTITUTIONS AND ADJUSTMENT POLICIES

Between 1980–86, Madagascar signed six stand-by agreements with the IMF. The first two were suspended in mid-term because the country failed to respect the performance criteria which were attached to the loans (in particular with respect to the obligation to reduce deficits). The next three (from July 1982 onwards) were carried to term. An additional one was approved in August of 1986. The central measures advocated by the IMF in these agreements included:

(a) Global strategies for reintroducing equilibrium: restriction of money and credit; devaluation: the tying of the Malgache franc to a basket of currencies, institutionalisation of a flexible rate of exchange, subject to revision every trimester and devaluations in relation to the basket of currencies; reduction of the deficit in public finances which included reductions in the investment budget and a ceiling of salary increases; reduction of arrears due to foreign loans and a ceiling on loans; abolition of subsidies for consumer goods (such as rice).

(b) Increases in agricultural prices.

(c) Progressive liberalisation of industrial prices.

(d) Progressive liberalisation of exchange controls and of the system of currency allocation.

From 1982 on, the CCCE implemented structural adjustment programmes which permit selective financing of imports and provide counterpart funds at the state's disposal with the agreement of the CCCE. These SAPs totalled French fr890 million for the period 1982–86. Most of the currency was used for inputs into industry and agriculture.

The World Bank provided credit assistance to industry (CASI) valued at $40 million in 1985 and negotiated another $60 million for credit assistance to agriculture (CASA) in 1986. As is the case with the structural adjustment loans of the CCCE, the CASI and CASA entail selective financing for imports. They also contain a wide range of conditionalities which are designed to alter the relative price structure to the benefit of agriculture (increases in agricultural producer prices) and export goods and the liberalisation of the economy (in particular the liberalisation of the internal rice trade). In its March 1986 economic memorandum, the World Bank attempted to outline a scenario for resolving the crisis, which included a plan for financing the proposed strategy.

THE EFFECTS OF ADJUSTMENT POLICIES

For the purposes of analysis we shall examine first of all, the effects of the overall policies introduced to re-establish an equilibrium, then the consequences of the selective financing of imports and finally, the initial observable implications of the measures for the reform of the price system and the liberalisation of the economy. It is nevertheless clear that the different dimensions of adjustment policies are inter-related: at the same time as its aims to re-establish an equilibrium in external finances, devaluation has the added objective of altering internal relative prices, to the benefit of agriculture and 'tradable goods'. Similarly, the selective allocation of foreign currency and of counterpart funds constitutes a powerful means for orienting sectoral priorities along the same lines. These new priorities finally aim to re-establish growth and to develop exports, and through this to assist in the reduction of deficits.

The Effects of Overall Equilibrium Policies

The statistics below contained in Tables 6.1, 6.2 and 6.3 provide a summary of Madagascar's economic performance since 1980. Positive results were obtained concerning the control of inflation,[4] the reduction of the deficit of the merchandise trade balance, and the balance of goods and services excluding the debt-service, as well as the reduction of the deficit of public accounts.[5]

TABLE 6.1   *The Evolution of Economic Growth and Inflation 1980–85*

	1980	1981	1982	1983	1984	1985
GDP*	100	91.4	89.7	90.5	92.4	94.6
Imports*	100	65.0	60.4	50.6		
Exports*	100	73.8	72.0	61.8		
Industrial production index	100	85.2	73.9	76.5	71.3	
Consumer price index†	16.9	26.1	33.0	13.1	9.8	10.0
GDP implicit price deflator†	15.0	25.2	28.5	21.6	9.7	11.2

* In constant 1970 Malgache francs.
† Annual growth rate.
SOURCE: World Bank, and INSRE (Institut de Statistiques Malgache).

TABLE 6.2 *Evolution of the Balance of Payments (in millions $ US, 1980–85)*

	1980	1981	1982	1983	1984	1985
Exports f.o.b.	436	332	327	310	333	278
Imports f.o.b.	764	511	452	378	352	336
Merchandise trade balance	−328	−179	−125	−68	−19	−58
Services net of interest on debt	−233	−161	−149	−127	−92	−87
Net private transfers	4	4	−1	−1	4	15
Balance of goods and services net of interest on debt	−557	−336	−275	−196	−107	−130
Interest on public loans	−22	−33	−47	−56	−83	−76
Interest on private loans	−18	−50	−39	−43	−41	−36
Interest on IMF loans	−2	−6	−11	−13	−13	−14
Total interest	−42	−89	−97	−112	−137	−126
Principal on public loans	−22	−96	−165	−96	−98	−106
Principal on private loans	−21	−14	−16	−100	−32	−43
Principal on IMF loans	−5	−9	−1	−4	−24	−33
Total principal	−48	−119	−182	−200	−154	−182
Total debt service*	−90	−208	−279	−312	−300	−316
Gross financing needs [(6) + (9)]	−647	−543	−554	−508	−398	−438
Current balance of payments [(6) + (7)]	−599	−425	−372	−308	−244	−256
GDP	3,265	2,904	2,848	2,837	2,383	2,329
Exports of goods and services	518	398	382	358	394	354
Debt outstanding (disbursed)	1,020	1,452	1,660	1,890	2,050	2,200

*Before Rescheduling.
SOURCE: World Bank, *Country Economic Memorandum*, 1986.

TABLE 6.3   *Evolution of the Balance of Payments and the Debt as a Percentage of GDP 1980–85*

	1980	1981	1982	1983	1984	1985
Exports f.o.b	13.4	11.4	11.5	10.9	14.0	11.9
Imports f.o.b.	23.4	17.6	15.9	13.3	14.8	14.4
Merchandise trade balance	−10.0	−6.2	−4.4	−2.4	−0.8	−2.5
Balance of goods and services net of interest on debt	−17.1	−11.5	−9.7	−6.9	−4.5	−5.6
Debt service*	−2.7	−7.2	−9.8	−11.0	−12.6	−13.6
Gross financing needs	−19.8	−18.7	−19.5	−17.9	−17.1	−19.1
Current balance of payments	−18.3	−14.6	−13.1	−10.9	−10.2	−11.0
Debt outstanding (disbursed)	31.2	50.0	58.3	66.6	86.0	94.5
Debt service as a percentage of exports of goods and services*	17.4	52.3	73.0	87.2	76.1	89.3

*Before rescheduling
SOURCE: Based on Table 6.2

On the other hand, the new-found equilibrium was achieved at the high price of very severe deflation: import-rationing; a drop of 10 per cent in the Gross Domestic Product, 29 per cent with respect to industrial production; a drop in exports; and a decline in investment levels. In 1982–83 gross fixed capital investment calculated in constant francs was one third lower than previous levels for the years 1970–75.

Average per capita consumption in constant francs dropped by more than 15 per cent, the purchasing power of the minimum guaranteed industrial income declined by more than 25 per cent and civil servants' salaries dropped by almost 50 per cent. Many consumer goods industries, despite the decrease in their potential, had to reduce their production for lack of outlets.[6]

The debt service increased rapidly while Gross Domestic Product declined (in constant Malgache francs and even more so in dollars), with the result that needs for overall financing, as expressed as a percentage of the Gross Domestic Product, did not decline but, rather, rose to 19 per cent. As a result of the increase in the debt-service and the drop in exports, the ratio of the debt-service before rescheduling, continued to increase, reaching 89 per cent by 1985. The amount of the debt disbursed continued to rise and reached 95 per cent of the Gross Domestic Product in 1985.

Deflation resulting from the shortage of currency and adjustment policies has had a particularly severe impact on Madagascar, in that it has directly affected both the level of demand and production through the scarcity of inputs, the absence of investment in the renewal of capital stock, disorganisation and deterioration in the transportation and distribution networks. The structural weaknesses of the Malgache economy (low levels of investment, weak internal articulation, weak growth of exports) have made the country particularly vulnerable to this shock, which in turn intensified these weaknesses. Several of the policies chosen by the international financial organisations (and notably the introduction of structural adjustment policies and then the CASI and CASA) have had the effect of mitigating the shock. On the other hand, in 1985 and 1986, the depressed level of demand became one of the principal barriers to the revitalisation of the economy.

Finally, the low level and lack of growth of exports, as well as their extreme vulnerability to internal disorganisation, meant that debt-service weighed particularly heavily in relation to the potentialities of the economy. Successive rescheduling has loosened the stranglehold somewhat but the above results clearly demonstrate that, firstly, it is necessary to find a more lasting solution to the problem of the debt burden; and secondly it is necessary to increase the levels of exports and activity in order to decrease the onus of the debt and to stop the process of pauperisation which has taken on alarming proportions among certain social groups.

The Effects of Selective Financing of Imports

Foreign currency credits which are allotted to finance imports (through the structural adjustment programmes (SAPs) of the CCCE, the CASI and CASA) have had a positive effect for the survival of the productive system. Whereas as a result of currency shortages, Malgache authorities sacrificed intermediate goods and equipment for social and humanitarian reasons in order to limit restrictions on the import of consumer goods (foodstuffs and rice in particular), the SAPs have supplied the financing for a minimum of inputs to agriculture, industry and transportation.

However, these credits, which represented roughly half the value of imports in 1986, constituted an extremely powerful tool for foreign creditors to progressively introduce new priorities in sectoral choices notably concerning: priority to agriculture and particularly to agricultural exports; priority to revitalising existing capacities; priority to export-oriented industries; and priority to solvent industries.

This new emphasis in favour of agriculture, currency generating activities and market economy indicators (which reflect an entire set of criteria diametrically opposed to those implicit in the strategy chosen in the 1970s), was accentuated with the implementation of the CASA and the CASI and the conditionalities which accompanied them.[7]

The Effects of Measures designed to Reform the System of Relative Prices and to Liberalise the Economy

These measures include a devaluation which is expected to modify the system of internal prices in order to favour agricultural producers (to the detriment of urban consumers) and to encourage an improvement in foreign trade. This is to be achieved through the introduction of measures to increase agricultural prices; the liberalisation of industrial prices; the liberalisation of foreign exchange controls; the progressive liberalisation of trade and, in particular, the liberalisation of the price and internal distribution pattern of rice.

It is expected that these measures will permit:

(a) an increase in production and exporting of agricultural products (in particular production and commercialisation of rice, production and export of coffee);

(b) a boost to industrial production as a result of the overcoming of bottlenecks (which are for the most part attributed to the poor management of the economy and in particular to the problem of the allocation of foreign exchange), and of the larger place to be attributed to market forces;

(c) the progressive re-establishment of foreign trade as a result of the boost to agricultural exports; the decrease in rice imports; a system of internal pricing more closely aligned with the principle of the comparative advantage of the moment and greater competitivity (as a consequence of devaluation).

It is still too early to evaluate the effects of all these measures. Nevertheless, a number of observations can be made with respect to the effects of devaluation, liberalisation of the rice trade, and the modification of relative prices in favour of agriculture.

The Effects of Devaluation

Between 1982–86, the Malgache franc was successively devalued by 75 per cent in relation to the SDR. Another devaluation of 20 per cent was decided upon in August 1986.

Despite its scope, the positive effects of these devaluations appear to have been rather limited, largely for the following reasons:

(a)   Initially, the increase in prices of agricultural exports in Malgache francs was funnelled toward raising state revenues and not producer prices.

(b)   The modifications in relative internal prices resulting from the devaluation were submerged in the movement of prices engendered by rationing, the rise followed by the partial absorption of parallel markets, and the movement of speculative prices which accompanied certain liberalisation policies (rice for example).

(c)   The notion of 'a balanced exchange rate' which allows for the re-establishing of equilibrium in external trade and commerce may be considered contentious firstly because imports have already been very much reduced and are now composed essentially of goods whose compression would profoundly alter productive potential. Secondly, the dilapidated state of the industrial productive system, and its high import content, bar the possibilities of companies becoming more competitive in the short term, except in the most rare cases, with respect to exports through the manipulation of exchange rates.

The principal results to be expected from the most recent devaluations are those which may arise from the increase in Malgache francs of agricultural prices to producers.

Increases in Producer Prices and the Priority given to Agriculture: the Problem of Coffee

Real producer prices for agricultural products continued to drop during the second half of the 1970s. This trend accelerated from

1980–82, as a result of high inflation which in part explains the stagnation or drop in production. Between 1975–82, production of most of the major crops (rice, coffee, cotton, cloves)[8] declined by roughly 40 per cent. The stand-by agreement of 1982 not only introduced a devaluation of 15 per cent, but also recommended an increase in producer prices for rice of 27 per cent, for cotton of 26 per cent, as well as for other agricultural products and notably coffee. Increases in rice and cotton prices were in fact implemented. They only partially counteracted the effects of inflation of the beginning of the 1980s.[9] On the other hand, the price of coffee (the major export) was only raised 4 per cent. This fact attests to the resistance of the Malgache government to the IMF policies and the government's preference to favour the public accounts, to the detriment of producers. This preference led to the following consequences. Firstly, far from contributing to the increase of producer prices, the devaluation was accompanied by a new decrease of real producer prices. The new price level was insufficient to make coffee commercially viable but only covered crops gathered hastily, subject to neither cultivation nor upkeep.[10] Secondly, the already poor ratio between rice and coffee prices was reduced further to 1:2.5 (while on the world market it was 1:10). Given this relationship, it was in the interest of coffee producers to cultivate their own rice rather than purchase it with coffee earnings. This of course led to strong competition in the allocation of labour time between these two products.

Under pressure from the IMF and particularly from the World Bank, coffee producer prices were raised in 1984–85, and especially in 1985–86, however less than the Bank would have liked, and the real price remained lower (roughly 20 per cent) than what it had been in the 1970s. On the other hand, as a result of increases in official prices, and especially liberalisation, the price of rice increased more rapidly so that the price differential between rice and coffee was again reduced.

The deterioration in coffee prices, first of all in real value and in relative value *vis-à-vis* rice prices, constitutes one of the variables explaining the drop in coffee exports (−35 per cent) from 1980–85. The consequences of this decrease were particularly serious in view of the fact that coffee represents approximately 40 per cent of Madagascar's exports. The drop may be explained because of the ageing of plantations, the almost irreversible deterioration of the former European plantations and the dilapidation of the transport and distribution networks. This deterioration of plantations and the existence of bottlenecks show, on the other hand, that while a necessary factor, substantial producer price increases and the re-establishment of a rice/coffee ratio which was more favourable to coffee would not be sufficient conditions alone to significantly increase the production and commercialisation of coffee.

The decrease in real producer prices and the deterioration of the economic environment are all at the root of the drop in production and exports of sisal, pepper, bananas (exports stopped in 1983) and groundnuts (exports stopped in 1975).

At the time of writing, only the increase in cotton producer prices, accompanied by vigorous development efforts seemed to have borne fruit, however, at a time when world prices were unfortunately falling, plunging this sector into deficit. The situation of rice will be examined below.

The Initial Effects of Liberalisation: the Case of Rice

The liberalisation of the internal commercialisation of rice was, without a doubt, a major issue in Madagascar in 1986 for the following reasons:

(a) the strategic situation of rice in Madagascar, the repercussions of price increases for consumers, on the standard of living of the urban population and on the demand for goods other than food products;

(b) the depth of the changes that liberalisation entails for the state's role in the economy, particularly with respect to its control over agricultural production and commercialisation;

(c) the importance of the political test of this operation for the entire process of liberalisation advocated by international financial institutions. A failure in this domain, sanctioned by the reactions of the population, could entail the strengthening of the position of those opposed to this process and an abandoning of this policy.

Begun in 1982, the process had achieved in 1985 the partial liberalisation of circuits of commercialisation and in 1986, their complete liberalisation. Only rice imports remained under the control of the administration and were subject to quotas. A buffer stock made up of imported rice was earmarked to weigh heavily on prices to consumers in the event that the price ceiling was surpassed. The objectives of liberalisation were to increase production and commercialisation through a boost in producer prices, and to achieve greater efficiency and lower costs of commercialisation.

The partial liberalisation of 1985 engendered heavy speculation and an explosion of prices on the free market. Prices reached 800 FMG/Kg as compared to the official price of 265 FMG. Complete liberalisation in 1986 provoked a soaring of producer prices, which more than doubled and even tripled (from 85 FMG to 250 FMG) and the same was true for consumer prices. The ceiling price was largely surpassed early in the season. Speculation occurred at all levels of the commercialisation process. Intervention, through the buffer stocks, permitted at the very last moment, (beginning of November) reducing the retail price in Tananarive close to the ceiling price (between 450 and 500 FMG). The stabilisation of this price (which already represented a doubling of prices for the consumer) in Tananarive, in other cities and in other agricultural regions, experiencing a deficit, represents a central issue for the years to come.

In the short term, the negative effects appeared to have gained the upper hand:

(a) At the level of producers, real prices showed strong improvement; on the other hand, the wave of speculation created a climate of uncertainty which is not necessarily beneficial to commercialisation (for it provokes an increase in security stocks held by producers), or beneficial for an eventual intensification of production (for uncertainty is not favourable to investment). The long-term consequences for production and commercialisation need to be examined more closely;

(b) the soaring of prices and speculation are disadvantageous to agricultural regions currently experiencing deficits, particularly for coffee producers and hence there has been a sharpening of competition between coffee and rice, or coffee and other food crops with respect to labour allocation;

(c) consumers have borne the brunt of these changes, in view of the fact that the price of other food crops has on the whole followed rice price trends. The heavy increases in food budgets have had a negative effect on the demand for other consumer goods;

(d) increasing speculation and its accompanying draining of capital are hardly beneficial for reform and revitalisation of the economy. Obviously the World Bank's strategy is premised on the assumptions that: speculation will eventually run itself out through self-regulatory competition precisely as a result of liberalisation; and that producer prices will eventually become stable at a substantially higher level than previously existed, stimulating an increase in production.

This optimistic vision nevertheless downplays the inflexible nature of the socio-economic structure and environment:

(a) The compartmentalisation and segmentation of markets (transportation problems, resistance and barriers caused by local administrations);

(b) the complexities of the social structure, the weight of notables, of the owners of rice mills; the complex alliances related to the administrative economic structure at the root of speculation;

(c) structural blockages in production which price incentives alone cannot remove.[11]

As we have emphasised several times, the outcome of this crisis is of central importance as much from an economic standpoint (the problems associated with the relative prices of rice and coffee, the draining of urban incomes and as a consequence, of the demand for manufactured goods) as from a political standpoint (more or less opposition to the liberalisation process). Its outcome will contribute to determining the feasibility of any of the scenarios for resolving the crisis. Consequently, two points in particular will merit close attention:

(a) the implementation of complementary measures which beyond raising producer prices, will permit overcoming the bottlenecks of production; these include credit, supplying of fertilizers, insecticides, plant samples, agricultural equipment and equipment for the maintenance of irrigation canals;

(b) the maintaining of quotas on imports at a sufficiently high level so that the buffer stocks can effectively fulfil their role of stamping out speculation.

Too rigid a policy with respect to these two points, imposed by the pressures from external constraints, would threaten the outcome of any strategy to resolve the crisis.

PROSPECTS AND CONCLUSIONS

The World Bank's Scenario for Resolving the Crisis

The March 1986 World Bank economic memorandum attempted to sketch out a scenario for resolving the crisis in Madagascar, based on compliance with adjustment policies advocated by the IMF and the World Bank (see Table 6.4). This scenario was premised on:

(a) a vigorous increase in exports (4.1 per cent annually between 1985–90, 5.8 per cent annually from 1990–95) principally as a result of the increase of agricultural exports;

(b) a renewal of growth (3 per cent from 1985–90, 3.6 per cent subsequently) engendered by agricultural growth (3 per cent, 3.6 per cent) and industrial growth (4 per cent, 5.4 per cent).

(c) a reabsorption of the deficit in the balance of goods and services, resulting from the increase in exports, the elimination of imports in foodstuffs by 1990, to be replaced subsequently by the export of rice and only a moderate increase of other imports (at the same rate as GDP increase);

TABLE 6.4   *The World Bank Scenario to Solve the Crisis*

	Growth Rates (% per annum)			Share of GDP* (%)		
	1980–85	*1985–90*	*1990–95*	*1985*	*1990*	*1995*
Gross domestic product	−0.9	3.0	3.6	100	100	100
Agriculture	2.3	3.0	3.6	42	42	42
Industry †	−6.5	4.0	5.4	18	19	21
Other sectors	−0.7	2.8	2.6	40	39	37
Consumption	−0.6	2.9	2.8	91	90	87
Investment	−9.0	1.5	4.7	14	13	13
Exports	−6.9	4.1	5.8	15	17	19
Imports	−15.1	2.1	2.6	20	20	19
Gross domestic savings	−1.9	4.1	9.5	9	10	13
GDP, per capita	−3.6	0.3	0.8	n.a.	n.a.	n.a.

* In constant 1985 Prices
† Includes Mining, Manufacturing, Construction, and Utilities
SOURCE: World Bank: *Country Economic Memorandum*, March 1986, p. 49

(d)   a plan for financing, which foresaw the continuation of a
       positive, although decreasing, net flow of capital which would
       cease by 1995, and which would be based on the rescheduling
       of debt on much more lenient terms than those which had
       been obtained up until then, notably 31-year loans of which
       nine years were differred at an interest rate of 2.8 per cent.

After such a long period of stagnation and growing deficits, this
scenario assumes a thoroughgoing reversal of the situation. In order
to achieve this it advocates the following measures: increases in
agricultural producer prices; devaluations; continuation of the process of liberalisation and deregulation, particularly with respect to
exchange controls, commercialisation, and transportation; and reform of the public sector (state corporations, banks) culminating in
reform, privatisation or closures.

In this scenario, the central element in the revitalisation of the
economy is based on better use of price incentives and a greater role
given to market forces, which are supposed to stimulate the productive system which at the time was very much under-utilised. This
process of recovery was to take place in large part without great
additional investments (the investment coefficient was to remain at
its 1985 level of 13.5 per cent and even slightly decrease until 1990)
which in fact meant a rapid decrease in the marginal coefficient of
capital.

As is the case with the World Bank's analyses, this study also
concludes that there must be an increase in exports and growth; that
in order to accomplish this, priority must be given to agriculture, and
that there is need for more favourable conditions of debt refinancing
in order that the burden of debt be tolerable.[12] The increase in
agricultural prices, reform and rehabilitation of banks and state
corporations, the implementation of market mechanisms in sectors
where administrative efficiency has been weak (commerce, transportation), reform and reduction of administrative procedures constitute
necessary measures for change. However, several comments concerning the feasibility of the proposed scenario are in order:[13]

Scenario Projections with Respect to Agricultural Exports

These appear realistic in view of the fact that they will on the whole
only achieve levels established in the 1970s. Nevertheless, even

assuming strong price incentives, this recovery may take longer than anticipated for the following reasons:

(a) the often irreversible ageing and deterioration of plants and plantations (of coffee in particular);
(b) the severe deterioration of the transport system including roads, and the fleet of trucks;
(c) the marked degeneration of commercialisation networks (transport, but also uncontrolled and excessive intervention by local administrations, speculation, insecurity) and the progressive peasant withdrawal from the money economy.

A number of conditions are necessary to permit the revitalisation of export crops:

(a) a lasting solution to the crisis concerning rice in order to permit a regular supply at stable prices to zones currently experiencing deficits and the establishment of relative prices favourable to export crops (particularly coffee);[14]
(b) a reinforcement of the activities of ODASE[15] in order to improve roads, to create permanent selling points for inputs, to facilitate commercialisation, to undertake training services and an extension of these measures so as to make them available to all productive zones.

Scenario Projections with respect to Rice

Scenario projections assume an end to rice imports and exports of 70 000 tonnes by 1995, which implies (barring a significant drop in urban consumption) a huge increase in the quantities sold. This increase is expected to result from the liberalisation of prices and circuits, accompanied by ensuring peasant producers easy access to consumer goods made available to encourage market exchange and to incite them to recycle the monetary incomes.

Recent studies[16] appear to show that the drop in the volumes sold since the end of the 1970s is not only a result of the commercialisation crisis but, equally, due to the serious problems in production which has been unable to keep pace with the continuing growth of the population. Sustained growth of production necessitates, in addition to price changes, an intensification of production and important back-up policies (delivery of equipment, inputs, plant samples, advisory services, credit) as had been the case during the large-scale operations of the 1960s in response to the deficit which occurred at that time, and are aspects which do not seem to have been taken account of more recently. It is also important to emphasise that the scenario projections are based on the assumption of a rapid and optimistic resolution of the actual crisis in rice production and exports.

The Level of Industrial Production

The sustained recovery of the level of industrial production under the conditions assumed by the scenario, appears highly unlikely for the following reasons. Firstly, the low rate of productive capacity utilisation on which potential recovery is premised, without a rapid increase in investment, is misleading. For, as a result of a long period of disinvestment (except for the new investments of 1979–80 which for the most part were unusable), and as a result of more recent upheavals, a large part of the country's potential capacity has been severely weakened. The lasting recovery of industrial activity presupposes a sustained effort to renew investments which would require a higher level of investment and imports of equipment than those which have been retained. Moreover, given the low level of imports of inputs in 1985,[17] it is difficult to imagine how sustained recovery of industry can be achieved without a proportional growth in imports.

Secondly, the level of demand is too depressed to allow the recovery of industrial production for the internal market. In addition, the priority accorded agricultural incomes mitigates against this potential demand (the consumer goods made available to incite market exchange earmarked for peasants are largely imported goods) and the increase in the price of rice will accentuate the squeezing-out effect on other consumer goods. Finally, one can hardly expect a significant short term increase in industrial exports, whatever the level of the exchange rate (productivity is too weak, import-content is too high, the costs for both internal and external transport are discriminatingly high). The above arguments cast doubt on the assumption of the scenario to the effect that the growth of industrial production will occur at a rate significantly higher than that of internal final demand.

The Projected Growth Scheme

The growth scheme proposed in the scenario for the next ten years closely resembles that of the Malgache economy in the second half of the 1960s: regular growth at a rate slightly higher than that of the population, led by growth in agricultural production (rice and other export crops) and even greater increases in industrial production. However, the constraints which accompany the scenario are more serious than those present in the 1960s:

(a) the rate of investment is slightly weaker (13.5 per cent instead of 14.5 per cent);

(b) import levels are lower and on the decline (from 21.3 per cent of GDP to 19.8 per cent in 1990, and 18.9 per cent in 1995) whereas the growth in the 1960s was accompanied by an increase in import levels of 21.5 per cent in 1965 to 25 per cent for the period 1969–71;

(c) the deficit in the balance of goods and non-factor services decreases and is wiped out, whereas throughout the 1960s it remained at 5 per cent of the GDP;

(d) demographic constraints have intensified since then (for example population growth, the urban population, the educated population seeking employment);

(e) growth during the 1960s resulted from the joint efforts of the administration (within which foreign technical assistance had a central place) and foreign capital, which dominated the trading economy, commerce, industry and banks. The country's economic and administrative fabric in 1985 appears to be much more disarticulated, the commitment of the principal agents to the new scheme of growth (which is radically different from that of the immediate past) must still be secured.

For these reasons, it may be feared that the manner in which the scenario attempts to resolve the crisis, that is by trying to combine recovery with the respect of external constraints, may prove infeasible and we may be moving closer to a prolongation of past trends whose negative consequences have already been detailed above.

The Difficulties Encountered by Adjustment Programmes

The difficulties encountered by adjustment programmes which are drawn up by foreign financial organisations, and which have as their dual objectives the re-establishment of equilibria and solvency on the one hand, and economic recovery through liberalisation and the restructuring of supply on the other, may be analysed around three themes. These are the problem of the timetable for adjustment and the loosening of external constraints; the problem of the permanence of structural weaknesses of the Malgache economy and the limits which this places on a strategy which relies on market forces; and the problems of resistance to adjustment and those resulting from the placing of the economy under trusteeship.

Problems associated with the Timetable for Adjustment and the Loosening of External Constraints:

As is the case with other countries which have implemented adjustment policies, Madagascar is confronted with the problem of the compatibility between policies designed to reestablish, as rapidly as possible, a situation of macroeconomic equilibria on the one hand, and on the other, the objectives of restructuring supply and restoring growth. The latter is absolutely necessary in order to be able to support the burden of debt and to avoid the continuing and dramatic impoverishment of certain sectors of the population.

To be sure, measures introduced as part of adjustment policies in order to achieve macroeconomic equilibria (and under the immediate constraint of currency shortages) in the short term, lead to the following:

(a) a compression of demand and in particular of urban demand;
(b) maintaining investments and imports at a very low level. With respect to the latter, this entails restrictions or quotas in one form or another;
(c) the state's disengagement from direct intervention in the economy and the compression of public expenditures.

Now the recovery of the economy based on liberalisation, is largely incompatible with too strict a rationing of imports. More specifically, in a country where the market operates very imperfectly and where, on a regular basis, one is aware of the dominant place of intermediaries, basic necessities become the object of speculation, as is well illustrated by the case of rice.

The revitalisation of agriculture presupposes, in addition to the increase in producer prices, the implementation of supporting measures (such as roads and development schemes) which are incompatible with the withdrawal of the state and drastic cut-backs in the means at its disposal.

The short term boosting of industry is not compatible with a compression of demand, priority accorded to agricultural incomes and the maintenance of investment and imports at such low levels.

Finally, the liberalisation measures and the restructuring of supply cannot be expected to have a decisive impact in the very short term for reasons which are physical (the time needed to restore roads, plantations, to make improvements in commercial circuits and to institute advisory and training services) and socio-political (widespread local and national resistance to liberalisation). Continuing deflation and increased speculation will inevitably strengthen such opposition.

The World Bank's scenario illustrates both the seriousness and the enormous difficulties of the situation. All delays which occur in the revitalising of exports and growth will only contribute to tightening the external constraints and increasing the relative burden of debt. In the absence of the shock absorber role which exists for other countries which are members of the Franc zone, Madagascar's currency shortages become immediate obstacles to production. Although in answer to this difficulty the scenario recommends rescheduling at conditions which are clearly more favourable than those obtained in the past, the weight of the financial constraints continues to have the upper hand over the measures to liberalise and restructure supply. Consequently, there is every reason to believe that the financial burden will compromise the anticipated results and consequently only serve to reproduce further constraints.

To avoid the complete regression of the economy and to successfully carry out the process of liberalisation and economic recovery, would require that a positive net flow of capital, substantially larger than that envisioned, be forthcoming. Nevertheless, this loosening of external constraints is a necessary condition but not a sufficient condition, as has been adequately demonstrated by the unfortunate experience of the 1978–80 period.

The Permanence of Structural Blockages in the Malgache Economy and the Limits to Market Forces

The structural weaknesses of the Malgache economy which had developed over a long historical period (low levels of accumulation, weak internal articulation, weak growth of exports, the importance of the place of intermediaries) were reinforced with the implementation of the strategy of radical change in the 1970s and during the period of austerity at the beginning of the 1980s.

The assumption underlying adjustment programmes is that liberalisation and greater reliance on market forces can progressively solve these problems. The solution in Madagascar, however, is far from obvious, because there the problem is not one of 'restoring market forces', as if they represented the natural functioning of the economy, but rather the introducing of a market dynamic in an economy where the market has been fragmented and deficient over a long time period and where it has clearly deteriorated for over a decade. At the very least this assumes firstly that the state be in a position to carry out its role as policeman, which is considered by the entire tradition of economic liberalism as a precondition for the proper operation of the market. The state must be able to guarantee the security of goods and individuals, and to check the abuses which might arise out of a situation of dominance. Secondly, voluntarist initiatives should be taken in the area of transportation and the regulation of commercialisation in order to unify the market and permit its proper functioning. From both these standpoints, comparison with the situation of grain markets under the old French regime is revealing: when the above conditions do not exist, liberalisation encourages the emergence of a situation of domination and soaring prices.

With respect to production, if it may be said that the regular operation of the market and the lifting or alleviation of the many administrative constraints are necessary conditions for revitalising the economy, it is equally true that the additional loosening of a certain number of bottlenecks cannot be considered sufficient without other supporting measures.

With respect to agriculture, these have been enumerated and include roads, measures designed to facilitate supplies and commercialisation, better supplies of plant samples, advisory services and credit. Solutions, aimed at resolving certain basic problems with respect to land and notably to limit rents, need also to be given consideration.

As concerns industry, due to the weaknesses inherent in the Malgache productive system which we have outlined above, and its weak position in the international environment, adjusting to the comparative advantage of the moment, coupled with successive devaluations do not represent sufficient conditions to ensure the recovery of the secondary sector. Opening up the economy under such circumstances would only contribute to destroying what still exists. On the contrary, it would appear more reasonable to implement selective measures in order to rebuild certain strategic sectors such as agro-business, building and public works, construction materials, small-scale mechanical activities and so forth.

The policy options raised by these issues are very concrete, as illustrated by the question of currency allocation. The choices include the creation of a system dictated only by market forces and criteria of solvency on the one hand, or the partial maintenance of a system of selective allocations in order to take account of priorities. The experience of the CCCE with its SAP programmes seems to weigh in favour of maintaining certain selective allocations according to priorities. The conclusions of the above analysis also go along these lines. Another important area of policy concerns the restructuring of tariffs, taxes and subsidies which has been prepared by the World Bank.

Finally, the stable operation of market forces and the development of the local market are not compatible with a highly skewed pattern of income distribution, particularly if the pole constituted by the highest incomes is linked closely to foreign markets rather than the internal market.

The insistence that the state must continue to assume various roles in order to ensure the optimal implementation of liberalisation policies and the strengthening of the market economy obviously raises difficult problems in a situation where administrative interventions have been discredited both locally and abroad. However, it would be short-sighted not to raise these questions.

Resistance to Adjustment and to the Trusteeship of the Economy

There is widespread opposition to adjustment policies and liberalisation from within the economy and from within the Malgache state. This opposition was illustrated by the attempt to delay increases in producer prices (principally of coffee), to delay or circumvent the liberalisation of the rice trade (local administrative opposition, speculation) and by the attempt to delay the restructuring of banks and state corporations. This opposition has its roots in both the desire to maintain certain advantages (sources of power and income) and also in the ideological opposition to the abandonment of the strategy which had been implemented to consolidate national independence and the Malgachisation of the economy. These resistances and conflicts of interest have ultimately contributed to the perpetuation of the dysfunctioning of markets and the disruption of efforts directed to encourage a renewal of production and exports.

International financial institutions however, possess powerful tools to quell opposition. These tools are proportional to the gross capital inputs which, in general, are tied to conditionalities and at times accompanied by the right to approve counterpart funds. Over the years, the interventions of the lending institutions have become more and more precise to the extent of placing large sections of the economies concerned under a quasi-trusteeship, sector by sector and firm by firm.

Even if the international financial organisations have achieved positive results in certain scattered sectors, the process they have instituted is not without risks and may very well stimulate strong opposition. Furthermore, one may ask, up to what degree of detail should such policies be pursued if a minimum of consensus amongst the principal economic and political agents concerned has not emerged, in order that the state may assure the conditions necessary to the process of liberalisation mentioned above (its policing role, the guaranteeing of the minimum conditions to permit market operations, support measures and so forth). It is extremely doubtful that greater and greater subordination of the economy will contribute to the emergence of such a consensus.

Notes

1. For a more complete analysis see G. Duruflé *et al.*, *Déséquilibres structurels et programmes d'ajustement à Madagascar* (Paris: Ministry of Co-operation, 1986) and G. Duruflé, *L'ajustement structurel en Afrique. (Sénegal, Côte-d'Ivoire, Madagascar))* (Paris: Karthala, 1988) pp. 151–193.
2. In Senegal the Muslim brotherhoods, and in particular the Mourides, played a crucial role in stimulating the endogenous development of the groundnut economy. In the Ivory Coast, societies such as the Baoulé or those in the North became organised around temporary migrations to the forest zones in order to develop plantations.
3. Ivorian industry retained a relatively sustained rate of growth in the 1970s as a result of the growth of the rest of the economy. But its share of the GDP declined after 1972.
4. Nevertheless, the 10 per cent rate in 1985 needs to be examined more closely. This statistic underestimates the effects of speculation on rising prices for domestic rice consumption and for other food crops. As a result of the speculative increases in the consumer price of rice and the other foodstuffs whose increase accompanied that of rice, together with the fall in incomes, rice and food in general occupy a more important place than that suggested by the manner in which the indicator is constructed.

5. The deficit of overall treasury operations decreased from 18.3 per cent of the GDP in 1980 to 4.2 per cent in 1985. However, this statistic does not include the deficit of public enterprises and state corporations, financed by bank loans.

6. Statistics do not account for either poverty or famine. See *Le Monde,* 22 November 1986, pp. 9–12.

7. Although it also supports the priority given to agriculture, currency-generating activities and solvent industries, the CCCE also accords particular attention to activities which may be qualified as strategic, even if they do not immediately satisfy the aforementioned criteria.

8. The two exceptions were vanilla and to a lesser extent sisal, the only products not to be caught up in this process of deterioration. The uncertainty concerning the extent of the deterioration is due to the uncertainty of the price index used to deflate.

9. For rice and cotton the real price of the 82–83 season reached the level of the 80–81 season, that is about 30 per cent lower than the price for the 76–77 season.

10. Jacques Richard, 'Identification des principales contraintes à la caféiculture dans le Sud-Est de Madagascar', Ministry of Co-operation (Paris: Bureau des Evaluations, November 1986).

11. J.M. Yung, 'Aperçus sur la filière riz à Madagascar,' Ministry of Co-operation (Paris: Bureau des Evaluations, November 1986) specifically pp. 104–106.

12. The tendential scenario, that is that which postulates the continuation of present trends (concerning the level of production, exports and conditions of financing), constructed by the World Bank in contrast to the scenario to resolve the crisis, rightly concludes that there will occur a cessation of payments and a collapse in production due to the rationing of imports.

13. These remarks are aimed at both exploring the possibilities and at finding solutions which, as emphasised by the World Bank reports, are the principal objectives of the exercise of scenario elaboration. In this respect, the World Bank's synthesis studies are of central importance and the Malgache administration deprives itself of a critical instrument in its negotiations with international financial organisations by relinquishing to these bodies, the task of defining macroeconomic coherence and projections.

14. The study cited of J. Richard emphasises that the central obstacle to the increase in production of coffee is the problem of food supplies for coffee producers. Because they are unable to purchase regular food supplies at reasonable prices, they centre their efforts on producing food crops.

15. ODASE: Opération de Développement Agricole du Sud-Est: the South-East Agricultural Development Scheme.

16. J.M. Yung, op. cit. (1986).

17. In 1985, imported intermediate goods stood at the same level in current dollars as in the 1975–77 period, which constitutes almost a 50 per cent drop in constant dollars.

7 Production and Commercialisation of Rice in Cameroon: The Semry Project

DOMINIQUE CLAUDE

INTRODUCTION

Between 1967 and 1983, during the high point of World Bank activity in rural development in the Cameroon, the Bank financed 18 agricultural development projects, nearly all of which were oriented towards export crops such as rubber, cocoa and palm oil. Most of the projects were carried out by semi-public corporations and were of an enclave type. The project under consideration here is interesting because it was conceived to serve the internal market. Moreover, it is a development project not a production project. This vast irrigated rice growing project, Semry (Société d'expansion et de modernisation tion de la riziculture de Yagoua), is in fact destined to produce rice for local consumption. For the lending agencies, as for the state of Cameroon, Semry represents one of the rare examples of successful rice farming in Africa.

In what follows, we shall analyse the project from the point of view of its two objectives – to assure the country's self-sufficiency in rice (enlargement of the domestic market) and to assure the development of the Yagoua region (impact on the peasantry).

We shall first examine the project's origin, as well as the context in which it was conceived. There is some ambiguity as to the objectives of the project that, in the final analysis, reflects the ambiguity of the country's agricultural policy. In this region of North Cameroon, characterised by growing desertification and drought, this vast irrigated rice growing operation appears at first sight to be the answer to development problems. The World Bank boasts of the project's technical success and the spectacular increase in peasant income. Apart from this technical concept of development which is shared by

MAP 2   The Semry Rice Cultivation Project of the Cameroon
SOURCE World Bank, Project Performance Audit Report,
Cameroon Second Semry Rice Project (Washington: June 1984) p. 21.

the lending agencies and the state alike, we shall analyse another reality: that of the peasants who are tenant-farmers on state land and have seen their general living conditions deteriorate. The analysis will also show the variety of responses from peasant groups to these new conditions and will demonstrate that far from being passive actors in development, the peasants have adapted in a very dynamic manner according to possibilities open to them. Moreover, as a result of having omitted to include women in its model of development, Semry has increased traditional inequalities in such a manner that women may now be described as 'the most exploited of the exploited', the consequences of which will weigh heavily on the future of the project.

In the second part, we shall see, through the problem of commercialisation, how the state short-circuits its policy of internal market development and how this problem reflects, in the final analysis, the contradictions within the state of Cameroon itself.

PRODUCTION

The Origins of the Project and the Ambiguity of Agricultural Policy

One of the most important agro-industrial complexes in the Cameroon, Semry was created in 1971 with the following objectives: to guarantee the country's self-sufficiency in rice; to improve the trade balance by permitting import substitution; and to create local added value and the development of the Yagoua region, a particularly underdeveloped area. It is important, first of all, to underline the origins of the project in order to show the continuity of colonial policy after independence and the foundations of this policy of self-sufficiency.

Rice farming in the Middle-Logone (Moyen-Logone) plains dates back to 1954, with the creation of the Experimental Modernisation Sector, whose mandate was to develop this crop, which was traditionally harvested in its wild state by certain of the local inhabitants. This decision on the part of the French authorities of the time, which followed upon rice growing experiments made by the Germans in the region, arose as a consequence of interruptions in imports of Asiatic rice after the Second World War. In this region, where cotton farming was impossible because of the floods during the rainy season, the *Société*, to which the responsibility was given, found itself entrusted with the mandate to develop the irrigable land, furnish the peasants with the necessary inputs and staff, and mill the paddy with a view to selling it in the country's urban centres.

Although North Cameroon had been designated as an exporter of cotton since the colonial era, there was room for a project oriented towards the internal market, as long as it did not compete with cotton. In creating Semry in 1971, the Cameroon government was merely pursuing this policy. Several factors mitigated in favour of the expansion of rice farming in the Cameroon with a view to achieve self-sufficiency in food: the drought of 1970–73, which exposed the vulnerability of an economy based on export farming, and the growing urban demand oriented towards imported models of consumption. The latter was doubtless a determining factor in that imports of rice and wheat showed a spectacular increase at the beginning of the 1970s. These rice imports came mainly from the Asiatic countries and were destined essentially for urban populations. The political weight of these groups was a determining element in the creation of the Semry project. Finally, the importance of North Cameroon in the system of legitimation of the Ahidjo government at the time is worth noting.

The Semry project was designed to encourage the expansion of the internal market. It forms part of the strategy for hegemony of the ruling class, initiated by the Ahidjo government and resumed and reinforced by the Biya government: in a word, to control the means of production and extraction of surplus. This aim in no way contradicts those of the World Bank, which notes in its report on the future of Semry:

> This rice production enterprise should be self-financing, efficiently managed and should be continuously on the lookout for ways of reducing overhead and other costs. In the end, it should even be possible for Government to dispose of part or all of its share capital in Semry to the private sector.[1]

The role of the state as a substitute for local private capital and as a means of reinforcing it is clear. More globally, the objective of the World Bank is to introduce its orientations into the Cameroon economy, that is, to defend the interests of capital in general. Following on the above quotation, one may read, with reference to its future participation in Semry:

> While the above are pertinent issues which will require continuous attention, the Bank, having withdrawn from the supplementary

financing of Semry, has lost some, if not most, of its leverage to play an active role in helping shape the future of Semry. This might not be immediately required; on the other hand, decisions in this field will not only determine the future viability of Semry, and thus of Bank-supported investments, but also the *shape of regional development in the North* [my italics].[2]

This policy, which seeks to be complementary to big capital and the national state, has taken form in a contradictory manner. More specifically, for the state of Cameroon, a certain ambiguity has always existed with respect to the final aims of the project and more precisely at the level of commercial policy.

Furthermore, there has always remained somewhat of a contradiction between the 'export' orientation of the project and the 'self-sufficiency' orientation of the Government's rice development policy. This contradiction has not yet been satisfactorily resolved.[3]

This ambiguity only reflects the hesitations of the agricultural policy as a whole. In fact, analysis of the Fourth and Fifth Development Plans (1977–81 and 1981–86) shows state hesitation between the old agro-export model and a development model based on the food sector as an engine of growth. The Fourth Plan, and more particularly the Fifth, places the emphasis on food self-sufficiency, while at the same time aiming at increased agricultural exports. These two very ambitious objectives may be documented by the level of investment allotment, as revealed by the following figures:[4]

	Fourth Plan	Fifth Plan
Export Sector	29%	40%
Food Sector	60%	30%
Integrated development projects	9%	28%
State plantation sectors	50%	42%

In the above, one may see an increase in investment in the export sector in the Fifth Plan. While for the World Bank the interpretation of the increase must be subject to caution, given the growing integration of the food sector and cash crops, it seems that the greater emphasis placed on the traditional sector does not appear to have materialised in reality. Some measures, such as the increase in prices paid to producers of the principal export crops, despite the stagnation of prices on the world market,[5] confirm this observation. Further-

TABLE 7.1   *World Bank Loans, Agricultural Sector 1967–83*

Sub-sector	Number of projects	Total loans ($ US millions)	%
Plantations	8	172.40	55
Rural development	5	62.80	20
Rice production	2	32.70	11
Stock raising	2	27.70	9
Forestry	1	17.0	5
	18	312.60	100

SOURCE: World Bank, *Project Performance Audit Report, Cameroon Second Semry Rice Project,* (Washington: June 1984, p. 2).

more, according to the World Bank, it can be noted, that there has always been a contradiction between the objectives stated in the Plan and their translation into reality.[6]

As for the World Bank's assistance in agricultural development, there is no ambiguity. Support for the export sector is clearly evident in Table 7.1 where it can be seen that 55 per cent of Bank loans have been destined principally for oil, rubber and cocoa plantations.

Annex I shows the detailed list of the 18 projects in the agricultural sub-sector. Total World Bank commitments for all of the Cameroon for the period concerned amount to US$800 million divided among 43 projects. Of this total, the Semry project absorbed $32.7 million.

The World Bank therefore operates on the basis of clearer choices than the state of Cameroon, which seems to waver between two models. Later, we shall see the contradictions in commercial policy that have emerged from this indetermination on the part of the state. As far as the peasants are concerned, however, the state and foreign capital have a very clear position that has never varied. The peasant is considered only as labour to be exploited and as a passive actor in development. In this sense there is no ambiguity; the state and foreign capital have created an alliance at the expense of the peasantry.

Description of the Semry Project

The first Semry project, created in 1971 at Yagoua (Semry I), was destined to develop 4300 hectares of rice farms and implied complete control over water supply. Given its success (4500 hectares were developed, the introduction of double cropping, greater yields than expected), a second, equally large, project was begun at Maga (Semry II) in 1978; and in addition, the realisation of the Logone and Chari Project (Semry III) in the Kousseri region was assigned to Semry in 1979.

In all, the Semry I and II Projects, which are the ones of particular concern here,[7] had absorbed CFA fr21 billion by 30 June 1984, of which 38 per cent was financed by the World Bank, 33 per cent by the Republic of Cameroon, 19 per cent by the French Caisse Centrale de Coopération Economique, CCCE, and 10 per cent by French public assistance, the *Fonds d'Aide et de Coopération*. For Semry III, it may be noted that at the same date, the cost amounted to CFA fr2.4 billion of which 36 per cent was financed by the Republic of Cameroon and 64 per cent by the European Development Fund.

Altogether, the achievements of the three Semry projects may be summarised as follows:

(a)   12 000 hectares of rice fields developed, of which 9000 hectares permit double cropping;

(b)   22 000 rice growing families, or more than 100 000 people directly supported by rice farming;

(c)   80 000 tonnes of paddy (harvested in 1983–84) and milled into 44 000 tonnes of rice;

(d)   an average yield per season of 5.4 tonnes per hectare in 1983–84 and 6 tonnes in 1985, or more than 10 tonnes per hectare per year on land that was double cropped (70 per cent of the total).

At the time, these represented the highest rice yields in Africa.

For the lending agencies, as for the state of Cameroon, Semry is considered an exemplary success. Thus, one may read in the World Bank's audit report:

Nevertheless, technically speaking, the project has been a great success. With transplanting generally accepted and new varieties having been introduced, yields are now expected to be higher than estimated at appraisal. Paddy production at full development would reach about 53,000 tons compared to the appraisal estimate of 47,000 tons. Fishing in the lake has produced substantial additional benefits. The reestimated rate of return is 20%. For irrigated rice development alone, the reestimated rate of return is 16%, close to the 15% appraisal estimate, with higher costs having been offset by higher yields. The number of beneficiaries is slightly higher than estimated at appraisal, and the project's multiplier effects, although not quantified, are likely to be substantial.[8]

As to the last point, Semry's impact on the peasants, Semry reasons in terms of the gross income derived from an average cultivation,[9] without reference to the peasant systems themselves. The success of this project (growth of peasant income, material and social infrastructure and research) conceals a more fundamental reality which we shall examine below.

The Peasants and Semry

According to the contract between Semry and the peasants, Semry manages the project and the operations are as follows:

(a) development of the land
(b) ploughing the rice fields
(c) management of the nurseries
(d) pumping and distribution of water
(e) maintenance of the irrigation network and infrastructure
(f) supplying fertiliser
(g) training and supervision of producers.

These services were provided in exchange for a fixed fee of CFA fr165 000 in the dry season and CFA fr135 000 in the rainy season. At the time, Semry bought and sold the crop. Peasants bring their labour, that is to say they finish the levelling and do the hoeing, make embankments, transplant the rice, weed, apply fertiliser, keep the land irrigated and harvest. This type of enterprise is well known. In such a system, peasants are workers of the state. They have lost all control over their labour power and are dispossessed of the means of production. Semry controls not only pre-production activities (infrastructure, irrigation), but those pertaining to production and post-production (sale of paddy). The supervisory role which dictates to the peasants the rhythm of ploughing, watering and drying is not an educational process, but one of strict control and enforcement. The social consequence of such a system is described as follows:

> On the other hand, one finds oneself in the presence of a peasantry totally dispossessed of their control over the essential elements of the system of production: land, labour, and techniques. They are masters – under supervision – of only that portion of the work that

cannot be done by machines, such as transplanting, weeding, and harvesting (insofar as it is not mechanised).

The process that has been introduced, in keeping with production objectives, is totally controlled by the technostructure. Yet in relation to the status that wage work normally entails, he [the peasant] assumes all the risks, but his remuneration is whatever is left over when he has paid his fees and possibly seasonal workers.[10] [Translated quotation]

The principle of distribution and utilisation of plots at Semry was established in 1971 as follows: Semry allocates 0.5 hectare, one plot or one 'piquet' for an indeterminate length of time to peasants applying for it. If the peasants fulfil their obligations to the *Société*, they receive the right of usufruct. It must be noted that theoretically women have the right to register as cultivators of a 'piquet'.

The question of 'piquet' allocation deserves some attention. In principle the 'piquets' are allotted by a Distribution Committee. In fact, the project largely ignores what happens at this level. In reality it is the local extension agents that determine the allocations. Priority was given to farmers (men) possessing the right of usufruct on land that had already been developed. Moreover, the texts do not specify the criteria (such as family work force, level of income) according to which several lots may be given to a single cultivator. The various reports concerning Semry underline that the phenomenon of accumulation of lots is very significant, an observation which confirms our own investigations.

One study has estimated that 87 per cent of Semry's revenues come from the difference between the cost of services and the fees paid by the cultivators.[11] This money serves to finance the administrative costs of Semry and the cost of the amortisation of equipment. The fee rate per hectare, usually the equivalent of two tonnes of rice per season, is judged by the peasants to be overwhelming. The break-even point for a peasant is four tonnes per harvest. At that level he pays more than 50 per cent of value produced to Semry. Thus, in 1985 a peasant producing four tonnes per hectare received:

CFA fr78 per kilo x 4000 kilos = CFA fr312 000
less fees (two tonnes) CFA fr156 000
Theoretical net income per hectare = CFA fr156 000
Theoretical net income per piquet = CFA fr78 000

This nevertheless represents a substantial monetary income, given the economic conditions prevailing in North Cameroon. It is estimated that the current income of Semry peasants is ten times greater than it was before the project.

If one examines the distribution of yields at Semry (rainy and dry seasons) in the best sections: 25 per cent of the peasants have yields of less than four tonnes per hectare; 25 per cent have yields of more than six tonnes per hectare; and 50 per cent are in the average range. On the other hand, in sections giving mediocre results, three-quarters of the peasants produce yields lower than the minimum in the dry season, as opposed to one fifth in the rainy season.[12]

The fee system favours high yields and penalises unproductive peasants. Its effect is to accentuate the differentiation amongst the conditions of the peasants: a large minority, obtaining yields of more than six tonnes, a middle category with results varying between five and six tonnes and a quarter of the peasants who are in the process of being marginalised.

The purchase price of paddy has scarcely changed over the years and has followed the rate of inflation exactly. Between 1955–76, the price of paddy paid to producers rose steadily from CFA fr14 per kilo to CFA fr28. Since then, prices have evolved as is shown in Table 7.2.

TABLE 7.2 *Prices Paid to the Peasant for Rice and Semry's Selling Price*

Year	Price of paddy	Price of white rice*	Amount Levied by Semry (CFA francs/ha/season) †
1976–77	35	90	–
1977–78	42.5	100	–
1978–79	42.5	100	–
1979–80	42.5	100	34 900
1980–81	55	120	55 000
1981–82	55	120	55 000
1982–83	62	145	62 000
1985	78	145	78 000

* Ex-Semry.
† Thus, a farmer practising double planting will pay this amount twice a year.
SOURCE: World Bank, *Project Performance Audit Report, Cameroon Second Semry Rice Project*, (Washington: June 1984) p. 22 and information gathered at the site.

A glance at the first column of Table 7.2 shows that in a nine-year period, the price paid to the peasant went from CFA fr35 to CFA fr78, an average increase of 12 per cent per year, that is the same as the rate of inflation. On the other hand, the selling price of Semry rice rose by 6 per cent per year on average, or less than the purchase price of paddy. The increase in the cost of paddy may be explained, especially in recent years, by the fact that the peasants prefer to sell their rice to merchants offering a better price than Semry.

For 1982–83, it has been estimated that Semry had created an added value of CFA fr7.2 billion. Of this amount, additional income distributed rose to 8.3 billion, which means that the state subsidised the project. Table 7.3 shows the distribution of income by economic agent.

TABLE 7.3   *Distribution of Income to Agents 1982–83 (CFA francs billions)*

Agents	Revenues
Peasants	2 862
Semry	3 913
Internal merchants	−110
Export merchants	1 625
	8 290

SOURCE: From Arditi, C., Baris, P. and Barnaud, M., *Evaluation socio-économique du Projet Semry au Cameroun, 'Conclusion',* SEDES, IRAM (Paris: November 1983) p. 111.

One can see that the chief beneficiary of the project is Semry, which received CFA fr3.9 billion, then the peasants, who saw their incomes increase by 2.8 billion. The project has also allowed for the creation of supplementary income for the merchants.

Under these conditions, it is not surprising that a significant black market has emerged. Thus in 1984, the price per kilo was CFA fr88, as opposed to CFA fr62 paid by Semry. In principle, peasants are authorised to keep 10 per cent of their harvest for their own consumption. In reality, the low prices paid by Semry result in peasants diverting their produce for sale to the merchants. Table 7.4 below shows the significance of this withholding of produce by the

TABLE 7.4 *Semry II, Production, Commercialisation, Retention*

		Total production		Commercialised production		Retention of rice	
		Tonnage	Yield per hectare	Tonnage	% of total production	Tonnage	% of total production
1979–80	* SP 79	1 706	2,47	773	45%	933	55%
	† SS 79–80	1 239	3,50	934	75%	305	25%
	TOTAL	2 945	2,82	1 707	58%	1 238	42%
1980–81	SP 80	5 349	3,43	4 652	87%	697	13%
	SS 80–81	4 720	4,56	3 934	83%	786	17%
	TOTAL	10 069	3,88	8 586	85%	1 483	15%
1981–82	SP 81	8 117	4,30	5 874	72%	2 243	28%
	SS 81–82	10 826	5,29	7 189	66%	3 637	34%
	TOTAL	18 943	4,82	13 063	69%	5 880	31%
1982–83	SP 82	11 407	4,81	10 435	91%	972	9%
	SS 82–83	16 007	5,32	13 514	84%	2 493	16%
	TOTAL	27 414	5,10	23 949	87%	3 465	13%
1983–84	SP 83	16 000	5,15	13 788	86%	2 212	14%
	SS 83–84	19 462	5,49	13 546	70%	5 916	30%
	TOTAL	35 462	5,33	27 334	77%	8 128	23%

* SP: Saison des pluies — rainy season.
† SS: saison sèche — dry season.
SOURCE: Semry, *Rapport d'activité 1983–84* (Yagoua: November 1984), Annexes.

peasants. With the very serious drought in North Cameroon in 1984–85, it is estimated that the peasants kept 50 per cent of their production to sell on the black market. In order to combat this phenomenon, Semry calls upon the administration and the police every year.

Besides the black market, the peasants have devised another strategy to fight against exploitation, which brings us to the issue of the distribution of 'piquets'. With the complicity of the local extension agents, the peasants, in order to avoid paying fees, abscond with the crop without paying the tiniest amount and then reappear at a new 'casier' or lot under a new identity. Those peasants who do not flee find their debt to Semry growing year by year. Table 7.5 illustrates the decline in the rate of recovery between 1982–84.

TABLE 7.5   *Fees Levied in Two Seasons: Dry Season, Rainy Season 1983–84*

Units	In weighted % of value				Loss on fees in millions of CFA francs	
	DS 1983	RS 1983–84	Total	1982–83	1983–84	1982–83
I. Semry I	81.1%	77.6%	79.6%	83%	205	163
II. Semry II	76.2%	67.8%	71.6%	92.3%	287	50
III. Semry III	95.9%	83.7%	91.6%	92.8%	11	7
Total weighted value	80.2%	72.5%	76.6%	87.1%	503	220

SOURCE: Semry, *Rapport d'activité 1983–84* (Yagoua: November 1984) p. 10.

The figures for 1985 were not available at the time of the study. One foresaw a considerable deterioration in the future situation at Semry.

Analysis of Peasant Reactions

The Massa at Semry I

If the forms of struggle we have outlined are common to the majority of peasants, it is important to underline that there exists a variety of reactions, depending on several factors. In fact, the peasants have adapted in very different ways to the conditions of rice farming, according to the availability either of land for other crops or of family labour power. We will take the case of the Massa at Semry I to illustrate the variety of prevailing conditions.

The pre-existing population at Semry I, the Massa, was relatively large: 43 395 inhabitants were counted in the 1976 census in the district of Maga[13]. The Massa population had no centralised power; the basic unit was the *zina* (concession or enclosure), which grouped together the head of the family, his younger brothers and their wives and children (between six and ten people). The head of the *zina* (the *bouzima*) possessed rights of usage over the land surrounding the enclosure. The system of production combined agriculture, stock raising and fishing, which guaranteed nutritional balance. The principle crop was sorghum (in the dry season) and *mouskouari* (transplanted sorghum) in the rainy season. One may distinguish, traditionally, three types of fields: the collective field of the *zina*, cultivated by all the members of the *zina*; a field for each household; and the women's field. Traditionally, the women do not participate in the work on their husband's fields, except for cash crops introduced by colonisation (cotton, groundnuts and rice). Moreover, their harvest belongs to them, because it is they who must assure the family's subsistence. According to C. Jones, 'the system seems to be such that a husband can mobilize his wife's labour – or the income from that labour – only if her labour generates a substantial cash income above and beyond what is needed to meet subsistence needs.'[14] This situation has been completely altered by rice farming, as we shall see.

The head of the *zina* benefits from the sale of cash crops and fish and owns the majority of the herd; hence his younger brothers depend on him to acquire wives. Apart from the women's crop, which is stored in their own granary, the eldest male manages the collective granary containing cereals produced in the collective fields; this granary constitutes a sort of reserve stock. A younger brother may own his own granary for the harvest from his own field or deposit his crop in his wife's granary. If he is not married, he will most often use his mother's granary. This division of the granaries reflects the control of surplus among the Massa.

One of the most important effects of rice farming has been the growing autonomy of the nuclear family. In fact, the collective sorghum field has disappeared to give way to the rice 'piquet' held by the family head. Traditionally the head of the *zina* had a right to all the revenue of the *zina*. Now, this right has been appropriated by the family heads. The other very important effect has been women's loss of autonomy. In fact, with the reduction in food production activities based on sorghum, women have lost their personal fields and have no choice but to convert themselves into labour power for their husbands. We will return below to this sexual division of labour that results from rice farming. Finally, we must mention that the reduction in stock raising activities, indeed, in some cases their disappearance, contributes equally to the overthrow of the traditional system at the social level, to the extent that the bride price, as a basic mechanism of social regulation, is about to disappear. Expressing as it does the wealth of the group and allowing younger brothers to acquire wives, its disappearance will inevitably have serious consequences. Moreover, the peasants have become dependent on a single economic activity and their nutritional situation has deteriorated. The possibility of turning to fishing and of raising livestock is at the root of two different reactions on the part of the peasantry.

In an enquiry into Semry I in 1980–81 (at Vele, Vounaloum to the east, and Widigué and Zebe to the west) C. Jones showed that the peasants situated in the east, wedged between the Logone River and the rice fields and disposing of less land to grow food and raise animals (but able to fish), have little choice but to cultivate rice, contrary to the people in the west. The latter, having more land available and being situated further from the rice fields, prefer to grow sorghum and, in the cash crop category, cotton and groundnuts, all of which permit higher incomes.[15] It seems, therefore, that the peasants cultivate rice only if they have no other alternatives. The factors mentioned are not sufficient, however, to explain why some peasants from west of the river practise rice farming nonetheless.

A determining factor seems to be the size of the family work force. The Massa family units disposing of a great deal of labour power as they are mainly polygamous families, have been able to manage the dual crop system: food and cash crops. The situation of less favoured family heads who cannot benefit from this sizeable work force has been more critical. It is important to underline the heavy manpower demands of rice farming. Rice cultivation is in fact highly labour intensive: the amount of time devoted to rice growing has been estimated at 195 work days per year for double cropping. Of 94 planters interviewed in 1976, 84 employed wage labour for transplanting, 31 for pulling up the plants, 27 for weeding and 20 for cutting. In 1986, the phenomenon had grown, particularly in transplanting (the peasant having quickly recognised the importance of this phase in the production of quality rice), which absorbs 40 per cent of the time. Moreover, the cultivation calendars for rice and sorghum overlap for all family production units.

After a decade of irrigated rice growing, a situation has been reached in which the smallest units of production grow only one rice crop and leave their 'piquets' to other claim holders (civil servants, merchants or peasants) able to employ wage labourers. Thus a veritable 'piquet' market has been created:

> These social categories (civil servants and merchants) using paid farm hands for the production of paddy exercise greater and greater control over the rice growing plots, to the detriment of the peasants, thus contributing to the latter's marginalization. There has thus been a slip in the objectives of the project, since the peasants whose land has been involved in the development ought to be the principal beneficiaries. Peasants who cannot obtain a rice growing plot because of growing urban demand have no recourse but to become wage earners on the lots. This evolution, which has been confirmed by various sources, is contrary to the aims of stabilizing the Massa peasants and establishing a 'stabilized' system of production.[16]

The phenomenon of plot accumulation thus appears as a result of the inability of some peasant units to carry on food and rice cultivation simultaneously. It has taken place to the benefit of civil servants and merchants who appropriate several plots under borrowed names in order to have peasants work on them. For obvious reasons, it is impossible to obtain figures on plot accumulation, but all observers agree in recognising the importance of the phenomenon of the conversion of civil servants and merchants into an agrarian bourgeoisie.

Migrants at Semry II

The problems enumerated above (competition between rice cultivation and food production and with fishing and stock raising, availability of family manpower) are found not only among the Massa, but also the Mousgoum and other small indigenous groups at Semry. They are at the root of the difficulties of Semry's development. We shall examine here the problem of migrants, which illustrates the hazardous nature of Semry in the long term. It appears in fact that this project of agrarian colonisation represents great difficulties with respect to the stabilisation of the work force because of the floating character of the majority of the population constituted by migrants.

At Semry II, the Mousgoum, the original inhabitants of the area, have to a great extent refused to participate in the project; hence the size of the migratory movement. It must be emphasised here that the conditions for the realisation of Semry II are different from those of Semry I, because of the construction of a 50 kilometre dike which permitted the creation of a 40 000 hectare artificial lake. It therefore became necessary to redistribute the indigenous population, the Mousgoum. The Mousgoum, who traditionally engage in fishing, have largely (half of the 44 000 Mousgoum in the 1976 census) refused to convert to rice farming. Either they remained in the partially submerged villages or settled outside the project's perimeter. Faced with the defection of the population and given the magnitude of the labour force required – 7000 families to work Semry II – an appeal had to be made for a strong contingent of Toupouri, reputed to be good workers, who supplied the majority of the migrants.[17] Table 7.6 shows the importance of Toupouri migrants at Semry II.

TABLE 7.6   *Number of Plots per Ethnic Group*

Rice Centre	Mousgoum	%	Toupouri	%	Others	%	Total
Pouss	880	90	–	–	100	10	980
Guirvidig	1 260	80	–	–	320	20	1 580
West Maga	360	10	2 250	70	740	20	3 350
East Maga	2 800	70	400	10	800	20	4 000
Total	5 300	53.5	2 650	26.7	1 960	19.8	9 910

SOURCE: Semry, *Rapport préliminaire d'évaluation du programme de structuration du milieu pour les 3 unités Semry,* (Yagoua: August 1985) Annex.

As may be seen, one rice cultivator in two is Mousgoum, one in four is Toupouri, one in five is from another ethnic group.

Among the Mousgoum of the area, as among the Massa at Semry I, lineages have an inalienable right of possession on their traditional lands. This fact is quite important since the numerous migrants in the area believe in the property rights of the first occupant. This fact, added to the complexity of inter-ethnic relations, is at the root of the instability in the area, because the Toupouri, among others, tend to return to their native villages. It is significant to note in this regard that three Toupouri were assassinated in a mysterious manner in 1985–86. One of them was one of the richest peasants at Maga and had just built a permanent dwelling, signifying by this very deed his intention of remaining in the area permanently.

Given the fact that their installation at Semry is considered temporary by the indigenous population, one may wonder why the Toupouri migrate to Semry.

The high cost of the bride price (CFA fr600 000 in 1985) prompts the young Toupouri male to turn to cash crops, allowing him to procure monetary income rapidly and thus acquire a wife and gain his independence sooner. Once he has accumulated the amount neces- sary for the bride price, he returns to his village to take up farming and raising livestock. This phenomenon contributes at the same time to the growth of the black market. In fact,

> Many young men leave their villages to spend a number of seasons at Maga building up their savings; beyond their instability, it is clear that they are the principal abettors of the black market, since they do not mind going into debt because sooner or later they will leave, while the black market permits them to double their income and thus save twice as fast.[18] [Translated quotation]

Semry's attitude, which consists of considering the migrants as a labour pool, is at the root of the instability of settlement.

As for the other ethnic groups such as the Chwa Arabs, Sirata, Fulbe, mountain people from the Mandaras Mountains, they consti- tute an unstable group as well, often preferring to establish them- selves outside the development and shuttle between the rice fields and their herds. In 1984–85, following the drought that raged in the Extreme North province, the demands for 'piquets' exceeded the supply. Thus at Maga in 1983–84, Semry registered 2008 newcomers for settlement in the vicinity of the new rice fields. Because of this, all the plots found takers, and several candidates were unable to find 'piquets'.[19] With the drought of 1985 we were able to note a massive movement of populations from the Extreme North province to the three Semry projects. Under these conditions it is possible that the populations will settle permanently. Thus, some Siraka and Chwa Arabs seem to want to convert to agriculture and are combining it with stock raising. If this factor, as well as the qualitative and quantitative shortages of land for millet, is the cause of migration, other factors deserve serious study notably from the perspective of in-depth sociological analysis. Let us remember, however, the vulnerability of the project, a vulnerability that is merely the counterpart of the technocratic vision of development that prevails at Semry.

Women

To the extent that rice is considered a cash crop, revenues are appropriated by the men, even if it is the women who are the chief participants in its production. It is estimated that the women's contribution represents 58 per cent of the work done on the 'piquets'. In exchange for the work of their wives, the men redistribute a little more than 10 per cent of the revenues from the harvest. It is not surprising that under these conditions the women have recently begun to abandon the work on their husband's plots in order to work as hired hands on other people's. This form of labour, traditionally know as *kerena* (work remunerated at the end of the day) is one of the most important sociological phenomena on the rice farms: women constitute 89 per cent of the *kerena* labour force. They belong to associations of 30 members each and form a united group. In 1986, for example, a husband tried to oppose the sale of his wife's labour power so that she could devote herself more fully to his 'piquet'. The women's group closed ranks to manifest their collective opposition to the husband, who finally had to give way.

It is mainly the work of transplanting that furnishes women with an opportunity to work as wage earners. Transplanting is difficult work necessitating a great deal of dexterity and patience. For a day's work at transplanting, women were paid CFA fr1000 in 1986. The phenomenon has grown so much that it now represents 20 work days per month.[20] It is difficult, however, to have these figures officially confirmed because the personnel at Semry are strangely silent on the issue.

One may wonder why the majority of women still accept work on the rice farms under such conditions. One of the determining factors is undoubtedly the size of the bride price, CFA fr600 000, that the husband has had to provide in order to acquire a wife: the women feel they should reimburse this investment.

Thus, Massa women are conscious that they represent an investment of a substantial sum of money by their husbands, and that this gives their husbands the right to mobilize their labour and appropriate their income . . . Yet the system is such that women are taught to value themselves according to the number of cattle which were given in return for them.[21]

Recently, women have begun to find alternatives to the system. At Maga (Semry II), for instance, a group of women have organised to produce groundnuts in a collective field. The women's responses to their over-exploitation deserves thorough study.

Response of Semry to Peasant Resistance

Faced with the peasants' strategies to escape exploitation through non-payment of fees and the parallel market in paddy, the *Société* envisages, on the one hand, the creation of cultivators' groups solely responsible to it monetarily and, on the other hand, mechanisation. As far as the latter point is concerned, the World Bank writes:

> On the other hand, Semry is seriously considering introducing advanced mechanized harvesting, threshing and collection methods, partly to increase yields even further but also to guarantee that a larger portion of paddy production is captured for milling by Semry.[22]

Thus, for example, the inter-seasonal threshing period conflicts with the peasants' food producing activities. Mechanisation would guarantee the capture of the entire harvest by Semry.

Mechanisation alone appears, however, insufficient to solve all the current problems. The *Société* thus envisages a redefinition of its relationship with the peasantry. It is interesting to see how Semry envisages this rearrangement in the future.

For a number of years, the World Bank has emphasised in its reports the necessity of creating village organisations. The continuation of its financing, like that of other lending agencies, is in fact conditional on this point, as well as on an increase in the price of paddy. In its audit report of 1984, the Bank's experts mentioned that one of the major constraints on the project, apart from the problem of marketing, which we will analyse below, was that of peasant participation:

In fact, the attitude of Semry towards the participation of farmers is rather paternalistic, a phenomenon not unfamiliar in settlement projects.
Farmers' participation should not be pursued as an ideological objective. Benevolent paternalism is not necessarily wrong, but it might be difficult to sustain in the long term as the project becomes more settled and the pioneer mentality no longer prevails. Aspects of farmer participation will require continuous attention in the future.[23]

In his progress report of 1983–84, the General Manager of Semry wrote:

Over the next few years, a great effort must be made by Semry to further motivate the population with a view to permanent settlement in a calm environment.[24] [Translated quotation]

This clearly shows that manpower instability poses a real problem for the *Société* in the future.
Launched in October 1983 under pressure from foreign lending agencies, the programme for the restructuring of the rice farming milieu has as its aim:

(a) to increase peasant productivity, which can be done only through a dynamic educational process. In fact, the local extension agents, who are difficult to find, are not very qualified or motivated and are often accomplices of the peasants in the misappropriation of the crop.
(b) to reduce peasants' fees, thanks to the programme of increased responsibility. Henceforth, the peasants will be responsible for the following operations: management of nurseries, distribution of inputs, rational and planned water management, maintenance of the secondary network, direct relations between peasants and middle and upper extension agents.

The result would be the progressive disappearance of local extension agents, monitors and storekeepers.
In fact, thanks to peasant structures, Semry hopes to recover 100 per cent of its fees by means of the identification of all rice farmers and collective responsibility. Semry's costs would diminish, while at the same time the quality of rice would improve (a higher percentage of marketable rice) which would raise the average price of the

commercialised product.[25] According to Semry:

> The fee, the collection, and the quality all reflect a common characteristic: the anonymity of the principal actor, the peasant. This results in a fixed fee, a lack of interest in the future of the lot and in the quality of the product, since everyone is treated in the same manner, whether he is a good or a bad rice producer.[26][Translated quotation]

In addition, the attitude of the peasants, who favour food crops, leads the *Société* to envisage the development and improvement of food crops and stock raising in the area of cultivation, the creation of pharmacies, sports fields, the construction of schools out of durable materials, and the creation of purchasers' cooperatives for basic commodities. These preoccupations, which go beyond rice cultivation, stem from the necessity of stabilising manpower in the area.

In 1983–84, the *Société* set to work at Semry I to identify basic social units and to group them together in the same rice growing lot (*casier*) as well as to negotiate with the peasants the transfer of duties.

In its work of 'peasant restructuring' Semry could not forget the chief element of the labour force: women. Hence the extra-agricultural training programme foresees the insertion of women in the community action decision-making process. Moreover, so that they may be able to devote themselves more to rice farming, the programme foresees a lightening of their domestic duties, notably through the acquisition of a millet mill, the greatest need of women in the North. The women of the village of Maroua, for example, were prompted to raise money to acquire a mill. Unfortunately, they were cheated by a merchant who delivered a used mill. It is interesting to note in this regard that the men did not want to participate in the work of constructing the building that was to house the mill. However, once the mill was acquired, they tried, unsuccessfully, to gain control of it.

The restructuring operation for the three Semry projects is expected to take five years. The major objective in regrouping is the reduction of the number of intermediaries for better control of the peasants:

> Finally, apart from all restructuring considerations, there are advantages in regrouping plots. We shall not reiterate all the different aspects, but we shall note its specific importance for

Semry II. In fact, this unit exhibits great instability among the migrant population; a large number of departures, returns, and temporary arrivals have been observed. Because of this, one does not quite know who is growing what. This certainly explains the rate of recovery of the fee (namely 82.8 per cent in the rainy season of 1983).[27] [Translated quotation]

The *Société* foresees, thanks to its programme of restructuring, a reduction in its disputes and conflicts with the peasants.

COMMERCIALISATION: FROM ECONOMIC SELF-SUFFICIENCY TO EXPORTS

The principal aim of Semry at its creation was to guarantee self-sufficiency in rice for the whole country. We shall see to what extent this aim has been realised and at what cost rice import substitution is achieved, as well as the contradictions it engenders.

Since 1976, Semry has been shaken by periodic financial crises which have arisen in part from the inability of the *Société* to market its production – crises that culminated in 1985 in the absence of cash to purchase the paddy harvest from the peasants. This marketing problem results essentially from the contradictions of government interventions: the government is hesitating between an export policy and a policy of development of the internal market. The aim of supplying the internal market implies protection of the local market in the absence of competitiveness of national production on the world market. In fact, the value of imported rice (CFA value, 1985) was CFA fr85 000 per tonne. If import duties are added it was CFA fr107 560 and CFA fr90 135 without duties (which is very important, given the amount of fraud). Once brought to North Cameroon, the rice is sold for CFA fr150–155 compared with CFA fr165 for Semry rice (transportation and storage included). It is immediately obvious that Cameroon rice cannot compete with imported rice however much the latter fluctuates in price. This is the reason Semry has had difficulty, since its creation, in marketing its production. It becomes obvious why the pertinence of Cameroon's rice import substitution policy comes into question. One alternative would have been to channel Semry investments into the expansion and improvement of millet production, which is the main crop of North Cameroon and the preferred crop of the peasants.

To resolve the problem of the competitiveness of Semry rice, the government instituted the twinning system in 1976: an importer is required to buy a proportional amount of the national product. This system has never functioned well. In 1983, imports were twinned at a quota of 17 900 tonnes for Semry. At the end of September 1983, only 9 815 tonnes had been taken.[28] Moreover, merchants imported quantities that were clearly larger than those authorised. In his 1982–83 progress report, the General Manager wrote:

The increase in the price (of Semry rice), in conjunction with the massive arrival of cheap foreign rice that was not re-exported to foreign countries as expected, in the end, exercised pressure on the local market and blocked sales almost completely as of December 1983.[29] [Translated quotation]

On 30 June 1983, 11 829 tonnes of white rice and 24 000 tonnes of paddy remained in storage, representing respectively values of CFA fr1 699 869 920 and CFA fr1 573 000 000.[30] This situation entailed other financial burdens, costs and losses (such as the cost of processing, disinfection, platforms, canvas covers, losses from water damage) estimated at CFA fr869 500 000.

At the time, enormous quantities of Asiatic rice bearing no relationship to national needs were unloaded at Douala. Between July 1982 and June 1983, these arrivals exceeded 318 000 tonnes.[31] These stocks were destined in part to be placed on the Nigerian market but, because of the collapse of the value of the Naïra, commercial transactions with Nigeria slowed down. In November 1986, after massive imports, the situation became catastrophic: 62 000 tonnes of paddy and 10 176 tonnes of rice were stored at the *Société*. Moreover, rice imports in the course of 1985 had been such that national consumption was assured for two years. Semry closed its mills and found itself unable to finance the following growing seasons. Consequently, not only was there no reinvestment of public funds, but the merchants themselves were threatened with bankruptcy.

The state has been forced to subsidise Semry regularly since 1976. In addition to subsidies, it has had to assume transportation costs in order to bring Semry production to urban markets in the Centre and South, the main consumption centres. A policy of subsidising rice could perhaps be justified in the context of food self-sufficiency.

However, Semry rice is partly exported. It was estimated that in the mid-1980s, 22 per cent of its production was sold in Cameroon, which means to say that the state was subsidising foreign rice consumption.[32]

National production of rice in the Cameroon is estimated at 50 000 tonnes and consumption needs at 75 000–90 000 tonnes per year. The complementary imports should therefore not exceed 40 000 tonnes. Now, some 200 000–250 000 tonnes of commercial rice, or five to six times the amount necessary enters the country each year. A portion of this rice is destined for neighbouring countries, mainly Nigeria, and a portion is sold on the local market – around 60 000 tonnes – of which 16 700 tonnes have been subject to tariff duties (1982 figures).[33] However, this rice is not exported through legal channels nor paid for in convertible currency. Thus, not only does the state subsidise Semry but it suffers losses at the fiscal level. Rice in transit is purchased with strong currencies by importers and resold in Nigeria to merchants who pay for it in CFA francs and, more generally, in Naïra. The value of currency leaving the country annually is estimated at nearly $40 million (190 000 tonnes at $210 a tonne).[34]

As we can see, the problem of commercialisation of rice arises from a conjunction of factors: large price differences between imported and local rice, the unloading at Douala of enormous quantities of imported rice theoretically destined for neighbouring markets but in part sold on the internal market, and the lack of control over merchandise in transit that can easily be sold in the Cameroon without having to be subject to import duties. Moreover, the policy of twinning is not respected and new import licences are granted, while purchasing quotas have not been respected.

It is surprising that the problem of rice marketing that has existed since 1976 had not yet found a solution ten years later. The World Bank favours the sale of Semry production on the North Cameroon market and in the countries of the sub-region (Nigeria, Chad, Central African Republic) and imported rice on the markets of South and Central Cameroon. However, it observes realistically that: 'This system of rice marketing and the semi-annual process of awarding quotas to rice traders has political connotations'.[35]

The political implications of the rice question in the Cameroon are many. To limit import quotas and have them respected runs counter to the interests of the commercial bourgeoisie and some bureaucrats who profit from the situation by 'selling' licences and forgetting to collect import duties.

There are eight large rice importers, mainly Fulbe from North Cameroon. These importers resell to Bamileke intermediaries who effectively assume control of internal trade. Fulbe and Bamileke constitute the backbone of the country's business bourgeoisie. The former were propelled by the Ahidjo government. As for the Bamileke, the Ahidjo government, just like the Biya government, never restrained their ascension:

> In the first years of independence, Mr. Ahidjo, his Minister Victor Kanga and the administration facilitated, for political reasons, the economic progress of the Bamileke traders by closing their eyes to numerous commercial, fiscal and customs irregularities. Afterwards, the government proved a little less complacent towards them (although it responded to their expectations by suppressing the toll on the Wouri Bridge, improving communications between the federated states, and restricting the number of departments subjected to the state of emergency); but at the same time it applied itself to the task of aiding the rapidly expanding Hausa (Fulbe) business class from the North.[36] [Translated quotation]

To oust them in favour of state capital would run counter not only to the government's economic project – the structuring of an internal bourgeoisie – but above all the aim of national cohesion, which depends on skilful ethnic balance. Although these two groups are part of the power structure and are part of the process of élite assimilation, the Fulbe have lost some of their privileges under the current regime; and the Bamileke, whose numerical and economic strength has always been feared, have never been at the centre of gravity of power. Without supporting them, therefore, the state is nonetheless unable to call their interests into question without introducing an element of destabilisation.

Another important factor in this equation concerns the civil servants who 'sell' licences and profit from fiscal and customs fraud. The traders' lobby carries all the more weight in that it shares in these specific interests. It is here that the problem of corruption as a mode of accumulation specific to dependent countries arises. These particularist interests exist in contradiction to the interests of the state bureaucracy as a class which are to make state capital bear fruit. In view of the importance of the stake which the rice market represents, the state has not been in a position to decide firmly in favour of a particular set of interests.

The state's hesitation is all the more explicable because it must face another contradiction. To assure the economic viability of Semry, the selling price of rice must be raised. It has been seen that the price of white rice and paddy are fixed by the government and that the price of paddy was raised from CFA fr62 to 78 in 1985, whereas the selling price of white rice has not moved. Since the increase in the price of paddy, Semry management has lodged a request for an increase in the price of rice with the Minister of Trade, a request that was not granted which explains the difficulties of the *Société's* treasury. The *Société* had to buy paddy from the peasants on credit at the time of the 1985 rainy season's harvest.

The increase requested by Semry was in the order of 24 per cent, which transmitted to the urban masses, would give rise to an explosive situation. To guarantee the peasants' production, the state has been obliged to increase the purchase price of paddy, but at the same time it finds it impossible to pass on this increase in the selling price of rice without risking massive protests from urban workers, who are the best organised politically. This rural-urban contradiction characteristic of African agriculture, is more difficult to resolve than the first. It explains why the working class is, on this issue, on the side of the merchants in favour of an open market policy. It is understandable that reconciliation of all these convergent and divergent interests can lead to fluctuations in economic policy and at times to paralysis of the state.

CONCLUSION

Rice cultivation in the Cameroon was envisaged from the time of the colonial era in a region where expansion of cotton production proved problematic. It aimed at satisfying a growing urban demand for an imported model of consumption. The project, taken up on a grand scale by the state of Cameroon in 1971, had as its aim the guaranteeing of self-sufficiency in rice for the entire country and the development of the North Cameroon region. The development of the internal market may be seen as part of an attempt by the local governing class and of capitalist interests to assert their hegemonic control through the expansion of the internal capitalist market. However, a certain ambiguity emerged from the start: rice as an export crop versus a food crop. This ambiguity, a reflection of agricultural policy as a whole, echoes the contradictory interests of international capital in Africa and those of the local dominant classes: namely the fact that there exists a complex political matrix made up of moving alliances of which some have interests linked to the export strategies of the large firms, while others are more concerned with the development of the local market.

Semry's achievements seem quite spectacular in technical, material and economic terms. Moreover, the peasant, who has been portrayed as the chief beneficiary of the project, has indeed seen his monetary income grow considerably. However, more careful analysis of peasant production and living conditions reveals the project's great vulnerability. Turned into a tenant on state land, the peasant is exploited on several levels: a very low and stagnant purchase price for his harvest and a rental payment that generally represents half of his production. Moreover, since traditional activities have diminished, the peasants have seen their quality of life reduced. The competition between traditional activities and rice farming doubtless explains why, until quite recently, the *Société* had a great deal of difficulty in recruiting candidates to cultivate all the land that was set aside for development.

The chief beneficiary of the project is Semry. Under such conditions, it is not surprising to note that the black market and the non-payment of fees are becoming more and more generalised. Beyond their very immediate struggle to conserve their incomes, the peasants react in various ways to avoid exploitation, depending on their means. For those who have the advantage of possessing land for food crops and stock raising, the attachment to Semry is marginal. Those peasants who may draw on substantial labour power practise dual production. The others have no choice but to work for wages on the 'piquets' of civil servants and merchants. Under these circumstances, one may understand the formation of a rural bourgeoisie composed of the most favoured social categories, which has emerged in a direct contradiction to the initial objectives of the project.

At Semry II, where the project has had to make a massive appeal to migrants, the reasons determining the installation of producers in the area and the conditions of life there, lead us to believe that their attachment to the project is only temporary, all the more so since they are considered by the indigenous populations as usurpers of the land. Until now, the great weakness of the project has been camouflaged by the high demand for 'piquets' prompted by, among other things, the drought in North Cameroon.

The most negative impact of the project has been the loss of autonomy and the over-exploitation of women. In fact, although they perform most of the work in the rice fields, they receive next to nothing in return. In addition, they have lost access to their traditional resources. The Semry project has therefore reinforced a traditional system of inequality.

As long as Semry's attitude of considering the peasants only as a potential labour force does not change, it is doubtful that the proposed methods of resolving the current problems can be satisfactory. In this regard, the new programme of restructuring the peasantry at Semry seems to be an attempt to counter peasant strategies and reduce operating costs.

Analysis of the project also reveals the dominant inter-class contradictions at work at Semry. On the one hand, the state must guarantee a return on international and public capital, which runs counter to the interests of the commercial bourgeoisie, the state's support group. The second part of this contradiction relates to the process of the formation of the ruling class founded on the appropriation of state resources. In fact, the corruption of the bureaucracy is a determining element in understanding the contradictions of commercial policy, which leads us to the conclusion that the state is short-circuiting its own policies. The interests of state capital, like those of international capital (the extraction of internal surplus), are opposed to the individual interests of the civil servants and, concurrently, the interests of the commercial bourgeoisie at this specific conjuncture.

These contradictions are nonetheless secondary in comparison with the relationship between capital and the peasantry. Here there is absolutely no ambiguity as to the necessity of exploiting the peasant labour force to the maximum. However, the peasants' resistance constantly obliges capital to redefine its strategies. At this level, international capital, not directly implicated in the internal contradictions of the local market, seems more sensitive to the long-term interests of capital in general; this would appear to explain certain pressures exerted in favour of reform. Finally, certain interests of the working class are indirectly supportive of the strategies of commercial capital, in so far as the interest of the former is to obtain rice at the best possible price.

The solution currently envisaged by the state and the World Bank, namely the marketing of rice in the sub-region, contradicts the policy of food self-sufficiency in the Cameroon and the development of the internal market – basic aims of the Fourth and Fifth Plans which were reiterated in the Sixth Development Plan (1986–90). Under the circumstances, the option in favour of taxing imported rice in order to counter dumping from Asiatic countries and the introduction of a more strictly controlled quota system would seem to be more appropriate measures to meet government objectives. Such measures however, if introduced, would imply that the situation of ambiguity, so characteristic of the state, had been overcome.

TABLE 7.7   *Annex I   World Bank Commitments 1967–83 (Loans)*

Project	Year of Approval	Amount in $ Millions
Camdev (rubber)	1967	18.00
Palm oil	1969–78	9.60
Semry	1972	3.70
Livestock	1974	11.70
Cocoa	1975	6.50
Niete (rubber)	1975	16.00
Plaine des M'Bo	1977	2.00
Socopalm II (palm oil)	1977	25.00
Rural development fund	1977	7.00
Camdev (rubber)	1978	15.00
Semry	1978	29.00
Zopi integrated dev. proj.	1978	7.80
Western Plains dev. proj.	1978	8.50
Hevecam (rubber)	1980	31.50
Livestock	1980	16.00
Northern Province integ. dev. proj.	1981	37.50
Forestry	1982	17.00
Palm oil/rubber cons.	1982	50.80
		312.60

SOURCE: World Bank, *Project Performance Audit Report, Cameroon Second Semry Rice Project* (Washington: June 1984) p. 1

Notes

1. World Bank, *Project Performance Audit Report, Cameroon Second Semry Rice Project* (Washington:Operations Evaluation Department, 25 June 1984) p. 22.
2. Ibid. p. 22
3. Ibid. p. 28.

4. World Bank, *Cameroon Country Economic Memorandum* (Washington: 1984)

5. Prices paid to producers of coffee and cocoa were raised by 6 per cent in 1982–83 and 12 per cent between 1983–84. For cotton, the increase was 17 per cent in 1982–83 and 11 per cent in 1983–84. Source: International Monetary Fund, Staff Report for the 1984 Article IV Consultation (April 1984) (Confidential).

6. World Bank, Economic Memorandum, op. cit. (1984) p. 45.

7. The Semry III Project, which is small (800 hectares), presents different characteristics from the other two: no centralised management, but rather the creation of small areas adapted to the size and location of the indigenous populations; self-sufficiency in food; and crop diversification (rice, sorghum, corn, market-gardening). In addition, the peasants are obliged to sell to Semry only enough rice to pay their fees (instead of nearly the entire crop).

8. World Bank, *Project Performance Audit Report*, op. cit. (1984) p. vi.

9. Between 1980–82, it is estimated that the average income of producers increased from CFA fr25 000 to CFA fr156 000.

10. Martine Audibert, *Semry: A Self-Assessment* (School of Economics of Aix-en-Provence, 1981) quoted in World Bank, *Project Performance Audit Report,* op. cit.,1 (1984) p. 55.

11. Arditi, C., Baris, P. and Barnaud, M., *Evaluation socio-économique du Projet Semry au Cameroun*, 'Conclusion, Mission d'évaluation', (Paris: SEDES, IRAM, November 1983) p. x.

12. Ibid. p. 19.

13. Semry, *Rapport préliminaire d'évaluation du programme de structuration du milieu pour les 3 unités Semry*. Period from June 1986 to June 1991, (Yagoua: August 1985) annex II.

14. Jones, C., *The Effects of the Intrahousehold Organization of Production and the Distribution of Revenue in the Participation of Rice Cultivation in the Semry I*, CRED, USAID (1982) p. 17.

15. Ibid. p. 6.

16. Arditi, C., Baris, P. and Barnaud, M., op. cit. (1983) p. vii.

17. Toupouri country, densely populated, is one of the great reservoirs of labour power for all large development projects in Cameroon.

18. Semry, op. cit. (1985).

19. Semry, *Rapport d'activité 1983–84* (Yagoua: November 1984).

20. Information gathered through fieldwork.

21. Jones, C., op. cit. (1982) p. 29.

22. World Bank, *Project Performance Audit Report*, op. cit. (1984) p. 21.

23. Ibid. pp. 20–21.

24. Semry, op. cit. (1984) p. 40.

25. One of the technical problems of the *Société* is the low quality of the product: 36.5 per cent of broken rice as opposed to 33 per cent of marketable rice.

26. Semry, op. cit. (1985) p. 10.

27. Ibid. p. 34.

28. World Bank, *Project Performance Audit Report*, op. cit. (1984) p. 16.

29. Semry, *Rapport d'activité 1982–83* (Yagoua: 1984) p. 12.

30. Ibid. p. 11.
31. Given the extent of clandestine trade, it is impossible to determine either the level of imports or the amount of rice in transit entering the Cameroon, as statistics on exchange at the borders were not available. Semry, *Marché et commercialisation du riz au Cameroun*, Report of the Mission, November 21 – December 16, 1983 (December 1983) p. 12.
32. Arditi, C., Baris, P. and Barnaud, M., op. cit. (1983) p. vi.
33. Semry, op. cit. (1983) p. 14.
34. Ibid. p. 22.
35. World Bank, *Project Performance Audit Report*, op. cit. (1984) p. 107.
36. Bayard, J-F., *L'Etat au Cameroun* (Paris: Presses de la Fondation Nationale des Sc. Politiques, 1985) p. 228.

8 The Politics of 'Adjustment' in Morocco[1]

DAVID SEDDON

Our role is to point out what needs to be done. The rest is up to the government . . . to decide how fast it wants to become efficient without falling apart politically.

(World Bank official, quoted in *African Recovery*, Issue 1, 1987)

INTRODUCTION

Over the last ten years, the government of Morocco has faced a dilemma. On the one hand, the structural problems of the economy, growing pressure from the IMF and the World Bank and the influence of other powerful interests both foreign and domestic, have led the government to adopt a series of measures which add up to a familiar package involving devaluation, cuts in public expenditure, a reduction of state intervention in the economy and the encouragement of private enterprise and market forces. On the other hand, the government has found it difficult until recently to implement its 'stabilisation' and 'structural adjustment' policies with the rigour that the two international agencies, aid donors and would-be investors would have liked to see. Reasons for this difficulty include: a continuing commitment to the war in the Sahara, strong pressure from certain sections of the middle class and organised working class to maintain a certain level of state involvement in the economy, and the danger that popular protest over measures threatening the welfare of the mass of the Moroccan people will turn into serious political agitation. Since 1987, however, the government appears to have committed itself more wholeheartedly to a programme of structural reform and privatisation.

In this essay, I examine the contradictory forces which act upon the Moroccan government and try to explain the often apparently vacillating position and practice adopted with regard to economic policy during a decade of recession and 'adjustment'. If we are to understand the politics of adjustment in the 1980s, however, it is

234

necessary to delineate, briefly, the main features of the Moroccan political economy as a whole as it has developed since independence in 1956. The first section of the essay, therefore, considers the early period of post-colonial reconstruction and the second, the second decade after independence. In the third section I examine the growing economic crisis of the late 1970s and early 1980s and the preliminary measures adopted to resolve the crisis. The fourth section explores the political and economic context of the programme of structural adjustment initiated formally in 1984 and pursued with hesitations until 1987 and more confidently thereafter.

FROM INDEPENDENCE TO A STATE OF EMERGENCY: 1956–65

The first decade after independence can be seen essentially as a period of post-colonial reconstruction from which the monarchy emerged in a commanding position politically, but presided over an economy in serious difficulties and a deeply divided society. Two distinct political phases can be identified: the first from 1956–61, during which the various class and sectional interests that had effectively shelved their differences in the struggle for national independence sought to exercise a decisive influence on future development; the second, between 1961–65, marked by the marginalisation of the more radical elements of the nationalist movement and the consolidation of the power of the monarchy and the conservative interests associated with it. This second phase ended with an economic and political crisis and the declaration by the king of a state of emergency. As regards the economy, it came during this first decade after independence to be characterised by a weak form of state capitalism in which an ideology of the free market was actively promoted (particularly after 1961) but in which private enterprise was supported by state intervention in most of the key productive sectors.

In the years before independence the Istiqlal (Independence) party had been able to hold together a variety of very disparate elements representing quite different class and sectional interests. However, political divisions became more evident once independence was achieved in 1956; one expression of this was the formation of, and growing support for, new political parties. Already in the 1940s a minority nationalist party, the Democratic Party of Independence (PDI), had emerged, which commanded a certain following during the 1950s, and participated in the first government of independent Morocco when King Mohamed V selected nine members of the Istiqlal, six members of the PDI, five independents and a representative of the Jewish community for his cabinet. The king, however, retained all legislative powers and refused to hold elections or allow a constitution to be drafted. He also began to encourage the development of explicitly royalist political groupings. In 1957, the Popular Movement (MP) was formed. This movement had strong roots in the rural areas and tended to draw its support from those hostile to the urban-based Istiqlal and PDI; it was royalist and particularly antagonistic towards the more radical tendencies within the Istiqlal.

Within the Istiqlal itself, divisions were growing. While party elders counselled a course of moderation and patience in dealing with the king, the left had grown alarmed at the increasing control exercised by the monarch over the state apparatus (notably the security forces and the ministry of the interior) and demanded restraints on the exercise of monarchical power. The left also began criticise more vigorously the government's economic strategy. After independence, a basically 'liberal' economic strategy was adopted. Instead of undertaking structural reforms the government concentrated on infrastructural development to provide the basic preconditions for private capital investment and economic growth. Investment in production declined, capital flowed out of the country as the French settlers withdrew, the level of imports contracted – and the economy stagnated. Paradoxically, stagnation enabled the balance of payments to be brought into equilibrium, albeit at a high level of capital outflow; despite the flight of capital and savings, and the drying up of incoming capital, the economic situation appeared superficially favourable as foreign holdings continued to grow and foreign reserves were used to finance the deficit on current account.

When, in early 1958, a crisis of government developed, following the resignation of the 'independent' prime minister over the right to organise freely in political parties, the left elaborated a set of conditions for continuing Istiqlal involvement in government. These included a commitment to economic growth and expansion, the institution of a constitutional monarchy, permanent guarantees of public liberties, a fixed date for elections, and measures to ensure Morocco's effective independence from undue foreign pressures. This was not accepted by the king or the party elders and a new government was formed in which only the minister of the economy represented the left. The left now began openly to attack the Istiqlal government, as did the Union Marocaine de Travail (UMT), the trade union grouping associated with the Istiqlal since its formation in 1955. In June 1958, strikes were staged throughout the major cities to express the discontent of the unions and their members with the government's economic policies and the absence of democratic rights. In November the minister of national economy resigned. In December 1958 the prime minister resigned and a new government was formed. The new government was more strongly influenced by the ideas of the left than of the 'old guard' and presided over the formulation of a national plan whose four major objectives were: agrarian reform as a prerequisite for agricultural development; industrialisation with considerable state intervention and direction; reform of the state apparatus, with Moroccanisation, austerity and streamlining, and democratisation as priorities; and the rapid provision of adequate schooling for all.

In September 1959 the Istiqlal split, and the Union Nationale des Forces Populaires (UNFP) was established to represent the more radical tendencies within the old Istiqlal. The UMT moved to create links with the new party, whose support came mainly from intellectuals, urban organised labour and the petty bourgeoisie. The most popular leader of the new UNFP was Ben Barka, who spoke in Marxist terms of the class struggle and saw the task of the UNFP as bringing together 'a synthesis of the three great forces of Morocco – the organised workers, the peasantry and the resistance'.[2]

As the new 'leftist' government began to formulate plans to bring the economy under more direct state control and to undertake radical structural reforms, and as the UNFP prepared for the promised elections, the king and the more conservative forces were working to consolidate the power of the monarchy and to undermine these 'socialist' tendencies. The split in the Istiqlal and the emergence of a popular leftist party, supported by the major trade union federation, constituted a significant threat to the monarchy and its control of Moroccan politics. In the same month as the formal establishment of the UNFP, the prime minister was obliged to proscribe the Moroccan Communist Party (PCM) on the grounds that it threatened the government and the monarchy. The PCM had been tolerated immediately after independence largely because of its insignificant numbers, its mild socialist programme and its consistent nationalism. Now, however, with increasing support for 'leftist tendencies' among the working class and the petty bourgeoisie, in particular among the intelligensia and students, it was banned. Early in 1960, the Istiqlal formed its own trade union, the Union Générale des Travailleurs Marocains (UGTM), with the approval of the king. When, early in May 1960, the prime minister called for increased government control over the national security forces and the UNFP achieved a surprise victory in elections to local chambers of commerce and industry, the king dismissed the prime minister, announcing that he personally would act as prime minister in the new government to guarantee national unity and stability until the elaboration of the constitution. His son, crown prince Hassan, was appointed vice prime minister in addition to his existing responsibility for the national security forces, including the Royal Army.

At the end of May, local elections – long awaited and long delayed – were held. In the country as a whole, the Istiqlal won about 40 per cent of seats in the local councils, with the UNFP gaining an impressive 23 per cent. The results showed clearly the UNFP strength among urban workers, state employees and the petty bourgeoisie of small commodity producers and tradesmen. However, only one UNFP member was brought into the new government formed by the king (as minister of agriculture) and the party continued in opposition. The UMT began to realign itself, initially adopting a 'non-political' stance. Its negotiations with the government during abortive attempts by the union of state employees to call a general strike during 1961 led many UNFP supporters and union members to recognise that the UMT had been effectively brought to heel. Over the next two years, the UMT became more clearly subordinate to the government and the palace.[3] At its third congress in 1963, the UMT announced that it was to be formally independent of all political organisations and have as its sole objective the welfare of the labouring masses. In the legislative elections that year the UMT refused to endorse UNFP candidates, merely advising its members to vote for 'progressive candidates'.

In February 1961 King Mohamed V died and his son Hassan became king. The only UNFP member of the government had resigned in January and Hassan now assumed the posts of prime minister, minister of agriculture, minister of defence and minister of the interior. In addition to direct control over key ministries, as monarch he had the right to appoint the government (including the secretary-general, secretaries and under-secretaries of state), the governors of provinces, district and sub-district officials, magistrates of secular and religious justice at all levels, officers of the army and gendarmerie, diplomatic representatives and other high-ranking state employees. During 1961 a new constitution was drawn up. The UNFP was the only party to oppose it, objecting to the secrecy involved in its preparation, the excessive powers retained by the king, and the ambiguities inherent in a government responsible, according to the draft constitution, to both king and Parliament. But the constitution was approved by a referendum in 1962 and preparations began for general elections.

Istiqlal cabinet ministers were now demoted to minor posts, which had the effect of swinging the Istiqlal behind the UNFP in its opposition to government policies. In January 1963 the Istiqlal published its 'manifesto for economic liberation' in which it called for 'an equitable division of the national revenue . . . to lead the country out of underdevelopment and to construct a classless society where social justice reigns . . . ' The manifesto also called for the nationalisation of credit, insurance, energy, transport, mines and basic industries, and urged that the land should be given to those who worked it. The Istiqlal, like the UNFP, was growing increasingly aware of the social and economic consequences of the stagnation of the Moroccan economy and the inadequacy of government economic policies. They clearly hoped to gain political capital from their forthright manifesto. But during 1963, the PDI, renamed the Parti Démocratique Constitutionnel (PDC), and the Mouvement Populaire (MP) joined forces with the Liberal Independents to constitute a coalition of pro-monarchical tendencies, the Front pour la Défense des Institutions Constitutionelles (FDIC).

The FDIC won a relative majority in the legislative elections held in April 1963 with 69 seats, while the Istiqlal managed only 41 seats and the UNFP 28 seats. The UNFP leadership claimed that the elections had been rigged and began to consider boycotting the subsequent local elections. But in June a meeting of all UNFP deputies and provincial secretaries was interrupted by a police raid and all present were arrested on suspicion of plotting against the king. Over the next eight months, 85 UNFP leaders and activists were held in gaol, brought to trial and the majority condemned to prison sentences. The UNFP leader, Ben Barka, was exiled. Throughout the country, UNFP supporters were harassed and intimidated. After the arrests both the UMT, which was to have fielded candidates in opposition to the UNFP, and the Istiqlal withdrew from the elections; as a result the FDIC ran virtually unopposed. But when, in June, the UNFP, still active despite the harassment of its leaders and membership, moved a motion of censure of government economic policy, the

Istiqlal voted for the motion and several of the FDIC, particularly those loyal to the MP, evidenced sympathy for it also.

Increasing political opposition focused on criticism of government economic policy, fed by growing concern at the social implications of what was developing into an economic crisis. The index of overall consumption in 1960 was 108 in comparison with the base year (= 100) of 1952, while the population had grown by 22 per cent over the same period; average consumption per head had fallen drastically, largely at the expense of the poorest classes. Unemployment had increased and during 1961 the major thrust of government intervention was towards the relief of unemployment. The plans of the 1958–59 government were revised during 1960: the agrarian reform was replaced by an inoffensive programme of agricultural development and the primacy of private enterprise in the industrial sector was emphasised in place of the earlier commitment to state intervention. New and openly 'liberal' positions were adopted after the way had been cleared by the promulgation of a new investment code in December 1960. From 1962 the original plan was officially abandoned. But these revisions and changes proved remarkably ineffective. By 1964 Moroccan GDP was still below the level of 1954. Production was roughly equal to that of 1958.[4] The volume of investment was around 13–15 per cent of production and remained badly distributed, with major emphasis given to administrative schemes and basic capital projects. Industrial production remained stagnant; exports other than phosphates failed to grow appreciably, while imports increased at a rapid rate. The steady drain of capital aggravated the already dangerous trend in the foreign trade balance and Morocco's previously impressive stocks of foreign exchange dropped between 1961 and 1964 from dirhams 860 million to 72 million. At the same time, the rate of growth in current administrative expenditure was maintained at around 5 per cent a year. Current public saving, which had still been at a high level in 1958, had been transformed into a considerable deficit by 1964. The economic situation was critical.

During 1964, the government decided to take action, and embarked on a series of measures designed essentially to reduce public expenditure, raise taxes and reduce imports. The announcement of these austerity measures, on top of the progressive deterioration in living standards and conditions for a significant proportion of the urban population in particular, triggered off a series of popular responses.

In January 1965 strikes by dissatisfied teachers led to large-scale street demonstrations in all the major cities. Teachers were joined by students and the unemployed. Over the previous year some 10 000 workers had been thrown out of work as a result of austerity measures adopted in response to the stagnation of the economy. In March, the UMT called a general strike, and massive demonstrations were organised. The ministry of the interior responded swiftly, sending in mobile security units to disperse the crowds. Several hundred arrests were made and the demonstrations developed into violent clashes with the security forces. According to some sources as many as 200–300 people were killed and many more hurt. In the same month, the exiled leader of the UNFP, Ben Barka, was condemned to death *in absentia* for his alleged involvement in a plot to overthrow the monarchy.[5] In a broadcast immediately after the disturbances, the king admitted that the economic situation was not promising and recognised that many of the demonstrators were low paid or unemployed. Nevertheless, he laid the blame largely on 'political factionalism' which made it almost impossible to develop coherent and consistent policies. In June, he dissolved parliament and declared a state of emergency.[6]

THE KING TAKES CONTROL: 1965–77

The state of emergency lasted almost five years, until the promulgation of the 1970 constitution; but the king was able to rule by decree without any elected legislative body between 1972 (when the constitution was revised) and 1977 simply by refusing to call general elections.

In July 1967 the king relinquished the post of prime minister, and during 1967 and 1968 there were eight major cabinet reshuffles, as he orchestrated the government so as to minimise the extent and depth of opposition. Considerable trade union and student unrest continued during this period, but the opposition parties remained muted, and in October 1969 municipal and rural communal elections were held in a somewhat freer atmosphere. The first local elections since 1963 were welcomed in some quarters – notably by the official opposition press – as heralding the end of the state of emergency and a revival of party politics. It soon became clear that this was not to be, for the most striking features of the 1969 elections were the blatant manipulation of the entire process by the local authorities and the overwhelming success of 'neutral' or non-party candidates approved by the authorities. The national results showed 70 per cent of those elected to have been registered as 'neutrals', with 14.5 per cent as Mouvement Populaire candidates, 13 per cent as Istiqlal and 2.5 per cent only from other parties.[7] In July 1970 a national referendum was held on a new constitution. Official figures claimed that over 98 per cent of the votes were affirmative, despite general opposition from the main political parties, the trades unions and student organisations. In August elections were held for a new single chamber legislature; of the 240 members, 158 were 'neutrals' and 60 were members of the MP. In the chamber of representatives, and throughout the country at large, the king appeared to have 'neutralised' the official opposition and effectively disarmed his critics.

But in 1970 several left-wing parties were formed – such as Ilal Amam, which split from the Party of Liberation and Socialism (the former Communist Party), and 23 Mars, which split from the UNFP – which were to provide a committed, if clandestine, opposition to the king and his government, in the name of revolutionary socialism, over the next 15 years. Also, between 1970 and 1973 student protest at government policies and the absence of free political life in Morocco reached a high point. Student strikes were almost permanent during this period and at the 15th congress of the Union Nationale des Etudiants Marocains (UNEM) in 1972, activists from the Ilal Amam and 23 Mars movements displaced the UNFP leadership which had headed the union since the 1950s. The government reacted by banning the UNEM in January 1973 and gaoling many of its leaders (some of whom are still in gaol).

In July 1971 there was an unsuccessful attempt to overthrow the king organised by right-wing army officers angered at the level of corruption in the royal administration and by the king's sophisticated policy of control over dissent on the left. During the months following the attempted coup, a series of conciliatory talks was held between the government and the members of Istiqlal and the UNFP, who had united to form a national front in July 1970, but the talks were unsuccessful. In March 1972 a new constitution was promulgated under which executive power was vested in the king; legislative power was to lie with a newly instituted chamber of representatives. On 30 April, however, the king announced that the chamber would remain dissolved and that elections for a new chamber were to be postponed.

In August 1972 another attempt was made on the king's life, apparently organised by General Oufkir, the Minister of Defence and Army Chief of Staff who had been responsible for the disappearance (and subsequent murder) of the radical leader Ben Barka in 1965. The king took over command of the armed forces and defence matters until appointing a new defence minister in March 1973. Elections were postponed indefinitely and the king formed a new cabinet in November 1973 without the participation of the official opposition.[8] Between 1973 and 1977, the king ruled supreme, ever mindful of the danger of political opposition and the threat of assassination.

In 1970, five years after the declaration of a state of emergency and one year before the first of the attempted coups d'état, one commentator remarked on the success, until then, of the king's efforts to contain the growing contradictions within the Moroccan political economy, but pointed out that 'the essential dilemma of such a monarch is to promote economic development without upsetting the delicate stalemate he ha(d) helped to maintain'.[9] The latter part of the 1960s, however, was a period of economic stagnation and growing inequality. In 1960, the poorest 10 per cent of the population accounted for only 3.3 per cent of the total value of consumption: by 1971 this had declined to a mere 1.2 per cent, reflecting the steady decline in the purchasing power of the poor. In 1971, the rate of unemployment was estimated as 35 per cent, with half of those recorded as unemployed being under the age of 24. Indeed, even the introduction to the 1973–77 five year plan stated that 'the overall improvement in living standards far from diminishing differentials in living standards has to a certain extent accentuated the differentials'. During the period from 1973–77, food prices rose by an average of 11.1 per cent a year, substantially faster than wages, and the social inequalities referred to in the five year plan intensified. An evaluation of the 1973–77 five year plan itself reveals gross regional inequalities in budget allocations, with the poorest and least developed regions receiving significantly less than the wealthier and more developed regions. Other aspects of the state budget envisaged under the plan suggest a commitment to further strengthen the advantaged sectors of the economy and restrain resources allocated to the weaker sectors.

The king recognised the political threat posed by growing inequalities within the country. During 1974 he held consultations with the military high command, ministers and party leaders to prepare an international campaign for the annexation of the Sahara, still under Spanish rule. In October 1974, on Morocco's initiative, the issue of the Western Sahara was debated at the United Nations and in December the General Assembly approved Morocco's suggestion that the matter be brought before the International Court of Justice to decide on Morocco's claim of sovereignty over the territory. In the atmosphere of national unity created by the Sahara issue, there was an upsurge in political activity. New parties were formed and existing parties reorganised. Divisions within the UNFP were formalised as the Rabat section of the party became the Union Socialiste des Forces Populaires (USFP), and the former Communist Party (founded in 1943 and banned in 1952 and 1959, and reformed under the name of the Party of Liberation and Socialism) was reconstituted as the Parti de Progrès et du Socialisme (PPS). Elections were promised for the following year. For a while it appeared that a genuine political liberalisation was taking place. But the elections were again postponed by the king, harassment of opposition parties continued and no opposition figures were invited into the government.

In October 1975, the day after the World Court ruled in favour of self-determination for the Western Sahara, the king ordered a 'peaceful invasion' of the Spanish territory; the Green March, which involved about 350 000 Moroccan civilians, was undertaken in a great wave of nationalist sentiment in early November. In the same month, Spain agreed to withdraw from the Western Sahara by February 1976 leaving the territory under joint Moroccan and Mauritanian administration, and Moroccan armed forces began an invasion from the north.[10] Within Morocco, all of the officially recognised parties, including the socialist and communist parties, supported the policy of annexation of the Western Sahara. Only some of the small left-wing movements, such as Ilal Amam, objected in principle; over 100 of the leadership and activists of Ilal Amam, were arrested during 1976 on charges of treason for their support for the Saharawi national liberation movement, the Polisario.

With such unprecedented national unity among the major parties and evident support for the policy towards the Western Sahara, the king felt sufficiently secure to hold the long-awaited elections. Municipal elections were held in November 1976, followed by provincial elections in January 1977, with elections to professional and vocational chambers in March. In June elections were held for the national chamber of representatives. The overwhelming majority of seats at all levels were taken by 'neutrals', mostly pro-government and conservative. Nationally, these 'independents' gained 141 seats while the Istiqlal won 49 and the MP 44; the USFP took 16 seats and other parties 14. The new government, announced in October, included former opposition members from the Istiqlal and MP, and one member of the UNFP – a former trade union leader – who was subsequently disowned by his party, which had boycotted the elections. The king appeared to have succeeded in his plan to combine the forms of political democracy with effective royal control, and to have either co-opted or suppressed all political opposition to his government.

But if the king appeared to have re-established political control, the Moroccan economy had clearly moved, during the first part of the 1970s from stagnation to crisis.

TOWARDS STRUCTURAL ADJUSTMENT: 1977–84

By 1977 Morocco was seriously in debt; substantial foreign borrowing had been undertaken to cover a current account deficit in the balance of payments of 16.5 per cent of GDP and a treasury deficit of 15.8 per cent of GDP. These deficits can be explained largely by the substantial public investment programme of the previous five years, the heavy expenditure on the war in the Sahara from 1975 onwards, the drop in the price of phosphates after a dramatic increase in 1974–75, and the growing bill for imports (mainly petroleum and petroleum-based products and foodstuffs, particularly grain).

In 1978, the government introduced a three-year stabilisation programme to redress the rapidly deteriorating financial situation and to decrease the growing trade deficit. This emphasised the need for stricter import controls and reductions in public expenditure. External events – including a decline in revenues from the export of phosphates and from migrant workers' remittances, the increase in international interest rates and the 1979 oil price rise – adversely affected this programme. But internal pressures also ensured that public expenditure remained high and imports continued to grow. By 1979, the war in the Western Sahara was estimated to be costing between $2 million and $5 million a day, and it was claimed that 'defence-related expenditure' accounted for no less than 40 per cent of the consolidated national budget.

The Plan for 1978–80 stressed the need for a reduction in regional and social inequalities, but again concentrated investment in the most developed industrial and agricultural regions and failed to redress the continuing growth in income differentials. Food subsidies were maintained, which slowed down the rise in the basic cost of living, but at considerable expense and with rather little effect on perceptions of continuing deterioration in the standard of living, particularly among the poor. Between 1973 and 1977 food prices had risen at an average of around 11 per cent a year, substantially faster than wages; and although the rate of increase slowed down somewhat between 1977 and 1980, the cumulative effect for the urban labour force was severe. The austerity measures introduced in 1978 were met by an initial wave of strikes in April and May. During 1978, eight USFP-led unions founded the Democratic Labour Confederation (CDT); by 1979 it had three more affiliates and was to grow in strength to become the most powerful Moroccan labour federation by 1981.[11] Throughout the winter of 1978 and spring of 1979 there were further strikes. These largely involved organised workers, often in the public sector – in textile manufacturing, transport, banking, the docks, the mines and the railways, and in teaching. The government dispersed their rallies, frequently with considerable brutality, but the actions gained increases in the industrial and agricultural minimum wage of 30 per cent and 40 per cent respectively, which in turn led to real wage increases. Unorganised workers and the growing mass of casually employed and unemployed did not benefit to the same extent from wage increases, and tended to experience a general decline in living standards.

At the beginning of the 1980s, the Moroccan government faced growing pressure from its international creditors to implement more far-reaching measures to reduce public expenditure, encourage private enterprise and investment, and promote greater efficiency in the allocation and use of resources. At the same time, the level of foreign aid and loans remained high, encouraging the government to postpone hard decisions, while within the country opposition to such measures as had been adopted continued to exert a real constraint on the implementation of stringent deflationary policies.

The 1981–85 Development Plan attempted to achieve a compromise, aiming at substantial growth within the economy (6.5 per cent a year) while at the same time cutting expenditure in selected 'nonproductive' areas. However, attempts during 1980 to make effective cuts in public expenditure, particularly in education – which accounted for nearly a quarter of the current budget – and in food subsidies, resulted in student strikes and in more widespread social unrest. In June 1981 price increases in a range of basic commodities (sugar, flour, butter and cooking oil) provoked general strikes organised by the CDT and the UMT. In Casablanca, the CDT strike turned into a more general demonstration against government policies as workers in both the public and private sectors were joined first by small shopkeepers and then by students and the unemployed from the shanty towns.[12] The social unrest brought special police units, the national guard and finally the army into action. In two days of clashes throughout the city over 600 people were killed.[13] Faced with such opposition to the austerity measures tentatively introduced, the Moroccan government hesitated to push ahead with more stringent policies, thereby incurring the disapproval of the International Monetary Fund and the World Bank. In the view of the latter,

> notwithstanding the difficulties confronting the economy, Morocco did not appear willing to introduce a comprehensive programme of policy measures which could have confronted the economic crisis. The shortcomings in the adjustment performance caused the IMF to convert a three-year EFF into a one-year Stand-By arrangement in 1982 and prevented the Bank from proceeding with a Structural Adjustment Loan at that time.[14]

Throughout the latter part of 1981 and during 1982, the government was mainly concerned to contain political opposition. But by 1982, Morocco's external public long-term debt (excluding military debt) had reached about two-thirds of GDP and 235 per cent of export value of goods and services, while the debt service ratio had reached 35 per cent. Early in 1983, the Moroccan government felt obliged to impose emergency import controls and budgetary cutbacks; but even so, efforts in the autumn of 1983 to re-schedule about $530 million of the debts owed to commercial banks ran into considerable difficulties. However, the results of the June 1983 municipal elections, in which pro-government, centre-right parties won decisively, were encouraging for the government. General elections for the chamber of representatives were postponed until September 1984 and a caretaker 'government of national unity' was formed by the king to replace the existing government which reached the end of its six-year mandate in November 1983.

In August, a programme of stabilisation was initiated, involving a 10 per cent devaluation of the dirham, fiscal and credit restraints, cuts in public expenditure and reductions in the level of food subsidies. In the five months between July and October 1983, largely as a consequence of price increases in August, the cost-of-food index rose 10.6 per cent, and the general cost of living index 8 per cent. With the experience of June 1981 still a vivid memory, the Moroccan government must have approached these measures with considerable trepidation, but the price increases of between 20 and 35 per cent produced no immediate political response. Indeed, even at the beginning of December it was reported that 'so far, the population has accepted the austerity measures and appears resigned to the lean years that lie ahead.'[15] In September, the International Monetary Fund formally approved the stabilisation programme initiated in August – a programme that it had itself recommended earlier – and entered into a stand-by arrangement for SDR300 million. Shortly thereafter, official creditors agreed to re-schedule external debt interest and principal payments coming due between 1 September 1983 and December 1984, as well as arrears as of 31 August 1983. Commercial bank creditors agreed in principle to provide comparable relief on amortisation. The total amount of debt relief obtained under these agreements for 1983–84 was estimated at more than $2 billion – including $575 million of relief on military debt. In November, a donors' meeting sponsored by the International Monetary Fund generated pledges of about $500 million for exceptional balance of payments assistance for 1983–84.

Official projections, however, indicated that the 1984 budget would be roughly a third less than the 1981–85 Development Plan projections, while the 1985 figure was thought likely to be 40 per cent below initial Plan forecasts. Just servicing the foreign debt would absorb at least 40 per cent of Morocco's hard currency income, while the visible trade deficit – reduced by around 27 per cent during 1983, largely by restricting imports and stringent measures to reduce domestic demand for investment as well as for consumption purposes – would remain uncomfortably high. The 'caretaker' government, headed by an administrator chosen for his lack of party affiliation and including representatives from the six most important political parties, was responsible for drawing up the economic programme for 1984. Given the bleak outlook and continuing pressure from the International Monetary Fund in particular to maintain tight control over expenditure, the government decided to reduce still further the burden of subsidies. A second round of price increases affecting basic commodities was implemented in December 1983 and the draft budget for 1984 contained proposals to raise prices again during the year.

The combination of the December 1983 price rises and advance publicity for the 1984 budget with its proposals for further cuts in subsidies and increases in student fees, coming on top of the increases of August, helped trigger off demonstrations in urban areas throughout the country. On 5 January 1984 high school students all over Morocco went on strike; clashes with the police were particularly serious in Marrakesh in the south. On 9 January demonstrations involving not only students but also thousands of the poor and unemployed took place in Marrakesh. Shops closed and there were spontaneous strikes in many factories and offices. Special anti-riot forces and army intervention units were rushed to contain the protests. As news of the demonstrations and clashes with the security forces spread, so too did the street protests. In Rabat they were quickly contained; Casablanca remained relatively calm. But in other towns, particularly in the south and in the north-east of the country large demonstrations and violence in the streets rapidly became a matter of acute concern to the local authorities, who responded generally with considerable brutality, even opening fire on protesters. On 11 and 12 January in Al Hoceima in the north-east students were joined by fishermen, sailors, port workers and many others, including women, in large and angry crowds. Clashes between protesters and security forces were violent and continued over several days, leaving some 40 dead in the town itself and its vicinity. After a few days of relative calm, major demonstrations broke out in two other northern towns – Nador (in the north-east) and Tetuan (in the north-west); here too high school students were at the centre of the protest, which nevertheless rapidly came to include large numbers from the poor neighbourhoods. Troops were airlifted into Tetuan, where the clashes were most violent and threatening, to reinforce the local police. It was several days before the fighting died down, and by that time the number of people killed was estimated at around 150. In all, some 9 000 people were arrested and as many as 400 people were killed, according to some sources, during the two weeks of 'troubles'.

On 22 January the king appeared on television to calm and appease the protesters and to reassure the population at large that the demonstrations were the work of a tiny minority of dangerous elements and were now under control. He also announced that there would be no price increases as planned in the 1984 budget. While there is little doubt that Islamic political groups and some of the leftist movements – notably Ilal Amam – were certainly involved, these were essentially demonstrations of popular protest, involving spontaneous actions by young unemployed or casually employed individuals from the poorest neighbourhoods of most towns where the 'riots' occurred. The regions most affected were the relatively disadvantaged north and south. The earliest major demonstrations occurred in Marrakesh, where the drought of 1983–84 had seriously affected the availability of food and the cost of living. The condition of the poor and unemployed in Marrakesh had deteriorated markedly over the winter; small wonder then that students were joined in protest at increases in fees and prices by others from the poorer quarters objecting to these increases. But mass demonstrations developed on the most significant scale and generated the greatest violence, in the north. This region, which had experienced Spanish colonial occupation between 1912–56, has suffered historically from considerable economic and social disadvantage in comparison with the rest of the country ever since independence. The integration of the former Spanish zone into the former French protectorate between 1956–58 caused great hardship and substantial increases in the cost of living for the population of the north. In 1958, and again in 1959, the region experienced massive social unrest. A commission of enquiry into the disturbances of 1958 and 1959 in the provinces of Al Hoceima and Nador revealed exceptionally high levels of unemployment, lack of support for agricultural development, inadequate economic and social infrastructure and poor and corrupt administration.[16] Over the next decade, very little changed; in 1971, when some 35 per cent of Moroccans were registered as unemployed, the rate of unemployment in Al Hoceima was 65 per cent; and an evaluation of the 1973–77 plan shows that the north as a whole, and particularly Al Hoceima and Nador, received very little investment. The national plan for 1978–80 stressed the need for a reduction in spatial and social inequalities, but again concentrated investment in the more developed regions in the west and centre of the country.[17]

But if the demonstrations were essentially spontaneous manifestations of underlying discontent and anger, and the involvement of political groups was extremely limited, the Moroccan government took the opportunity to initiate a systematic programme of arrest and interrogation which concentrated on known activists and on what were perceived as the most dangerous clandestine opposition groups.

Not only were the radical Islamic groups and leftist organisations like Ilal Amam harassed and attacked, but even the PPS and the USFP were apparently considered suspect. Approximately 2 000 persons were detained during and after the riots and many of these subsequently received prison sentences of up to 10 years, for 'threats to public order' and 'subversion'.

Apparently oblivious to the political repercussions of 'austerity measures', both the International Monetary Fund and the World Bank became increasingly concerned during 1983–84 to press the Moroccan government to implement policies that involved not merely the standard deflationary package for economic stabilisation, but a far-reaching structural transformation or 'adjustment'. The principal elements of such an adjustment programme would involve:

a shift to outward-looking trade and exchange rate policies; far-reaching reforms of price, credit, tax and regulatory policies to remove institutional and other obstacles to efficient mobilisation and use of resources in key productive sectors of the economy; considerable improvements in the efficiency of government investment; more cost-effective methods and better targeting of social programmes; and a thorough overhaul of the public enterprise sector.[18]

It was recognised that the implementation of the stabilisation policies and measures for structural adjustment would entail 'some transitional social costs' and that the benefits might not be felt until the end of the decade.[19] However, it was believed that the cost of *not* undertaking 'the required economic adjustments' would be greater in the long run.

The Moroccan government remained caught in the old dilemma, for to implement whole-heartedly the programme as prescribed by the International Monetary Fund and the World Bank risked further increasing social inequality within the country, and provoking the kind of unrest that erupted in January 1984 with possible longer-term political implications. It also implied a severe cut-back in resources allocated to the war in the Sahara, which had for nearly ten years constituted a major drain on resources (despite support from abroad which could be diverted towards covering the cost of the war), but which remained a central element of the king's strategy for maintaining control over domestic politics. But to persist in an economic strategy which failed to win the now vital approval of the International Monetary Fund and World Bank risked major difficulties with debt re-scheduling in the near future.

The Moroccan government had little alternative but to acquiesce to the demands of the International Monetary Fund and the World Bank and adopt a programme of structural adjustment. At the same time, all too aware of the political dangers inherent in such a programme, it was determined to move as cautiously as possible, until the domestic political situation was secure.

STRUCTURAL ADJUSTMENT: 1984–88

In January 1984, just as popular protest at the measures already implemented broke out in the streets in Morocco, the World Bank in Washington committed itself to assisting Morocco's programme of structural adjustment with an Industrial and Trade Policy Adjustment Loan (ITPA I). This loan was based on the assessment of Morocco's 'needs' provided by a Bank report on industrial incentives and export promotion which in turn was a logical development of an earlier (June 1983) Bank report on priorities for public sector investment. In 1984 also, the Moroccan government formally initiated a five year agricultural sector adjustment programme in response to the worsening macroeconomic situation, the continuing poor performance by the agricultural sector and pressure from the International Monetary Fund and World Bank. Following a joint IMF-IBRD economic updating mission to Morocco in 1984, a Consultative Group meeting was held in Paris in January 1985, and five months later agreement was officially reached on a Bank sector adjustment loan for agriculture. Adjustment in agriculture was explicitly viewed as one element in a total package of policies, the general objective of which, according to the Bank, is a transition from inward-looking import substitution to outward-orientated export expansion.[20]

During the period 1983–84 the rate of growth in GDP averaged around 2 per cent a year, reflecting in part the impact of the essentially deflationary stabilisation programme on consumption and investment demand and in part the effect of two years drought on the agricultural sector. The government budget deficit was reduced from 12 per cent of GDP in 1982 to about 7 per cent in 1984, although this resulted largely from a sharp reduction in investment outlays. Import growth was restricted by the reduction in domestic demand, while the share of exports and gross domestic savings rose appreciably. The current account of the balance of payments improved somewhat, but largely as a result of debt relief obtained from Morocco's official creditors; the net inflow of public medium and long-term capital tended to decline over the two years.

As the government tightened its control in the economic sphere, it also became evident that it had managed to survive the popular protests of early 1984 and to re-establish its control over political life through a judicious mixture of 'stick and carrot' – the former against the clandestine political groupings and the latter for the official political parties. Legislative elections were held in September and despite widespread gains by the centre-left USFP the chamber of representatives was once again dominated by centre-right, essentially loyalist parties, which between them held 206 of the new total of 306 seats. In October the king invited the leaders of the six main parties to submit their planned programmes to enable him to form a new coalition government; in the meanwhile, the previous 'government of national unity' remained in office. When a new government was formed, it included the four main centre-right parties (the Rassemblement National des Indépendants – RNI, the Union Constitutionelle – UC, the Mouvement Populaire – MP, and the Parti National Démocrate – PND) and excluded the Istiqlal and the USFP (both of which had been represented in the former government). The prime minister – who was retained from the previous government of national unity – presented the government's programme to the chamber of representatives in April 1985. The major elements of government policy were privatisation, the decentralisation of health and education and reforms in the civil service and the education system.

Towards the end of 1985, the Moroccan economy seemed at first sight to be in a better position than during the previous two years: a bumper harvest and the continuing fall in oil prices had helped to reduce the bill for imports, GDP grew by around 4 per cent, receipts from tourism had increased substantially and the value of remittances from workers abroad had also risen. In September, the International Monetary Fund indicated its approval with an agreement to a new Stand By arrangement whereby Morocco had access over the next 18 months to a facility worth some $230 million, as well as a compensatory financing facility for cereal purchases worth about $130 million. Shortly after the IMF package was announced, an agreement on terms referred to by the Moroccan finance minister as 'favourable' was reached with the 11 member Paris Club on the re-scheduling of $1 billion in medium- and long-term debts. Finally, the 1983–84 re-scheduling agreement between Morocco and the commercial banks (considered virtually complete at one time in early December 1983) was eventually signed in October 1985.

However, the trade deficit worsened in 1985 and barely improved in 1986. Although exports grew in 1985-86 the growth was almost entirely in raw phosphates and phosphate products, with manufactured and agricultural goods showing considerable weakness, and the bill for imported cereals remained very high. Foreign reserves were low – barely sufficient to cover one month's imports. Finally, the impressive growth in GDP achieved during 1985 and 1986 depended to a substantial degree on two exceptionally good harvests resulting from unusually favourable weather conditions: in 1986 the growth in GDP of 5.7 per cent was underpinned largely by growth in agricultural output of 15 per cent. The improvement in the balance of payments situation was heavily reliant on a favourable conjuncture combined with the willingness of the banks and the IMF to continue to lend and re-schedule. The World Bank estimated in 1985 that Morocco's debt service would rise to nearly $0.5 billion by 1986; while a study at the same period by the London-based International Economic Appraisal Service forecast that Morocco's debt would rise to $14.5 billion in 1986 and $17.5 billion in 1989, and its total financing requirement (principal repayment plus current account deficit) would increase to $3.1 billion by 1990. The Moroccan government confidently predicted that it would be able to service its now very substantial debt but others were less sanguine.

In 1986 the World Bank reported that 'preliminary data suggest some slippage in fiscal performance in the first half of 1985 and disappointing results on external trade', which led it to suggest that 'stronger corrective measures would be needed to keep the stabilisation programme on course, including in particular, restraining current expenditure and reducing subsidies on foodstuffs and public services'.[21] Internal domestic pressure resulting from the effects of the deepening economic crisis exacerbated by the implementation of stabilisation and structural adjustment programmes go a long way to explaining the Moroccan government's failure to keep down public expenditure in the way that the World Bank would have liked. It was, for example, recognition of the desperate plight of the vast majority of small farmers in rain-fed regions during the drought years, entirely

unable to respond to the 'incentives' provided through the process of
structural adjustment, that led the king in May 1985 to promise
tax-exemption for farmers in drought affected areas, even if this
would lead to a 10 per cent reduction in government tax revenue in
coming years. The political dangers of drought combined with
increases in the basic cost of living in the most disadvantaged regions
had been revealed in January 1984. Restrictions on public expenditure associated with the austerity programme had affected the
government's ability to make any inroads into the growing problem
of unemployment – in 1984, out of a planned 44 000 jobs, only about
half were actually created; while the rising cost of living (up by nearly
10 per cent during 1985), particularly the increasing relative and
absolute cost of basic foodstuffs (up by nearly 13 per cent during
1985) – resulting in considerable part from the measures adopted
under the structural adjustment programme – had adversely affected
whole sections of the working class and also public sector employees
belonging to the lower middle classes. According to the USAID
country development strategy statement for 1988, ' . . . per capita
incomes are continuing to decline. Morocco is no longer a middle
income country, and per capita GDP has dropped from US$631 in
1981 to US$515 (at current prices and exchange rates)'. If average
incomes have declined, it is largely because, at the lower end of the
spectrum, the poorest sections of the population have experienced a
considerable decline in incomes.

In September 1985 (after the general cost of living index had
jumped nearly 4 per cent and the cost of food index 5.7 per cent
during August alone), to forestall any organised expression of
discontent, the government announced a 10 per cent rise in salaries
and wages for industrial and agricultural workers – the second rise in
that year; an extra 5 per cent was granted to civil servants. However,
the trade unions continued to press for more substantial wage
increases for their members – mainly in the organised sector – and
the number of strikes and other forms of industrial action continued
to be high through the period from 1984–86.

During the autumn of 1985, the government took action once again
against the clandestine political groupings which appeared most
threatening. In August, 26 members of Islamic Youth were charged
with plotting to overthrow the monarchy and to establish an Islamic
state; 14 were sentenced to death in September. In October a further
28 people were charged with membership of another clandestine

Islamist group – the Moudjahedine Movement, and with subversive activities. In February 1986 27 left-wing activists of Ilal Amam were imprisoned for subversion.

In January 1986, Morocco failed to make the first payment of $85 million due to foreign commercial creditors under the October 1985 agreement with the Paris Club, and was only bailed out by a loan from the Al Ubaf Bank of Bahrain. In February, the IMF suspended its stabilisation programme and called for discussions regarding the renegotiation of the loan agreement reached in September 1985. The IMF was concerned that the Moroccan government had failed to implement 'sufficiently rigorously' the major elements of the package upon which this loan was conditional. In addition to fundamental weaknesses in industry, trade and agriculture, the IMF was concerned at the budget deficit, the failure to control the growth of credit and the corresponding expansion in the supply of money, and the insufficient reduction in public expenditure, including food subsidies. It was particularly concerned at the failure to make the payment due to the Paris Club.

Under these circumstances, the IMF looked with extreme disfavour at the Moroccan government's announced plans to increase public expenditure and investment and run a larger deficit during 1986 and thereafter. In addition to a proposal for an increase of 67 per cent in investment, the Moroccan government had stated an intention to increase by 30 per cent its spending on the occupation of the Western Sahara and its military operations against the Polisario. Proposals for 1987 indicated clearly where the government estimated its priorities to lie: national defence was to receive the equivalent of $860 million in recurrent and capital expenditure (about 16.5 per cent of the total); only education was to receive more. Agriculture, considered a priority within the strategy for economic development, was to be allocated less than half that earmarked for 'defence'. Debt service provision for domestic floating debt and for foreign public debt was planned to rise by 80 per cent.

These plans for an expansionary budget in 1986 with only a slight contraction thereafter were shelved, however, after negotiations with the IMF, which had become extremely concerned at the budget deficit, the failure to control the growth of credit and the expansion of the money supply. The budget deficit in 1985–86 at between 9.1 and 9.4 per cent of GDP was well above the IMF target of 7 per cent, while the growth in the supply of money, at nearly 18 per cent was considerably over the IMF target of 10 per cent. The confidence expressed by the Moroccan government in its plans for the state budget for 1986 and 1987 and founded no doubt on the apparent strength of the economy during 1985, was not shared by its creditors or by the international agencies.

In the event, policies geared towards tighter control of spending and gradual reform of the fiscal system helped bring the treasury deficit down,[22] limit the increase in the money supply[23] and reduce overall government spending.[24] The budget policy actually implemented during 1986 was directed towards reducing the deficit, in large part by cutting government expenditure, particularly capital expenditure, in order to satisfy the IMF and other creditors. A reduction in the level of imports (10.5 per cent down in 1986) partly due to a fortuitous reduction in the cost of oil imports and a drop in the cost (but not the volume) of wheat imports, and measures to initiate a programme of systematic privatisation also characterised the Moroccan government's practice during 1986.

All this evidently encouraged Morocco's creditors and restored lagging faith in the government's capacity to restructure and reform the economy in the direction clearly laid down by the IMF and the World Bank. In mid-December 1986 a new stand-by credit of SDR230 million ($280 million) was agreed by the IMF for a 16 month period. Negotiations for the rescheduling of the $1.8 billion worth of medium and long term commercial debt due between 1985 and 1988 were also completed in December (the terms were a rescheduling of payments between January 1991 and January 1997 at an interest rate 3/16 per cent above Libor), and short term debt worth $640 million was also rescheduled on a revolving basis. In March 1987, a new Paris Club agreement on bilateral debt was signed to cover $1 billion worth of principal and interest payments due between March 1987 and 30 June 1988. The March agreement also dealt with a further sum of $300 million which had been rescheduled from 1984 and which was now to be deferred for four years until 1990. During 1987, the Moroccan government made it clear that it expected to receive further international support since, by virtue of the Seoul 1985 IMF communiqué, it is one of the heavily indebted Third World countries to receive aid under the $20 billion Baker Plan.

The World Bank was also clearly impressed by the Moroccan government's commitment during 1986 and 1987 to follow the IMF prescriptions and to implement the first stages of a far-reaching structural adjustment in all sectors of the economy (trade, industry, agriculture) reducing the level of public expenditure overall. Introducing the World Bank's fiscal 1987 report, made public in Washington in September 1987, the Bank's vice-president for Europe, the Middle East and North Africa declared that Morocco was 'well-poised' for economic success as a result of its economic stabilisation programme. Although Morocco remained the Bank's second largest debtor after Turkey (with $2.07 billion worth of loans still outstanding), the Bank was prepared to increase its lending during 1987 to make Morocco its third largest recipient after Turkey and Pakistan (with $577.3 million in that year alone). Major loans included $240 million for the restructuring of state enterprises, $245 million for infrastructural development (in telecommunications and sewerage and water projects) and $70 million to aid export industries.

Economic performance in terms of GDP growth during 1987 was disappointing, largely due to a fall in cereal output from 7.7 million tonnes in 1986 to 4.2 million tonnes. This, combined with stagnation in the crucial phosphate sector, meant that GDP growth was probably around 2 per cent in real terms, as against 5.8 per cent growth in 1986. But measures to reduce public expenditure were certainly effective; in the period January to May 1987, state expenditure fell by 18.6 per cent in comparison with the same period the previous year, largely as a result of substantial cuts in capital expenditure and investment, down by more than 70 per cent on 1986. By contrast, private investment was up 17 per cent by the end of the first eight months of 1987 in comparison with the same period in 1986. Inflation was kept down – half year figures for 1987 suggested that the retail price index had only risen 1.5 per cent and end of year figures indicated a rise of around 2.4 per cent, in comparison with 8.8 per cent in 1986 – largely as a consequence of the marginal increase (0.3 per cent) in food prices. The cost of living index rose by only 1.9 per cent between December 1986 and December 1987, according to official figures, in comparison with a rise of 4.6 per cent in 1985–86.[25] Agricultural prices actually fell by 2.2 per cent and food industry prices by 1.2 per cent in 1987.[26] The ability of the government during 1986 and 1987 to hold down the rate of inflation, particularly as regards food prices, was clearly important in preventing the growth of social unrest. But rising unemployment and an effective freeze on wages since the early part of 1985 meant that conditions for the urban poor in particular had been deteriorating, albeit not in the dramatic and spectacular fashion of the late 1970s and early 1980s.

Also important was the government's evident ability to control the level of political opposition in the country at large. Centre-right and loyalist parties now predominated and held the majority of seats in most elected assemblies and councils, with the exception of some of the larger cities, such as Casablanca, where the USFP had gained ground. Support for the old Istiqlal appeared to be declining. The government's general strategy in the political sphere was to maintain and consolidate the essentially loyalist support of the official opposition parties, while at the same time permitting to a limited degree the expression of different opinions on economic and social matters. Its strategy with regard to the clandestine opposition groups was to increase its surveillance and control of known activists, to intimidate and harass those committed in their hostility towards government policies, and to attempt to persuade those who might waver and abandon their active commitment to fundamental opposition under pressure to do so. Throughout 1986 various clandestine groups were subjected to thorough investigation, and from February – when 26 members of Ilal Amam were imprisoned for their involvement in the January 1984 'bread riots' – to November – when three members of the new Marxist-Leninist group, Al Qaaidiyin were imprisoned for their membership of the illegal organisation and for disturbing public order – there was a series of arrests. At the same time, four members of Ilal Amam, who had been in jail with sentences of between 22 and 32 years for endangering state security and disturbing public order, were pardoned in December 1986 after they had affirmed their loyalty to the state and renounced their links with the movement. Also in December the king approved the idea of a subvention of dirhams 20 million to be made available for distribution among political organisations and trade unions and their associated journals. This was, ostensibly, to ensure that they 'fulfil the role allotted to them under the constitution', although fears were expressed that the subvention could become a further means of government pressure on the more critical opposition parties and unions.

Some of the resentment felt by opposition parties and trade unions over the rigid limits on democratic expression imposed by the government surfaced in late November 1986 during the second national congress of the Democratic Labour Confederation (CDT), Morocco's most left-wing union, closely associated with the USFP, when it was claimed that the government had removed effective political and trade union rights. In the same meeting, the union denounced the government's economic policies and the country's dependence on the IMF which, it was claimed, was mortgaging the country's future.

Despite these criticisms, however, the level of effective opposition to government policies remained low during 1987, and government confidence in its ability to maintain its control over the political as well as the economic sphere grew. Throughout the year, the king announced a series of amnesties and pardons, designed to undermine any criticism of the government's harsh treatment of political opposition. The 40 political prisoners who remained of the 173 leftists of the Ilal Amam organisation found guilty at the notorious Casablanca trial in 1976 for actions construed as treason (largely because of their rejection of Morocco's claim to the Western Sahara) were informed that a royal pardon could be obtained by recanting on their previous position. By mid 1987 a total of eight had been released – four in December 1986 and four at the beginning of the year. In the autumn the king called for national unity around the banner of Islam. At the same time, however, a series of arrests of political activists, involving particularly Islamic militants and student union leaders, took place in the late summer and into the autumn.

The government faced the prospects for 1988 with confidence. In his initial budget statement in November 1987, the minister of finance predicted that GDP growth in 1988 would reach 4–5 per cent while inflation would be held to 6 per cent. He expected that the current account deficit could be restrained, as in 1987, at around 2 per cent of GDP and the overall budget deficit to around 6 per cent of GDP, in part by improved economic performance, particularly with respect to export growth, but in large part by tight control on public expenditure, strong restraint on import growth, and strict limits to price and wage inflation. The 1988 Finance Law was passed at the end of 1987 despite opposition within the Chamber of Representatives to measures described as 'anti-social' and as 'failing to respond to the aspirations of the overwhelming majority of the population'. Salary levels were to be frozen, despite a 10 per cent increase in the minimum industrial and agricultural wage rates; there would be cuts in state sector employment (but growth in jobs within the defence administration and to a lesser extent in education); state investment would be cut by around 20 per cent; and there would be increases in VAT (value added tax) which would be levied on products and services previously exempt. The net effect of these measures, it was argued by the opposition, would be to reduce the real incomes and standard of living of large numbers of lower-income earners, particularly in the public sector.

The approval of the 1988 Finance Law at the turn of the year, together with the privatisation measures approved by the Chamber of Representatives in April 1988 demonstrate that the Moroccan government and the king were determined to press ahead with a substantial re-structuring of the economy. In part, this commitment was a response to pressure from the World Bank and the IMF, but it was also a result of the conviction that the reforms had a substantial measure of support within the country and that more fundamental opposition to the government's policies had been effectively controlled and limited. The government had high hopes for Morocco's economic performance during 1988 and its forecasts envisaged a growth in GDP of between 4 and 5 per cent with a real possibility that the current account might even move into surplus. In short, the government now felt confident about its ability to pursue the programme of structural adjustment.

Externally, the debt problem remains; and rescheduling will be essential if the debt service ratio is to be kept manageable. Negotiations with the IMF with regard to a further stand-by credit arrangement to follow on from the agreement which ran out in March had begun by mid-1988. Given the level of official commitment to adjustment, and the control exerted over the basic elements of fiscal and economic policy by the government, it seemed likely that the international community would provide the necessary support for refinancing of the foreign debt. Internally, while undoubtedly opposition remained to the government's economic policies for reform, as well as to its broader strategy for economic and social development, such opposition was muted and apparently well under control. There was reason to believe that the proposed reforms had the support, by and large, of the middle classes, particularly among those sections likely to benefit from the expansion of the private sector.

However, for the poorer sections of Moroccan society, particularly those in the disadvantaged regions, economic insecurity, generally deteriorating conditions and lack of access to recognised channels of political expression remain the lived reality, providing a fertile environment for social unrest and popular protest. Unemployment was still high at the start of 1988, and despite the nominal increases in the minimum industrial and agricultural wage rates of January 1988 real wages and incomes had declined for many. Food prices appear to have been kept steady during 1987 but as further cuts in subsidies on foodstuffs and other basic commodities were implemented official concern grew regarding the situation of the poorest social groups, particularly in the urban areas, and the implications of a further deterioration in their living conditions.

One of the main reasons for concern on the part of the Moroccan government about the deteriorating situation of 'the poorest social groups' is the potential for social unrest and for more organised political protest. After the riots of 1984, the security services became extremely assiduous with regard to the surveillance and control of political groups likely to be involved in agitation and protest, and financial support for the internal security forces was increased.

In 1985, the Moroccan government requested the World Bank to undertake a study of possible compensatory measures to be directed towards 'low-income groups' for the period 1985 to 1990. The proposals made by the World Bank in 1986 centred on direct food assistance programmes, including food-for-work. In December 1987, the World Bank agreed a second loan for the structural adjustment of the agricultural sector; under the programme envisaged in the loan agreement, some 3.5 million Moroccans would receive free food or food-for-work, in comparison with the 1.8 million actually receiving such assistance. Food subsidies would be deployed to target the poorest groups in particular and would concentrate on food items considered of high nutritional value.

Not only the World Bank, but other international agencies have now come to recognise what are euphemistically called 'the social costs of transition' predicted as an unavoidable part of the process of structural adjustment and economic reform under IMF and World Bank auspices. Not only has UNICEF made its view clear, in its report on 'Adjustment with a Human Face' (1987), but in May 1988 a report published by the IMF itself recognised that poor people have been hurt by the policies it has pressed on Third World countries, such as devaluation and cuts in government spending. The report suggested that 'the more adjustment efforts give proper weight to social realities – especially the implications for the poorest – the more successful they are likely to be'.[27] Some bilateral agencies clearly agree. At the beginning of April 1988, the USA signed an agreement with the Moroccan government for a food programme worth $60 million for the period 1987–89. The programme provides for the purchase of foodstuffs such as flour, wheat, edible oil and milk. A part of the sum will finance 'social projects' through the Moroccan National Assistance and National Promotion (food-for-work) programmes and through the Water and Forest Resources Department.

It is doubtful, however, that the kind of measures envisaged in the World Bank proposals for 'targeted assistance' or the USAID programme will be sufficient to change the situation of the poorest social groups in Morocco. Only a commitment to a very different kind of structural reform – involving a substantial redistribution of resources to the poor and a genuine democratisation of Moroccan politics – would do so. In the absence of such a radical structural reform, which in 1988 appeared further from the government's mind than perhaps at any time over the previous thirty years, the problems of social disadvantage and deprivation and of political marginalisation will remain and even grow. It is predictable that, despite harassment and repression, the more radical clandestine groups, and particularly those with an Islamic ideology, will continue to attract support. The growth of support for the USFP is perhaps also an indication of the remaining potential for serious critical opposition to government policy. In the short term, however, for the majority of the poor, the most probable form of expression of growing discontent and resentment will be that of the spontaneous upsurge of protest punctuating periods of apparent acquiescence and docility.

Notes

1. My thanks to Bonnie Campbell and to Tony Barnett for their comments on an earlier draft.
2. In fact, by 1959 very little remained of the resistance, particularly after the brutal suppression in January of the last rural rebellion associated with the Army of Liberation in the north of Morocco by the armed forces under crown prince Hassan. For details see Seddon, D., *Moroccan Peasants: A Century of Change in the Eastern Rif. 1870–1970* (Folkestone: William Dawson, 1981) pp. 176–82.
3. Government pressure had weakened the UMT commitment to play an aggressive role in support of the organised working class, in large part by threatening to withdraw state support for UMT officials' salaries and to oblige them to share their rent-free accommodation with other unions, like the UGTM.
4. In terms of constant prices, prices having risen about 20 per cent during the previous six years.
5. He was murdered later in the year, in France.
6. Article 35 of the Moroccan constitution permits the monarch to

declare a state of exception under which he may rule by decree for an indefinite period.

7. Seddon D., op. cit. (1981) p. 287.
8. The opposition parties were asked to collaborate with the government and to cooperate in supervising general elections. Both the Istiqlal and the UNFP demanded in return that a number of substantial political reforms be adopted, which were unacceptable to the monarch as they included curtailing the king's powers and guaranteeing political freedom.
9. Waterbury, J., *The Commander of the Faithful* (London: Weidenfeld & Nicolson, 1970) p. 318.
10. Seddon, D., 'Morocco at War', in R. Lawless and L. Monahan (eds), *War and Refugees: the Western Sahara Conflict* (London and New York: Frances Pinter, 1987).
11. Representing teachers, phosphate workers, postal workers, health employees, sugar and tea workers, water and electricity workers, petroleum and gas workers and some railwaymen in 1978. In 1979 workers in the tobacco industry, agricultural workers and employees in municipal administration were also represented.
12. In 1981, the World Bank estimated that well over 40 per cent of the Moroccan population was living below the absolute poverty level, the majority of these in the urban areas.
13. Seddon, D., 'Winter of discontent: economic crisis in Tunisia and Morocco', *MERIP Report*, no. 127, 14, no. 8 (1984) p. 13.
14. IBRD, *Report and recommendation of the president of the IBRD to the executive directors on a proposed loan in an amount equivalent to US$100 million to the Kingdom of Morocco for an Agricultural Sector Adjustment Loan*, IBRD, report no. P-4032-MOR/CNR 2590 – MOR, (Washington: 1986).
15. *Financial Times*, 1 December 1983.
16. Seddon, D., op. cit. (1981) pp. 176–81.
17. Seddon, D., op. cit. (1984) pp. 7–16.
18. IBRD, op. cit. (1986) p. 4.
19. 'With population growth of about 2.5 per cent per annum, GNP and consumption per capita which have been essentially stagnant since 1980, are not likely to show much improvement in real terms until the end of the present decade. Stabilisation policies and measures to increase efficiency will initially be reflected to some extent in depressed domestic demand, increased unemployment and some decline in real incomes, particularly the real income of urban population, government employees and workers in the less competitive industries' (IBRD, op. cit. (1986) p. 7).
20. Seddon, D., 1988 'Structural adjustment and agriculture: Morocco in the 1980s', in S. Commander (ed.), *Structural Adjustment and Agriculture* (forthcoming, 1988).
21. IBRD, op. cit. (1986) p. 4.
22. To Dh7.5 billion in 1986 in comparison with Dh10.6 billion the previous fiscal year: a reduction from 8.9 per cent of GDP to 5.6 per cent.

23. Which had risen at the end of 1986 by 15.9 per cent instead of by 17.7 per cent the previous year.
24. Down from over 35 per cent of GDP in 1985 to 33.6 per cent in 1986.
25. Between 1972–73 and 1978–79 the cost of living index rose, on average, between 10 and 15 per cent a year; between 1979 and 1980 it rose by 13.5 per cent; between 1980 and 1981, by 11.9 per cent; between 1981 and 1982, by 8.2 per cent; between 1982 and 1983, by 12.9 per cent; between 1983 and 1984, by 7.4 per cent; between 1984 and 1985, by 9.7 per cent.
26. Food prices rose only 2.6 per cent between December 1985 and December 1986, compared with an increase of nearly 13 per cent during 1985.
27. *Financial Times*, 28 May 1988.

Bibliography

A NON-COMPREHENSIVE BIBLIOGRAPHY OF EXISTING CASE STUDIES

Archimede et Leonard, Carnets de l'Association Internationale de Techniciens, Experts et Chercheurs, (Paris: AITEC 1985) no.1 (Mali, Madagascar).

Baer, Werner and Due, John F. (eds), *Brazil and the Ivory Coast. The Impact of International Lending, Investment and Aid* (Connecticut: Jai Press, 1987) 225 pages.

Bangura, Yusuf, 'Structural Adjustment and the Political Question', in *Review of African Political Economy* (December 1986) no. 37, pp. 24–37. (Nigeria.)

Bassett, Thomas J., 'The World Bank in Ivory Coast', in *Review of African Political Economy* (September 1988) no. 41.

Brown, Richard, 'On Assessing the Effects and Rationale of the IMF Stabilisation Programme in Sudan since 1978', working paper, sub-section on 'Money, Finance and Development' (The Hague: Institute of Social Studies, 1984) no. 12.

Campbell, Bonnie (ed.), *Political Dimensions of the International Debt Crisis* (London: Macmillan, 1989. (Sudan, Senegal, Ivory Coast.)

Canadian Association for the Study of International Development, CASID, Fourth Annual Conference, 'Global Transformation and Development' (University of Windsor, Canada: June 1988). (Zambia, Mozambique, Ivory Coast.)

Carlsson, Jerker (ed.), *Recession in Africa*, background papers to the seminar: 'Africa – Which Way Out of Recession?', Uppsala, September 1982 (Uppsala: Scandinavian Institute of African Studies, 1983). (Ghana, Ivory Coast, Malawi, Zambia and Zimbabwe, Tanzania, Mozambique.)

Cornia, A.C., Jolly, R. and Stewart, F., *Adjustment with a Human Face, Protecting the Vulnerable and Promoting Economic Growth* (Oxford: Oxford University Press, 1987) 2 vols. (vol 2 Botswana, Ghana, Zimbabwe).

Cournanel, Alain, 'FMI en Guinée: un programme très contestable', *Le Mois en Afrique* (Paris: June-July 1985) pp. 69–76.

Davies, Robert and Sanders, David, 'IMF Stabilisation Policies and the Effect on Child Health in Zimbabwe', in *Review of African Political Economy* (Sheffield: April 1987) no.38, pp. 3–23.

Development and Change, Special Issue, vol. 17 (July 1986) no.3 (Tanzania, Zaire, Sudan, Kenya, Malawi and Mozambique.)

Duruflé, Gilles, *L'ajustement structurel en Afrique* (Paris: Karthala, 1988) (Sénégal, Côte d'Ivoire, Madagascar.) 205 pages.

Green, Reginald H. and Xavier Kadhani, 'Zimbabwe: Transition to

Economic Crises, 1981–83: Retrospect and Prospect', *World Development*, vol. 14 (1986) no. 8.

Green, Reginald H., 'Unmanageable. Towards Sub-Saharan Debt Bargaining?', in Stephany Griffith-Jones (ed.), *Managing World Debt* (UK: Harvester-Wheatsheaf, 1988) chapter 9.

Havnevik, Kjell, (ed.), *The IMF and the World Bank in Africa, Conditionality, Impact and Alternatives*, seminar proceedings, no. 18 (Uppsala: Scandinavian Institute of African Studies, 1987). (Nigeria, Sudan, Zambia, Sub-Saharan Africa.)

Helleiner, G.K, 'The IMF and Africa in the 1980s', in *Canadian Journal of African Studies*, vol. 17 (1983) no.1. pp. 17–33.

Helleiner, G.K. (ed.), *Africa and the IMF* (Washington: International Monetary Fund, 1986).

Helleiner, G.K., 'Stabilisation, Adjustment and the Poor', *World Development*, vol. 15 (1987) no. 12. (Tanzania.)

Hoogevelt, Ankie, 'An Open Letter to the IMF', in *Review of African Political Economy* (Sheffield: April 1987) no. 38, pp. 80–86 (Sierra Leone.)

Hugon, Philippe, 'La crise économique à Madagascar et l'intervention du Fonds monetaire international', in *Canadian Journal of African Studies*, vol. 20 (1986) no. 2, pp. 186–218.

Hutchful, Eboe (ed.), *The IMF and Ghana: the Confidential Record* (London: Zed Press and Institute for African Alternatives, 1987).

Institute for African Alternatives, 'Africa: the IMF and the World Bank' (London: September 1987). Conference proceedings, to be published. (Guinea-Bissau, Zambia, Nigeria, Uganda, Senegal, Ivory Coast, Sudan, Ghana, Lesotho, Tanzania, Zaire, Zimbabwe, Burkina Fasso.) Institute for African Alternatives, IFFA, 23 Bevenden Street, London, N1 6BH.

IDS Bulletin, University of Sussex Special Issue on the Berg Report (January 1983).

Journal of Development Planning 'Sub-Saharan Africa: Towards Oblivion or Reconstruction', R.H. Green (ed.) (1985) no.15.

Kayizzi-Mugerwa, Steve, *External Shocks and Adjustment in Zambia*, Department of Economics, Gothenburg University, Göteborg, Sweden, 1988.

Korner, P., Mass, G., Siebold, T. and Tetzlaff R., *The IMF and the Debt Crisis. A Guide to the Third World's Dilemma* (London: Zed Press, 1986), (Sudan, Zaire, Ghana.)

Kydd, Jonathan and Hewitt, Adrian, 'The Effectiveness of Structural Adjustment Lending: Initial Evidence from Malawi' (University of London, Wye College, and London: Overseas Development Institute, 1985) mimeo, 72 pages.

Lawrence, Peter (ed.), *World Recession and the Food Crisis in Africa* (London: James Currey, and *Review of African Political Economy*, 1986). (Tanzania, Sudan, Tunisia and Morocco, Zaire, Nigeria, Zimbabwe.)

Libération Afrique (Paris: November-February, 1983) nos. 15–16. (Zaire.)

Loxley, John, 'The World Bank and the Model of Accumulation', in Jonathan Barker (ed.), *The Politics of Agriculture in Tropical Africa* (Sage, 1984) pp. 65–76.

Loxley, John, *Debt and Disorder: External Financing for Development* (Boulder, Colorado: Westview Press, 1986).

Loxley, John 'Alternative Approaches to Stabilization in Africa' in Helleiner, *Africa and the International Monetary Fund.* G.K. (ed.) (IMF, 1986) pp. 117–147.

Loxley, John, *Ghana, Economic Crisis and the Long Road to Recovery* (Ottawa: North-South Institute, 1988) 64 pages.

Loxley, John, 'Structural Adjustment Programs in Africa: Some Issues of Theory and Policy' (1988, to be published) mimeo, 21 pages. (Ghana, Zambia.)

Ravenhill, John (ed.), *Africa in Economic Crisis* (London: Macmillan, 1986).

Rose, T. (ed.) *Crisis and Recovery in Sub-Saharan Africa* (Paris: OECD, 1985).

Singh, Ajit, 'Tanzania and the IMF: The Analytics of Alternative Adjustment Programmes', *Development and Change*, vol. 17 (The Hague: July 1986) no. 3.

Timberlake, Lloyd, *Africa in Crisis: The Causes, the Cures of Environmental Bankruptcy* (London: Earthscan 1985).

Torrie, Jill (ed.), *Banking on Poverty. The Global Impact of the IMF and the World Bank* (Toronto: Between the Lines Press, 1983). (Tanzania.)

Young, Roger, *Zambia, Adjusting to Poverty* (Ottawa: North-South Institute, 1988) 52 pages.

Uganda Economic Study Team, *Economic Adjustment and Long-Term Development in Uganda*, Government of Uganda/International Development Research Centre (IDRC) (Ottawa: July 1986).

United Nations Economic Commission for Africa, *The Abuja Statement* (Addis Ababa: June 1987).

World Bank, *Accelerated Development in Sub-Saharan Africa* (Washington, DC: 1981).

World Bank, *Towards Sustained Development in Sub-Saharan Africa – Joint Program of Action* (Washington, DC: 1984).

World Bank, *Financing Adjustment with Growth in Sub-Saharan Africa, 1986–90* (Washington DC: 1986).

Index